THIS LITTLE ICHNOLITE OF MINE

A MEMOIR

by Martin Settle

Legacy Book Press
LLC

Camanche, Iowa

Memory, native to this valley, will spread over it like a grove, and memory will grow into legend, legend into song, song into sacrament.

—Wendell Berry

TABLE OF CONTENTS

POEMS BY THE AUTHOR

I dedicate this book to the city and people I grew up with on the banks of the Mississippi River. You have given me a mythology rich in adventure and imagination.

PROLOGUE
THIS ICHNOLITE OF MINE

"A writer—and, I believe, generally all persons—must think that whatever happens to him or her is a resource."
—Susan Sontag

Quincy, Illinois, is more than provincial — it is preserved in amber like an insect. The architecture of the city points to a time when it once was prosperous. Brick homes in crumbling disrepair that overlook the river still maintain an elegance of once being inhabited by a thriving merchant class. Today they are inhabited by the poor or abandoned altogether. Then there are the mansions off of Main Street that were built and maintained by rich industrialists at the turn of the 19th into the 20th century. Some of those have given way to being divided up into apartments, and in one case, a dormitory. The original aristocracy has long ago died, and their companies have often died with them or moved elsewhere. The downtown is filled with old brick bastions that still have their old names fading on walls like pictographs of an extinct people.

Mark Twain mentions in his *Life on the Mississippi*, written in the 1850s, how Quincy was once a city of great promise and commerce:

In the beginning Quincy had the aspect and ways of a model New England town: and these she has yet; broad, clean streets, trim, neat dwellings and lawns, fine mansions, stately blocks of commercial buildings. And there are ample fair-grounds, a well-kept park, and many attractive drives; library, reading-rooms, a couple of colleges, some handsome and costly churches, and a

grand court-house, with grounds which occupy a square. The pop-
ulation of the city is thirty thousand. There are some large facto-
ries here, and manufacturing, of many sorts, is done on a great
scale.

The town I grew up in a century later in the 1950s and 60s was still around thirty thousand with little of the industrial potential it once had during Mark Twain's life. Decay had set in in many sectors of the town. Of the multiple causes of this decay, the most profound was Quincy's location. Whereas once riverboat and barge traffic made the town thrive, it became increasingly less relevant in the era of railroads and trucks. Quincy was bypassed by modern highway systems and the railroads. Major industries moved out because they needed to be closer to distribution centers and more concentrated populations. And while Quincy tried to maintain itself, it became a victim like many cities in the rust belt.

For you, that may sound like a sad story. Yet I thrived in Quincy's demise. For all my life, I have had an intimate relationship with decay. Maybe it's a genetically programmed predisposition to be a hunter-gatherer of junk. My brothers all had the same addiction of combing alleys, trash sites, and abandoned houses to find treasure: rusty nails that could be straightened and reused, porcelain pans to build a fire under, and pieces of tin that sounded like thunder. The riverfront with all its abandoned industries and railroad parapher-nalia were rich ore for children who thought they were combing the ruins of a lost city (which, of course, we were).

Rust, peeling paint, smells of musty wood, sharp-edged broken windows, and collapsing porches — none of these discouraged our ardor for exploring and collecting. What about lockjaw from step-ping on a rusty nail, what about infections from cuts, what about germs? Irrelevant. Perhaps, that is why when I first saw the paint-ings of Ivan Albright in The Art Institute of Chicago in my early twenties, I identified with his sense of beauty poignantly hidden in the deterioration of people and things. That was my Quincy, and Albright's painting "That Ichnolite of Mine" provided me with a fo-cus of how I felt about time held in decaying abeyance, like a leather suitcase in an attic. I had seen in real life not only the decaying objects that Ivan Albright depicted but also the deteriorated people. I know the Ida living in the lost elegance of the Newcomb Hotel as she is portrayed in Albright's "Into the World There Came a Soul Called Ida." I know that farmer's wife next to the wood stove in "The Farmer's Kitchen." I've seen the spent flesh of the soldiers at Soldiers Home in "And God Created Man in His Own Image."

"That Ichnolite of Mine" by Ivan Albright

An ichnolite is a fossil footprint. The remnants of a golden age in Quincy sink slowly into a sedimentary layer. Soon what we were will be lost like the sea deposits that made our bluffs. One of the reasons for my writing this book is to make a fossil that could be found by later generations, just like I have found with wonder the crinoids and trilobites in the limestone of our area. Mark Twain, whose childhood was only 15 miles away from Quincy, has certainly made a footprint of dinosaur proportions about his own time. Of course, without even trying to be humble, I seek a lesser remembrance for my childhood city. The question, then, becomes — is a blip of time (1950s and 60s) spent by an obscure person on an obscure bend in the river worthy of remembrance? I have convinced myself that it is.

First of all, on the imaginative level, I believe there is a sense today that such a provincial and parochial existence is something to be disposed of as soon as possible. In general, our present culture tells us to eschew the ordinary and go out and encounter the unique and awesome. You should travel to Athens to see the Parthenon, take a Viking cruise down the Danube, and watch the running of the bulls in Pamplona. That you would stay in one small place on earth is viewed as a deprivation of the imagination.

In my book, I would like to put forth a challenge to the myth of the dullness of a small city. I find plenty of dullness everywhere I go. Being stimulated every minute is a kind of restless dullness. My imagination was never stultified by my small-town existence. The people, their stories, the nooks and crannies of the town and surrounding areas, the religions, the soil, etc. all held their mysteries and abilities to move the imagination. This dullness that people point to in small-town existence is more a matter of failure of imagination by the outsider than anything inherent in the place.

I think the people and the stories found in this memoir will satisfy your imagination in a Dickensian way. "The little people" are not little people at all. The uneducated can be wise; and the educated can be fools. There is always and everywhere in small towns someone like Emily Dickinson, untraveled and unknown during her lifetime, that looks out her window and is sustained by all she sees and hears. I know that I have seen her behind laced curtains as I walked the city as a child.

Writers very often try to keep something of the past alive. My memoir does this, but it does more than mere preservation — it tries to point out what was lost with an eye to the present and future. Each chapter in my book ends with the heading "Backward Forward." In essence, these conclusions try to suggest parts of the past that can bring insight to what we have become and what we could do to change. For instance, a friend of mine said to me, "I don't know if your childhood is possible anymore." Is this a good or bad thing? I have two chapters in my book, "Play: Ways and Means" and "Play: The Games A-Foot Or A Yard," about childhood and play. These chapters certainly beg to be compared with children being raised in the present. How does the child surrounded with electronic media fare with the past child surrounded with nature? Do we need to make adjustments to the experiences introduced to children in the future? "Backward Forward" after each chapter is my commentary of what parts of the past might be relevant today and tomorrow.

What qualifies anyone to write a memoir? Too often today, I find that publishers and agents only want memoirs that are sensational — Ten Years as a Sex Slave, [Fill in Celebrity's Name] Battle with Addiction, Working in the Trump White House, etc. My memoir does not qualify under the categories of famous, infamous, or sensational. My memoir is about the love of a place, and its "ordinary" people. To write such a memoir in the present milieu requires something that just doesn't happen as often — bonding with a place and experiencing homesickness.

As places become everywhere or anywhere and as people become increasingly mobile and mobile-phoned, places are not blanketed with legend and mythology. I cannot see my childhood city without the patina of stories. Others who come to Quincy see an exhausted Midwestern town that matches the muddy waters of the Mississippi River. But I see it as of yore as rich as the medieval castles.

Pity me not. Perhaps, my memoir may make you pity yourself for not having a similar sustaining sense of home. Maybe today's opioid crisis, mass shootings, and suicides are the result of current feelings of displacement. Commercial wealth, after all, does not provide belonging. Where is home? Whose stories do we continue to tell?

My ancestors, the Settles, who were once a bright thread in the fabric of Quincy history, are all gone. We were not the movers and shakers of Quincy. We were not the salt of the earth kind of people. I don't think anyone would have called us "good." We were bartenders. We were entertainers. We were rascals. And we were fun.

This memoir is my ichnolite on the alluvial shores of the Mississippi River. Sediment turning to fossil — pick it up or dismiss it, skip it across a creek like a stone, or keep it in a cabinet as a curiosity like a geode with a dull cover and crystals inside.

1325 Lind Street — The Omphalos

CHAPTER 1
PLAY: WAYS AND MEANS

"The highest poetic endeavor has its inception in the child's need to be what he wants to understand, and to express that knowledge in some outward form."
—*The Ecology of Imagination in Childhood* by Edith Cobb

"Marty, Larry, Kirby, come out and play." Early morning and outside our bedroom we were being serenaded by Richie Higgins or the Meyers brothers, or Clive Courty or Steve Hull or combinations thereof. That's how it was done in our neighborhood if you wanted your friends to come out to play. You could do this because people did not have air conditioners. You could do this because people had screens on their windows to stay as cool as possible at night. We knew where everyone's bedroom windows were. So, we sang through the screens our invitations to play. No knocking on doors or ringing doorbells or phoning.

There were no organized activities. I don't remember ever having an adult appear in our neighborhood play group. We usually assembled under a tree until some inspiration moved us, and then we'd be off like autumn leaves in a breeze. The menu for the day could include a variety of activities from just roaming alleys to baseball games in the park nearby to building camps to playing cards. We were unsupervised and could appear in a variety of places like quanta — some with permission, some without.

Neighbors were not surprised or upset if we went through their backyards (except "Old Lady Walbrink," who liked to keep her yard pristine; even the weeds were afraid of her.) Sometimes we popped up at the lumberyard for materials, the parks for baseball games, the brickyard for war, the college campus to explore, or Soldiers Home to catch crawdads. At all these places, adults hardly gave us a second look — just kids at play; leave them be.

It would be easy to assume that parents were blissfully ignorant of the dangers that their children might encounter. Au contraire. The Depression generation knew all the bad things that could happen to children: infected cuts that could lead to lockjaw, pneumonia that still killed, polio, falls from trees, drowning in the river, etc. These were toughened people who had been through two World Wars, poverty and rationing, adjusting to a new country (my mother was a child of immigrants), work-related deaths, and more. One of the most salient features of this generation was their lack of self-pity. It was not a blissful ignorance of danger that allowed them to let their children run free; it was the belief that their children needed to be able to be toughened up by independent experiences.

The traditional gender roles and the economy at the time contributed to this free-wheeling, child-rearing, lifestyle. Fathers went to work all day with little time for children but, unlike today, they were capable of earning enough money to keep the family afloat financially. Mothers stayed at home and took care of the domestic business of cooking, cleaning, child rearing, and "husbandry" (my special usage for the servant qualities wives provided for their husbands).

In the 50s, taking care of the house and children was a lot of work. For example —maintaining clothes. There were no electric washers and dryers. The women in our neighborhood washed clothes in a tub with a scrub board, rinsed and squeezed them out by either twisting them or running them through hand-cranked rollers (one step away from going to a creek and beating your clothes on a rock). Drying them entailed taking baskets of laundry outside and hanging them in the sun. Every household had clotheslines outside stretched between two T-shaped posts. I could always tell it was Monday when I looked up the block to see the neighborhood's sheets billowing like a Spanish armada. I can still picture my mother with a bag of clothespins in a pouch and three or four in her teeth, draping our underwear over the line and fastening them with clothespins (it was no secret what kind of underwear everyone on the block wore.)

This weary chore of washing and drying was followed up by the equally onerous task of ironing the laundry. There was no permanent press at this time. Housewives stood for hours at an ironing board with a soda bottle filled with water. The bottle had a shower nozzle, so that it could be used to moisten the cloth before ironing. They did this without having the luxury of watching TV, as there were no TVs. Finally, they patched and sewed clothes, adding another level to just this single area of responsibility — maintaining clothes and linens for the family.

My two brothers and I were often not allowed to be inside the house and be underfoot. Mom would shoo us out the door and tell us not to come back until lunch. She was not about to entertain us and had no suggestions of what we should do to entertain ourselves. She didn't completely ignore us, however. Occasionally, she brought out snacks with Kool Aid, which we enjoyed on the shaded backsteps. And even though we thought she wasn't paying attention, she did have this "second sight." No matter how nonchalantly we walked by her, trying to sneak something out of the house, she'd just take a glance at us and say:

"Stop. Look at me. You're hiding something."

"No, Mom. Just got a drink of water, and now I'm going back out to play."

"What's that bulge in your pants?"

"Oh, that. Well, that's just Dad's wire cutters and nail punch. I didn't think he'd care if we used them."

"I see. Put them on the table."

How did she do that! It definitely dissuaded me later in life from ever becoming a thief. If I were on *Mission Impossible,* I'd be caught in the first two minutes of the show.

Thus, the mothers without a lot of the time saving devices did not have time to play, nor did the fathers feel up to playing much with their children after an exhausting day at the factory that often entailed more than forty hours a week. As children of lower middle-class families, you had to create your own fun and games in the neighborhood. And we did.

Serendipitous Play of the Alley Ways

A day of play in the summer had many parts. One of the parts had to do with just roaming. I call this kind of play *serendipitous* play. You never knew what you might come upon or whom you might come across to make your day interesting. It was opportunistic. Of all the places we roamed, I would say alley ways were our favorite. Our main focus, however, was on the alley's edges. It was like looking at what had washed up on a river's shores. Many people put things at the alley's edge that they were going to throw away or, perhaps, use in some remote future. These items we viewed with an eye to future uses.

Stacks of boards with the nails still in them could be taken back to our neighborhood for nail recycling and camp building. Once I remember building a teepee with burlap bags our neighbors were throwing away. Round garbage can lids made for great shields and, if we armed ourselves with sticks, we could re-enact Viking raids. We never stole the lids, but we did batter them up quite a bit. What we did steal was backyard fruit.

Many of the people of the Depression grew fruit trees in their backyards to supplement their food supplies: apples, apricots, pears, cherries, and peaches. From the alleys, you could raid these trees of their largess. We knew early in life about forbidden fruit, and the fruit stolen from these trees often tasted much better than anything our mothers bought from the store. Approaching fruit trees from the alley gave us the advantage of a furtive raid. We would strip fruit from the side of the tree facing the alley, which hid us from view of the owner's house. Occasionally, we were caught in the act. Mrs. Hartsell would come after us wielding a rake with the fury of a wounded animal. But we easily avoided her blows and went laughing up the alley. Another neighbor Mr. Smith tried to keep us from his fecund apricot tree. Never have I experienced apricots in such profusion or with such flavor. We'd watch his house until he drove off to work (he was an old bachelor), then we would take over his tree like a flock of starlings. We would sit on the branches and rain down seeds for an hour. Too often, I ate myself to sickness and spent the rest of the day with a stomachache.

One day we came across a fruit we had never seen before. It had a nice, smoky orange color and was as large as a golf ball. When we were about to raid it, the owner appeared. I'll let my poem tell you the rest:

Persimmon Tree in Eden

Mr. Smith's apricots
a delicate orange in profusion
called to us like a waterfall
we scouted his departure
then took the tree
away from the squirrels
seeds rained down from limbs

polished red Hartsell apples
required military maneuvers
hiding behind the garage
then crawling on bellies to tree base
fruit tasted best
when we outran Mrs. Hartsell
wielding her rake

we were aware of all
the subtleties of pears –
russet, yellow with red blush,
and green hard enough
to take out a tooth
we knew peaches that were spotted
and wouldn't give up their seeds
we felt invulnerable in our stealth
with getaway abilities
of spider monkeys

Then we came upon a strange fruit
smoky orange, plump,
smaller than an apricot
the owner surprised us
before we could run

he praised the persimmon's sweetness
he picked and offered each a fruit

"bite large" he said
and he smiled
watching our awakening
to a bitter moral order

If you haven't tasted ripe persimmons, you do not know their mouth-puckering power. They are filled with tannin and very bitter. In order to be eaten, they must be bletted, that is, progress beyond ripening to the rotting stage. Needless to say, that from our encounter with persimmons, we learned to be a little more discriminating in our choice of fruit and a bit humbler about being able to outfox adults.

My brothers and I had a particular stretch of alley that intrigued us more on an aesthetic level rather than utilitarian. The alley abutted a machine shop, which had old rusty engines and parts that would spill out into the alley. Since we had no mechanical knowledge or familiarity with engines, we found these rusty parts as archeological totems left behind by some extinct race. They were just as interesting to us as finding seashells on a beach. We collected these and marveled over their shapes and wondered what purpose they had originally served. You would think this alley would be picked clean after a while, but it amazed us that there was some new object with a numinous glow to be put in one of our treasure, cigar boxes.

What is most amazing about this alley of forgotten engine parts is that it had a profound significance on the futures of my brothers and me. This is the part of serendipitous play that defies some of the logic of organized play. We cannot know what we come across unthinkingly that will imprint itself upon our minds. The collecting of metal objects in an alley led to my present avocation as an assemblage artist — an unexpected result that only makes sense in retrospect. The mystery of objects is one of the foundations of assemblage art. The first time that I saw Joseph Cornell's work, I immediately understood what he was all about, and I wanted to emulate him.

As I search in dumpsters and in the streets for junk to make my sculptures at 73, I am a child again, and I feel the wonder of every object having an otherworldly existence. Andre Breton, a founder of surrealism, said, "Beautiful as the chance encounter of a sewing machine and an umbrella on an operating table." This is what my sculptures are about — building unusual habitats for objects so that we can truly see them in a different light.

My brothers, too, found their futures influenced by their alley days. My brother Larry ran an antique store until he retired. This career required him to go through other people's junk in yard sales, estate sales, auctions, and furniture cast away on the side of the road. This work resonated a lot with his childhood, and his "job" seemed more like play.

Although my brother Kirby has not made any avocation or vocation out of junk, he has always combed the thrift shops for art, books, and clothing. He could easily afford all these things by paying full price. But why do this when he can immerse himself in other people's throw-a-ways and find treasure.

We continue to be the three musketeers of the alley ways, even as old as we are. Who could have predicted that? Who could have decided that ferreting things from alleys could be a good career path and should be introduced into the educational curriculum? No one, course, yet not having a parent behind us telling us not to roam the dirty alleys and pick up rusty and moldy objects allowed us to deeply engage in an activity that led our imaginations to higher ground. The imagination often does not have any poverty.

The Games A-Foot Or a Yard

There was a whole host of games we played, and we were never given the rules by grownups. Either someone had learned the game somewhere else, or we made up the rules, or made up the game. We played the major national sports of baseball, basketball, and football. Of these three, baseball reigned supreme in the fifties, and we played it the most.

We were a ragtag group with ragtag equipment when we played baseball very similar to the baseball team in the movie *The Sandlot*.

A neighborhood baseball game required the contributions from all the participants — gloves, bats, and balls. If it weren't for black electrical tape, most of these games wouldn't have been played. The life of a baseball in our group was long, indeed, because once we beat the cover off, we wrapped it in electrical tape and continued to use it. It was the same with cracked bats, whose lives were extended with electrical tape. Occasionally, someone would contribute a new ball. After all of us taking a sniff of its new leather and getting a feel for the ridges of its lacings, we proceeded to beat the hell out of it, until it became old before its time and had to be swaddled in black tape.

Location was another problem. First of all, we played hardball, finding softball too sissified for our tastes. When we could, we'd go to nearby Berrian Park to play. We usually made our own ball diamond, using trees and sticks as bases. At the far end of the park, there were official ball diamonds, but these were directly in the sun and often taken by older boys before we got there.

Often, we just played in our backyards. Backyard baseball was fraught with danger. Knocking out windows, for instance, and then having to retrieve the ball from a neighbor's house. That usually entailed repayment and a lecture. Baseballs occasionally entered into a fenced-in yard with an earnest watchdog. Weeds and gardens ate up baseballs, and we often had to spend inordinate time trying to find out where a ball was hiding — we could ill afford to lose a ball because there was not another. Finally, we had to find a place that had a natural backstop for pitched balls. We never had a catcher because the equipment was too expensive and, without equipment, the position was too dangerous. I remember once someone trying to be a catcher ended up getting 15 stitches on the side of his head because he got too close to the batter.

The Settle backyard fit the bill nicely for pick-up baseball. We had a corner lot with a street on one side of our playing area, eliminating windows and gardens on one side. The brick wall of our house made a good backstop and the brick garage on the far side of the yard stopped line drives from going too far. We played so often in our backyard that grass did not grow for years on our pitcher's mound, batting box, and bases.

Besides games that required equipment and fields, we played many games that seemed to sweep our fancy for a limited time. One summer, we were intensely interested in hopscotch. All hopscotch required was rocks — a rock to draw the hopscotch shaped on the sidewalk and a pitching rock for each player. King of the Hill was another non-equipment game. We had banks along our backyard, which enabled us to have one or more persons to claim they were king of the hill. The rest of us would rush them to cast them to bottom of the hill to replace them as king. Yes, it was a Tide Laundry Detergent commercial moment after a session of King of the Hill.

If it were really too hot to engage in physical activity, we'd gather under a shade tree to play a variety of card games or to take out our baseball cards and make trades with the others. Those that had new cards still wrapped up would have the pleasure of opening them to see if they had Stan Musial, Mickey Mantle, or Willie Mays. Then, we'd chew on the flat, pink rectangles of bubble gum provided with the pictures. I can only describe this bubble gum as industrial; it was one step away from being a building material or tiling for a shower. To work a piece of ball card, bubble gum into a chewable wad meant breaking it into shards in your mouth that often painfully punctured your gums. Then, you ground these shards into smaller particles that eventually adhered liked putty. After all that work, the taste of the gum lasted about five minutes.

Other games that were played often were marbles, hide-n-seek, tag, and statue. Unfortunately for us, we had an all-boy neighborhood. This anomaly does not allow me to comment on games that girls played. I *can* tell you there was quite a distinction between girl and boy games at the time. Even our recesses at school separated boys and girls. However, there was some overlap. As I've pointed out, we loved hopscotch, even though that game in general was relegated to girls. Also, we loved jumping rope, but only as individuals. We never had a person on each end of a rope with one, two, or more jumpers in the middle reciting some rhyme. That was strictly for girls.

Without trying to make a comprehensive list, I think the salient points about these games is that we refereed ourselves, and we were facile in adjusting any game to our needs and circumstances. Secondly, we had an array of ages and talents playing these games. In our group there was a five-year gap between oldest and youngest. Also, we had a steep differential in talent, not only because of age but because of physical impediments — being overweight or having poor vision; and psychological impediments — no passion for sports but deeply interested in other areas of our activities where he could shine (building, mechanical knowledge, camping, etc.). All these variations were accommodated, although sometimes somewhat embarrassingly when choosing sides (there were no adjustments made to make you feel better, if you were chosen last). We did not need official leagues to play. We had a league of our own.

Foul Is Fair and Fair Is Foul

"Foul is fair and fair is foul" is a line from *MacBeth* spoken by the witches. In the context of the play, it's about *MacBeth* not being able to distinguish between appearances and reality. But I have appropriated the quote for a different context — baseball. How do you *fairly* determine if the ball that was hit is a *fair* ball or a *foul* ball? Without umpires and referees in our games, we had to make these decisions ourselves, and we had methods to do so.

First of all, fairness is a concept that runs deep in children. They come by it not only through adults but even from their primate past. Studies by Sarah F. Brosnan and Frans B. M. de Waal have revealed that brown capuchin monkeys have strong sense of fairness and won't play a game if they think it isn't fair. So, you can believe when children devise their own rules, they must be fair, else players will quit, and there were no players in the wings to take their place.

We had various rhymes to insure the fairness of most processes. These rhymes were a means to make sure decisions were made by chance and, thus, were fair. Here's an example:

Aka baka soda baka, aka baka doo
Aka baka soda baka, out goes you

There were variations on this:

Aka baka soda cracker, aka baka boo -
Aka baka soda cracker, out goes you!

One person would say the rhyme and point at a different person as he said each word. The last person pointed to was selected for a particular reason: he may be *it* in a game of tag; first to choose sides; first to sit out a game, if the sides were unequal; be the person to use an extra glove that was available, etc. The same rhyme could be used to determine a foul or fair ball, if there was no consensus.

Another of these rhymes was:

One potato, two potatoes, three potatoes - four
Five potatoes, six potatoes, seven potatoes - more
Eight potatoes, nine potatoes, ten potatoes - all
One, two, three, four, five, six, seven, eight, nine, ten

Every time you say a number and a potato, you point to a person as well as the number at the end of the line. The last line requires you to point for each number.

All of these rhymes came from England and Ireland. I say this in preparation for the next rhyme, which can be blamed on the Brits for its racist element. Thankfully, this was eventually eliminated in the U.S., but not before we learned the racist part.

Eeny, meeny, miny, moe
Catch a [N-word] by the toe
If he hollers let him go,
Eeny, meeny, miny, moe
My mother told me
To pick the very best one
And that is Y-O-U

The N-word in this rhyme was later replaced (and with good reason) with "Tiger." (As a side point about the Brits and the N-word,

Agatha Christie first published her book *And Then There Were None* in 1939 under the title *Ten Little N-words*. It was changed when it was published in the States a year later.)

Besides rhymes, we had other ways to make fair decisions — drawing straws or sticks. The person that got the short straw was selected or eliminated. The bat toss was a method used to see which team would bat first in baseball. This entailed throwing a baseball bat in the air with another person catching it as best he could with one hand in the middle of the bat shaft. Then an opposing team player would wrap his hand above the other person's hand. They would climb up the bat with their hands alternating. When they reached the top of the handle, the person who had room to cover knob was the winner.

Weapons of Least and Most Destruction

We LOVED the idea of war. We loved playing games that assimilated battle. Since we were post-war Baby Boomers, our imaginations were full of the gallantry of war. There were reminders everywhere of WWII. Army surplus was everywhere — canteens with olive canvas belts and pouches; ammunition satchels, which my brothers and I used for school bags; army helmets and liners; metal ammo boxes; and more. Army surplus stores flourished. Many of our fathers were WWII veterans, and we went to parades with them and watched them proudly marching. All of us wanted to follow in this great tradition of the warrior.

We'd take over the entire neighborhood and the park nearby to play our war games. We had real helmets and fake guns. Hiding behind garages, in trees, and below embankments, we'd each try to seek and destroy the enemy. The surprise attacks resulted in few deaths; we would refuse to die at distances greater than a yard from a shooter, always assuming our enemy had very poor aim. But if we did die, let's say by a pinecone grenade, it was very dramatic with writhing in agony on the turf or doing acrobatic leaps before hitting the ground.

The green plastic army soldiers in classic poses of heaving a grenade, shooting a bazooka, or shooting from a prone position were popular toys in less expansive games of war. Everyone had some items to add to a small, pretend battlefield, including tanks, cannons, battleships, and war planes. We supplied all the sounds that went with the shooting, explosions, airplanes being shot down, and killing.

Larry, Marty, Kirby — Reporting for duty, Sir

"Cowboys and Indians" was another game that filled our minds with weaponry and epic heroics. Cap-gun six shooters were popular as well as bows with suction cup arrows. While it was hard to get people to be Nazis (if we had to, we'd resort to one of the choosing games mentioned above), it was easy to get people to be "Indians." Many liked the stereotypic stealthy ways and war whoops of the Native Americans and felt no compunction about capturing the invasive cowboys and tying them to a clothesline pole, ready to be roasted. Our sense of who "Indians" were or what to call them had not entered into the consciousness of the times.

While the games above required toy weapons, we all wanted the real deal. And most of us had ready access to and ownership of things that were weapons or were dangerous and could be easily used as weapons: hatchets, bows and arrows with metal tips, firecrackers (cherry bombs and M80s), slingshots, knives, BB guns, pellet pistols, rifles, and shotguns. Oddly, it never occurred to us to use them against each other. The demarcation of their usage was clear and sacred: war games meant fake weapons; real weapons meant no war games.

The most ubiquitous of dangerous objects was the pocketknife. A pocketknife was almost a requirement for a boy from first grade on. My playmates all had a variety of pocketknives from Case and Buck knives to Switch blades, which friends and relatives brought back from Mexico. We played a number of games using our pocketknives, our favorite of which was Stretch.

Rules of Stretch

Stretch had two opponents facing each other about two to three feet apart with their legs together. The person going first tried to stick his pocketknife in the ground about 12 inches to the side of the feet of the other. If the knife stuck upright, the opponent had to keep one foot planted while "stretching" the other to the knife. Then it was the other person's turn, and he tried to stretch his opponent. When you both were stretched, there was a way that you could return to your original, unstretched position: you had to stick your knife between the legs of your opponent. Of course, if you didn't stick your blade upright, you remained stretched. The game ended when one of the players could not be stretched any farther.

Kids practiced sticking their knives in the ground. This was good for your aim and good for your knife, as soil was better to clean your blade with than any commercial product. The better you were with sticking your knife, the better chance that you had to win at Stretch. Also, it helped if you were flexible and could do the splits. As a middle-aged adult, I tried to teach Stretch with my pocketknife to the children of one of my friends. The mother almost passed out when I had them try to stick the knife between each other's legs. Times change, and "Mr. Marty" was not always a welcome guest to houses with children.

Besides games, we whittled on sticks with our pocketknives, usually sharpening the ends of sticks to make more knives or spears. Knives with damaged handles were good for sticking in trees. Over time, I got quite good at throwing a knife at a vertical target. Again, a skill that today's parents don't want me passing on to their children. Did kids receive cuts from using their knives? Indeed, they did, but nothing requiring stitches; only mercurochrome and Band-Aids. No big deal.

Blade weapons captivated the imagination of many boys in my time. Besides pocketknives, we had arsenals of other kinds of knives: machetes (some from WWII in the Philippines), Bowie knives, hunting knives (my brother Kirby had one with a deer hoof handle), serrated fishing knives, combat knives, and throwing knives. Some had scabbards that fit on your belt. Most of these knives weren't very useful, but we coveted their possibilities for "self-defense."

The knife I coveted the most, but could not use for play, was the dagger that my father brought back from Germany. It had a metal scabbard and a handle made of wood that was carved to fit the hand. On the handle was an eagle with the Nazi swastika in its talons. When you took out the blade, which fit snuggly and required some effort to get out of the scabbard, you could see embossed on the blade the words "Alles Fur Deutschland" (All is for Germany). The SA dagger was not only beautifully designed, but it had the mythology of my warrior father behind it, who took it off a soldier he had killed entering into the city of Metz. Occasionally, I got to show my friends this knife, and we all sat worshipfully around it, knowing its history.

To BB or not to BB

Anything that delivered a projectile was highly valued in our tribal society. Some were homemade like rubber guns that stretched pieces of bicycle tire tubing across a wooden gun shape. These ultra large rubber bands were released by a clothes pin, but they had very little potential to hurt anyone. However, sling shots made with the same materials could deliver quite a blow. They could put out an eye, shatter a streetlight, or kill a bird. The ammunition for these was plentiful because the alleys were full of rocks of the right size.

A real rite of passage, though, was getting your first Daisy Red Ryder BB-gun, levered action like the rifles of the Old West. Even though a slingshot was more accurate and probably delivered a harder blow, the bb-gun was a "real" rifle to us and just one step away from graduating to the capital B — Bullets. A companion to the bb-gun was the pellet pistol that looked like a real .45 pistol. Armed with both of these, there was a propensity to want to hunt something. Looking back, I wish we had had more supervision in this area because some of our sadistic tendencies seemed to be released by having guns in our hands. Stinging stray dogs and cats with bb's is something we never did with slingshots, but we did with our air rifles. Also, killing birds (again I say this with the greatest distaste) was something we liked to do. Thankfully, these weapons were about as accurate as a blunderbuss.

If you've read Jean Shepherd's book *In God We Trust: All Others Pay Cash* or seen the movie based on the book, *A Christmas Story*, Ralphie, the main character represents most boys' desire for a bb-gun in this time period. Most mothers protested with the same words as Ralphie's mother, "You're going to put somebody's eye out." But this was not a problem in our group, since we never shot bb's at each other.

The Incident

Of course, BB-guns would never ultimately satisfy our yearning for real weaponry. Our raison d'être was having our own real rifle or pistol, which was the real demarcation between childhood and adulthood. I had friends that had .22 rifles and shotguns, but they were never allowed to play with them like they could a ball bat or pocketknife. But they did hunt with their fathers and in this sense got to experience some real action.

My father was not a hunter, but we did have a sweet, little Browning .22 semi-automatic rifle. It had a walnut stock with a notch on the side to slide in bullets. My father kept it broken down in a case in a closet. There were occasions when he took us out to shoot, but these were rare. They didn't begin to satisfy my craving to squeeze off shots accurately at targets 50 yards away. That was the primary cause of "the incident."

I call it "the incident" because it should have been one, but it wasn't. One summer day when I was bored, I decided I was tired of waiting for the next time to shoot. Why not, I thought, take the rifle out for a spin myself? Stealthily, I went to the closet where the rifle was kept, took it out of its case and assembled it. Even though my father thought he had hidden the packages of .22 long shells, I knew right where they were in his sock drawer. I put a box of these in my back pocket. My next problem would be trickier — to get past my mother, who could always psychically tell when I was up to something.

I needed to create a diversion of some sort and what better resource than a younger brother? Younger brothers could be talked into about anything with a bribe, and my middle brother Larry was more than willing to help me out if he got to shoot. He distracted our mother with some bogus problem while I slipped out the screen door with gun and ammo. It wasn't long before we were walking down 12th Street, a main street in town, with me carrying the rifle on my shoulder like a parade soldier. We were not sneaking around in any way, but bold in our unconscious violation of societal norms.

Perhaps it was because these were the days of boys hunting that no one stopped us. Or maybe people didn't associate gun violence with young boys. Whatever the reason, no one questioned what we were doing as we made our way to the creek behind Soldiers Home. It was here we began to shoot anything in sight — old cans, bottles, rotting stumps, squirrels, and birds. We had no concept of what the "mile range" meant on the package of bullets when we raised the rifle to shoot a bird off a telephone wire. I still cringe today when I think what kind of repercussions could have occurred with a bullet flying randomly for a mile. There were plenty of innocent people within that range who could have been injured or killed.

When we ran out of bullets and were satiated from shooting, we walked home in the same fashion, and again we were not deterred by any adult. When we got home, I cleaned and oiled the gun as I saw my dad do (the cleaning materials were in a third place). Then I put everything back in its place (I couldn't replace the bullets, but there were enough packages that my father wouldn't be aware that one was missing). I thought to myself that no one would ever be the wiser. And it was true — my brother and I got away with a kind of Ferris Bueller's day in the sun, and we were wise enough to never try such a thing again.

As adults, Larry and I told my father what we had done. Even twenty years later, he was angry at us and self-castigating about how his role in not being more careful in his storage of bullets and gun. For a moment, my brother and I were children again and were awaiting some punishment to be meted out.

Another Genesis Story

Ironically, Abel was the name of the first young person to tragically die while I was in school. He was a contemporary, and he came to his demise not through a disgruntled brother but a shotgun. If you thought I have been a bit flippant about the dangers of guns, I am quite aware of their finality. Bill Abel was just entering his junior year in high school. He was a charming guy — smart, athletic, and popular. Certainly, he had before him a life of great promise. But he stepped into another world when he went hunting with his buddies, a common activity for teens in Quincy. He violated one of the rules of hunting and paid for it with his life: never lean your shotgun against a barbed wire fence when you're crossing it. Abel did just that on September 8, 1963; the barbed wire caught the trigger, and Abel went to the land of Nod. His blood cried out to me from the ground at the time; my romance with the gun began to disintegrate.

The death of William Abel on September 8, 1962, was regarded by all the students of Christian Brothers as the tragedy of the year, especially by his Junior classmates. The high regard with which Bill was held will insure his constant remembrance in their prayers.

Correlations Past and Present

I think what is interesting about this era of lust for weaponry for boys is that for the most part it did not translate into adulthood. I cannot correlate my childhood love of weaponry with a continuing romance into adulthood. After high school, my brothers and I and friends pulled away from the imaginary roles of warrior and began getting into more salient needs: girls, for instance. Most girls were as impressed by a weapons' collection as we were about a collection of Barbies. Our careers did not tend toward the military or law enforcement, where we realized we could be killed, but to tamer pursuits like teaching, engineering, social work, biology, etc. A more informed resistance to war became a hallmark of our response to the Viet Nam War.

If you look at the Baby Boomers in general, they were the first American generation that balked at war, protesting in large numbers with some ex-patriating to Canada. The Viet Nam war was a war of disillusionment for my generation. In my experiences in the army, I did not find highly charged patriots ready to die for their country. What I found was more drugs than I did when I was in college. The realities of war were made prominent by the first TV coverage of a war. The horrors of war replaced the gallantry, and fewer wanted to participate as they saw themselves as cannon fodder.

Today I ignore much of the chatter about the evil influences of violent video games. If such games were available when I was a youth, I would have attached myself to them like a limpet. And yet, I think the same results would have occurred — growing up and realizing that the way of strength in life is finding a career, a spouse, and a family. These run deeper in the psyche than the love of violence.

On the other hand, I do believe that a baptism of a sort occurred with Columbine. For certain individuals these images run deep, and there has been little success in erasing them from the collective unconscious. In my day in school with both gun availability and the accepted love of weapons, no one contemplated taking out their anger on classmates and teachers with guns. We definitely did not have better teens at the time, and we definitely had many reasons for hating our fellow students and teachers, but we had no images created by Klebold and Harris to fire up our imaginations. In this sense, Columbine was like a 9/11 in our society, and it changed the rules of the game.

Backward Forward

"Marty, Larry, Kirby" began our day as it ended our day: with our mothers calling us to supper. It was the way of all mothers in our neighborhood to stand on their stoops and call their children's names, a kind of reveille for the end of the play day. Do this today and you would be disturbing the peace.

The important part of our days of play was that we were left to our own devices. I have come across children today that have schedules that are more complicated and filled than my professional life was — swimming lessons, computer camp, guitar lessons, soccer camp, play date with Billy, eat out, etc. There is little time in their schedules for "fruitful monotony" as Bertrand Russell would call it. Aimless roaming on one's own and unsupervised play with other children seems to open up the imagination more than time spent with electronic devices.

Was the past a better way to raise children? I'm always reluctant to say we had it better than another generation. My father and mother thought they had it better, and my daughter, despite the fact she's only thirty, looks down on the childhood of those following her. When I get together with my contemporaries, we bluster about our values and virtues and decry those of the succeeding generations. In our hearts, though, I think we try to suppress what was not good until we hardly remember the downsides to our times.

The Old Man Speaks through QuickTime

I was of the middle era
somewhere between the heart and brain
we still knew the chestnut tree
but we knew more of paper

I grew up by a creek with speckled trout
each house had a yard
each yard a garden
garter snakes fed on grasshoppers

I have seen the sun set
without the rainbow of engines
I have counted the Dipper's stars
as neighbors talked on porches

I have swum naked in the pasture pond
that became the shopping mall
I have eaten wild apples
once I was bitten by a wedged-head snake

I have known storytellers
who spoke only in the darkness
and I have felt wilderness
surround the town

but you, my children, and children's children
will not know Sabbaths
rituals of the moon.
your fast days will be fast

wherever you go
there is the light switch

fireplaces that burn
without wood

you bring space with you
there is no far, no near
you wonder like Lapps
information is your caribou

I have not lived to tell you
what is right or what is wrong
or to tell you one life
is better than another
there is danger in all life
in all ages, in all moments
no one I am certain
can ever escape this

carry my thumb drive like a shaman
carries an ancestor's bones
load my image to speak once a year
dance by the monitor's light

my ghost will say
it is more valuable
to know what you have lost
than what you have gained

my parents are in the ground
they come to me in dreams
speaking like fallen apples
pressing their lips to the earth

I shall not tell you all my grief
in electronic bites
but I counsel you
remembering soothes more than forgetting

does not the sea make death into a beach?
are not your genes castles of ancestors?
the silicon that was once sand
becomes the channeling chip

I am with you in all data
I am absence answering to your one

I am a footprint on alluvial shores
moons scratched on mastodon bones

keep this ritual until herds return to the plain
the gods are but flickering shadows of ourselves
measure yourself by the past's faithfulness
this is the span of my palm

CHAPTER 2

LAST CHILDREN IN THE WOODS

"In the space of a century, the American experience of nature has gone from direct utilitarianism to romantic attachment to electronic detachment."
—from *Last Child in the Woods* by Richard Louv

"These were the woods the river and sea / Where a boy / In The listening / Summertime of the dead whispered the truth of his joy / To the trees and the stones and the fish..."
—from "Poem in October" by Dylan Thomas

In 2005, Richard Louv published his best-selling book called *Last Child in the Woods*. It confirmed what I already knew — that children today are separated more profoundly from nature than at any other time in history. This separation is not an arithmetic separation but a geometric progression. The confluence of so many changes in the U.S. has resulted in a leap to a quasi-human species, *Homo electronicus. Homo electronicus* can stay indoors in front of some kind of monitor for long periods of time. It can stay outdoors for extended periods of time as long as its monitors are shaded. It can walk with monitors. *Electronicus* explores and discovers with monitors. It socializes with monitors. Monitors carry its memory. It encounters adventure with gaming monitors.

The labyrinth of the brain of *Homo electronicus* has been reconfigured by the use of computers and smartphones. I like to think of these new technologies in terms of mythology where Daedalus (the consummate archetype of the inventor) designs a labyrinth to contain the monster the Minotaur. In my case, I see the mother boards as labyrinths and the screens that hold the children captive as the "Monitaur." The Monitaur eats the brains and imaginations of our sacrificial young. It does not require much research to conclude that these technologies have affected memory, attention span, cognitive abilities, addictive behaviors, social and emotional development, and sleep cycles. The human brain's neuroplasticity allows it to alter itself to these electronic experiences — the young are caught in a synaptic maze that has never before existed.

I try not to be too critical of this brave, new world and try not to put my childhood experiences up on a pedestal of nostalgic superiority. Maybe I'm so out of touch that I join the ranks of all the old fogeys of history, who are always perturbed by the new generation. Maybe this is the new, evolutionary destiny for humans — to become cyborgs. All I can say is that the break with nature is something significant for me and that, if we are heading for a society that is part flesh and part robot, I would choose to retain my unaltered body unto death. I do not wish to be a part of this evolutionary path of the machine.

Night Sky and Windows to the Soul

Progress is a word that has been used to describe our pathway toward a culture that has less and less to do with the natural environment. Many see the new electronic technologies in terms of progress and better than nature. Yet I think in order to appreciate and evaluate what you have, you need to be aware of what you have lost. Some of these losses can be subtle and elusive for those that have never experienced them. For instance, the night sky.

What awe was available when I was a child and looked up at the night sky! An uncountable proliferation of heavenly bodies — stars, constellations, planets, and the trail of the Milky Way. Our minute position in the universe was confirmed in the vastness of the galaxy and our sense of mystery/god became heightened in this immensity. To lose this was not like losing reception on the television set. It was like losing the Grand Canyon.

I did not require a great deal of training nor a telescope to lie on my back at night and gaze in wonder at the night sky. It was a profoundly spiritual experience available to most people in the United States. But with polluted air and the ambient light of most communities, it's rare for our imaginations to be filled with the firmament. Today, I feel this loss deeply, living in Charlotte, North Carolina, where I can never look into the edge of the Milky Way Galaxy. Mostly I see the tattered light from a few countable stars trying to compete with savaged air and streetlights. The planes going to and from our airport have outcompeted the stars and fill our minds with our own lesser creations. Now it's only when I go to darkened beaches or mountain heights that I can see the North Star clearly and orient myself to the mystery of a universe that is receding faster than the speed of light.

Besides losing the night sky, another loss for our times is the loss of night itself. Without other forms of entertainment, neighborhood families were out a lot at night. The adults sat in lawn chairs and the children careened all over the neighborhood, checking in occasionally for food or drink. We played in the night's coolness, we collected lightning bugs, and we rolled on the ground, becoming food for chiggers. When the socializing ended, we were called in to prepare for bed.

Bedtime was not a clear demarcation between inside and outside. Without air conditioning and pollutants, we slept by screened-in windows. You could smell the night and its ever-changing odors. The breezes brought news of a storm, and the rain's patter was better than any lullaby that I've ever heard. The crickets told of shorter days until the coming cold, the owls proclaimed their authority in the kingdom of darkness, and distant train whistles worked into your dreams with longing for lands far away.

I feel so claustrophobic today when I close the windows at night. We keep out the abused air, we have tamed the temperature, and we listen to the hums of refrigerators and central air. If it rains, we do not know until the next day. We are not signaled to awaken with the morning cacophony of birds. We, indeed, are becoming one with the inside; we are becoming one with the machine. While many find the dream of living on a starship like Star Trek's *Enterprise* an ultimate goal for humanity, I find this thought to be my ultimate, indoor nightmare. I slept better as a child and deeper because I felt connected to the outside world and nature.

Sheltered Childhoods

The impulse to build shelters, I believe, runs deep in our DNA. We are almost as compelled to do it as birds are compelled to build nests. As children in the 50s, we were obsessed with making a dwelling of our own. We built teepees, tree houses, huts, lean-tos, and even attempted underground dwellings. Our designs depended on the availability of castaway materials, which could be branches, used boards, poles, canvas, burlap bags, cardboard, tin sheets, and more.

Comfort was a relative concept in our designs. Living conditions in our shelters would have been grounds for Children and Family Services to take away children from parents. For us, our sweatboxes were always ten degrees hotter than the outside air, and the insect life thrived with ants, spiders, and mosquitos abounding. But, if you built a hut of your own, you looked upon it as a five-star hotel. To add to the discomfort was always the central fire hearth. Fire still held for us the glow of ancient ancestors — a source of power. Whatever we cooked over the fire, which were mostly hot dogs and marshmallows, was delicious. The water from our corroded canteens was delicious.

The amount of time one could spent in these was limited. We'd get bored quickly after the construction, the initial ritual fire in the firepit, cooking food, playing cards, and laying down ragged blankets for beds. Soon it was time to go and make forays to see what we could find for home improvements or what kind of tribal adventures we could have before our return.

One of our favorite building sites was a large lot on the other side of the road from Berrian Park. The lot was overrun with small locust trees, all six to ten feet high. The foliage was dense, and the locust limbs were full of thorns, which we liked essentially because it kept other kids out. We enjoyed using our axes and chopping out a clearing and then bending and binding uncut saplings to make a structure. The chopped-up trees we weaved into the frame for a covering of our hut. The advantage of this location was that it was near a park, so that if we wanted to, we could store bats, balls, and gloves in our shelter and go over to the park and play baseball when we were bored. But the greatest advantage of our location was that it abutted a brickyard.

The brickyard was on a hill overlooking our jungle below. The cinder blocks were stacked into uneven walls about twenty feet high. For us, these were castle walls and parapets. We liked to make raids on the castle, scaling its walls and brandishing sticks that we had sharpened with our pocketknives. The enemies were the yard employees. They shouted at us to get off the stacks of bricks because we could get hurt. They occasionally made attempts to go after us and drag us down, but we were far too nimble for them. We leaped from stack to stack with the agility of mountain goats. Finally, the enemy just gave up, which left us to turn on each other with sword fights and mock deaths falling off the wall.

The brickyard provided us with another activity that oddly became a passion — rock breaking. It sounds like what people do in prison. Again, no adult could have told us to do this; it would have seemed like a punishment. But we relished going to the brickyard's sand pile and digging out the large rocks. Wherever the yard got their sand, it was always mixed with an array of larger, disposable rocks of all shapes, sizes, and material. We would squirrel them out onto the concrete road and hit them with a sledgehammer. Sometimes we had to hit a rock three or four times before we split it to see what was inside.

Seeing what was inside was what goaded us on from rock to rock. We looked mainly for diamonds, rubies, sapphires, or flecks of gold. Once in a while we would find an ugly rock about the size and shape of a human brain — a geode. Splitting open a geode was a real surprise because the ugliness on the outside belied the diamondlike crystals that filled the inside. Of course, we thought these were diamonds and stored them in our camp as treasure. The geode has always provided me with the metaphor of what could be inside a person's brain unbeknownst to people outside. Who knew from outside appearance if the person I looked upon as ugly could be inside like a crystal palace?

Our camp building had reached its pinnacle and decline after we decided to build an underground village. The impracticality of it never entered our minds. We had no thoughts of how we would brace it or light it — all we knew was that the first step was digging a tunnel. As we sweated with picks and shovels in an empty field, a man in a city truck came by and stopped.

"Do you boys know you're digging into a gas line?"

"What's a gas line?"

"It's a pipe filled with flammable gas that goes to homes that burn gas for stoves and heat. If you hit that line with a pick, you could let all the gas go. And you might even blow yourselves up with a spark."

That was the last camp we ever attempted. Our utopian dreams seemed to fade after that, and we were, after all, getting older with other interests taking priority. I'm sure we would have gone on full tilt had the movie *Swiss Family Robinson* came along after this. No camp builder could have resisted this enclave of paradisiacal bliss, adding the possibility of romance with a girl to our building obsession.

Once Upon a Flora/Fauna

Roaming about in parks, overgrown empty lots, woods, meadows, creeks, ponds, river banks, cliffs, etc. led to many sensual encounters. It would be difficult to estimate what these encounters did unconsciously for us. Our "senses" of the world — the images we maintained in our minds, the background sounds in our heads, the feel of breeze and trees, the smells of decaying organic materials, and the taste of wild foods — came together in an unnoticed ecology that held together our experiences.

Encounters with Animals

Unplanned meetings with wild animals are significant moments. They run deep into the psyche, with a combination of fear or wonder. Each creature is a mystery and has a long history with humanity. Snakes, for instance, are especially provocative in our imaginations. I would say we are wired to avoid snakes. We see snakes before we "see" them. If I am walking and there's a snake shape in front of me, I jump before my conscious mind determines whether it's a snake or not. It may be a stick or a vine, but my subconscious warns me quickly.

In our play, especially near creeks and rivers, we often ran into snakes. The first thing we always did was to identify the snake. Wedged heads, hourglass patterns, and orangish color meant copperhead. We gave these a wide berth, which didn't mean we left them alone. We'd either drive them away with long branches and stones or kill them.

By far the greater number of snakes that we encountered were non-venomous — garter snakes, blacksnakes, water snakes, puff adders, and corn snakes. Even though some of them were not venomous, it didn't mean they wouldn't bite you or be aggressive. You didn't have to surprise a group of water snakes to be bitten; they would come for you. If you were in their territory, run. Often we'd find snakes that were either strangling a prey or snakes with jaws unhinged swallowing its victim whole. It was a lesson that nature has nothing to say about cruelty. Snakes must do what they do to eat. They give no mercy to the cute chipmunk going down its gullet. It's prey for snakes; pray for the human world. The following poem is about this ethical dilemma for humans and god:

Swallowing Whole

parting grasses near a tree bole
I open a curtain to an ancient scene –
black snake coiled around a chipmunk.
the chipmunk's mouth curled
in agony of last prayer.
merciful man
what to do.

deus ex machina
I could unravel this drama
with my hands unwinding the twists
head to tail,

or like Alexander simplify the tangle
with my knife.

in a youth
unattuned to tragedy
I would have watched this drama
siding with prey,
prejudiced by myths
of deceiving serpents,
and fangs in the heel.

but I have seen the vulnerability of snakes
shedding skins,
helpless as strangers passing through.
or jaws unhinged
unable to plead their cases,
like witches of Inquisition.

this alimentary script says
that we eat our prayers
that mercy may be an injustice
that the abstractions we mouth
do not exceed the next meal.

I do not stay for the climax,
or the darkened tunnel toward death
— and life.
swallowing whole is a paradise
difficult to accept.
best to walk away
as God does.

Another creature that came to our attention one day was a strange elongated, black fruit, hanging from a branch on a tree. It was about fifteen feet above us and, in order to knock it down, we used a clothesline prop. I remember striking it fairly hard, and it plummeted to the ground. I was shocked by what hit the ground — it had shape-shifted into a creature with the most hideous face I had ever seen. The face was black with pointed ears and a mouth with needle teeth that hissed out a high-pitched sound. My mates stampeded off, while I remained standing confronting this grotesque animal. All I knew was that I couldn't let it up, whatever it was.

So, I kept hitting it and hitting it until it was dead. I had seen bats hunting in the twilight, but I had never seen one so up close and in a defensive posture in daylight. I needed no movies after that to teach me about what the perception of horror might make one do. I have a guilt that still resides in me for panicking and killing that helpless animal.

Creatures to encounter resided in all kinds of places in the nature we explored. To search them out was a matter of knowledge and faith that they would be there. There is a squirrel's nest and, if we take our slingshots and shoot into it, it will come out. There must be crawdads in this pond, even if we can't see them. Then we'd tie pieces of raw chicken giblets to a string and cast it in the water. We had faith they would come nibbling, and we could haul them in. Perch will be in this shady spot in the stream, even though we can't see them. The chipmunk will have another exit to its burrow — look and you will find it. Dig here and you will find earthworms and grub worms for fishing. The V-shaped tracks in the snow lead to the rabbit's burrow — lock and load your shotgun. Everywhere there were signs to "ferret" out life, and one was always learning a new visual/verbal vocabulary for the behaviors of each kind of creature. As Paul Shepard, the nature writer, has written, "Every child is committed to the use of animal images in the shaping of his own consciousness because thought arose in the past as an interaction between different animals and between people and animals."

Encounters with Plants

If you're a child of the woods, one of the first plants that you must identify is poison ivy. Taxonomy becomes a part of your life when you realize you might have to spend a week with itchy, running sores. There was always somebody in our group that had wandered into a patch of poison ivy and had to wear their pink badge of discourage, Calamine Lotion. Remember: three leaves with a prominent center leaf notched on both sides and the attendant leaves notched on one side like a mitten. Remember: it can be a vine or a small plant; as an old vine, it has hairy stems that snake around the tree. We were experts about poison ivy. We could even identify the look-alikes of boxelder and Virginia creeper and roam among them with impunity.

Another plant that could get your attention as you were roaming in fields and meadows was stinging nettle. Often, we had our shirts off in our explorations. If you happened to wade through a patch of chest high nettle, it wasn't long before you were on the run like you were being attacked by a swarm of bees. You would try rolling in the grass to make the pain subside. Soon a blistery rash arose on your skin that lasted for about three days.

Stinging nettle was a plant that had an evolutionary mechanism to dissuade grazing animals from feeding on them. The plant was hairy on both leaves and stems. Some of the hairs were specialized to break off and pierce skin like a hypodermic needle filled with poison. Needless (or Needles) to say, we were always on the alert for the nettle's saw-toothed leaves shaped like elongated hearts, the small flowers on top that came out of the leaf axils, and the fine deadly hairs that covered the plant.

Other plants that we kept an eye out for were plants for which we had special uses. Cattail and mullein flowerheads dunked in kerosene made for good tiki torches. Ragweed, despite its prominence as a major source of pollen that caused "hay fever," were used as spears in late fall when they had lost their leaves and became straight shafts from six to ten feet tall. If you pulled a ragweed stem out of the ground, its taproot was pointed, and the feeder roots provided just the necessary weight for a projectile. Crabgrass made for the best whistles held between thumbs. Pokeberries could be used for ink, and milkweed for glue.

The most exciting and enduring of my encounters with wild plants were their edibility. Free food! No grocery store or farmer as the middleman but offerings right off the vine. I agreed with Nigel Calder when he said, "Eden was no garden, but a gathering paradise." Without toil, I could eat my way through a hike and bring back food for the family.

I never saw *weeds* as evil as many do today. Each had its particular properties and usefulness. Wild garlic, dandelions, chicory, and English plantain were edible, so why spend time killing them in your yard to establish some kind of grass fascism. Weeds were nature's cornucopia. Those raspberry and blackberry vines weren't weeds; they were snacks on hikes and brought home to my mother to make jams. The same with wild strawberries that grew by the old railroad tracks. They were smaller than the domesticated variety, but twice as sweet. You had to be able to distinguish them from cinquefoil and mock strawberry, which had very similar leaves with yellow flowers instead of white flowers. The berries of mock straw-berry while not poisonous were bland and dry, and their seeds were on the outside of the berry instead of inside.

The wild grape had both berries and leaves that were edible. But, unlike the wild strawberry, the wild grape had some look-alikes that were toxic. The berries and leaves on Canadian moonseed looked very similar and both were poisonous. Exacerbating the problem was the fact that they often grew in the same places. I'd always squeeze a purple berry to see if it had just one seed and if that seed was crescent-moon shaped (moonseed; no eat). Pokeweed, also, presented a problem because people made poke salad, so you would think the purple, grapelike berries would be edible. Not so. If I were to choose a fruit to replace the apple tree in the Garden of Eden, I would choose pokeweed. Their berries looked terribly delicious to me as a child and so much like juicy, purple grapes. It only took one try to realize they were toxic and thankfully not deadly in such a small quantity. I lived a wiser Adam after that.

Before I move on to trees as a source of food, I can't forget the one fungus in my litany of wild edible foods. I include it because it was such a grand prize to those who discovered its haunts — the mighty morel. Anyone who found a patch of morel mushrooms never reveals their location. As mushroomers would say, "I could tell you where I found them, but then I'd have to kill you." The other saying that mushroomers told us was, "There are only two kinds of mushroomers — the bold and the old." That was drilled into my head. It was so to speak my "morel compass," and I never experimented with eating other funguses. In our area, the mo-rels were gray to black, about an inch or two high and grew in villages. My mother could fix them like no one else. She'd bread them and fry them lightly. They were juicy with an indescribable, earthy flavor.

The real windfalls of edibles came from trees. Walnuts and hickory nuts could be found in great numbers. Collecting the walnuts in their chartreuse hulls made for stained and smelly fingers. I loved the strong odor of walnut hulls and, even if I weren't collecting them, I liked to rub them against my hands and arms to carry the smell with me. If we brought a bunch of nuts home, we set up shop with a building block, hammers, and small picks. We'd break open the nut on the building block and pick out the meat. Usually, it was a lot of work for not very much meat. We tried to eat acorns, the meatier nuts of oaks. Of course, they were extremely bitter. We didn't know you had to leech them of their tannin before they were fit to eat or make flour with. The white oaks could be palatable raw, but just barely.

Besides nuts, trees provided us with wild fruit. A number of rogue apple and pear trees survived in nearby forests and meadows. The fruit was usually smaller and mottled but could be gathered in great quantity. The apples usually had a biting taste to attest to their wildness. Wild pears had a tendency to be hard and were good for compotes. Both fruit trees had a tendency to be short and branchy because of their battles with deer that chewed off their extremities.

Once I remember collecting crab apples and squeezing them with a hand press juicer. To get just a quart of juice required what seemed to me a thousand little apples. I recruited my two younger brothers to help with the squeezing. To this day, they have never forgiven me for giving them such a tedious task. But I was determined I was going to make crabapple wine. With some sugar added, I kept the juice in a mason jar for a year (I had almost forgotten about it). When I finally opened it, the brew inside was murky and not exactly inviting. It had a strong smell that opened up my nostrils. There could be no doubt that it had alcohol in it because when I tasted it, it made my hair stand on end. Whoa, baby! The strong taste, however, did not spoil the joy I felt in having made my own alcohol. *Maybe I'll go into business*, I thought.

Besides the practical purposes of providing food, kindling, and building material, let me say unequivocally, trees are the plants that own my soul. They were parents and elders overlooking our childhood activities. We gathered beneath their embracing shade to play games, build objects, make fires, chatter idly, and swing in hammocks. We were aware on some level of their beauty — the shimmering leaves of cottonwoods in the sun; the spectacular colors of sugar maples in the fall; the maples' samaras dropping on our head like grace; the spreading, regal crowns of oaks; and the cool, soft padded oases of pine forests. In the evenings on the horizon, the inky, silhouettes of trees joined heaven and earth.

I have kept faith all my life with trees. For me, they are like friends, and there are trees that I still visit when I return to Quincy. There are, also, trees whose absence saddens me as much as the death of a loved one. Like Thoreau, I could tramp "...eight or ten miles through the deepest snow to keep an appointment with a beech-tree, or a yellow birch, or an old acquaintance among the pines."

My father's generation suffered and mourned the loss of the chestnut tree; for me, it was the loss of the elm tree. Both trees were swept away by blights — huge and magnificent trees brought down to their stumps by ineradicable fungi. The Berrian Park elms, 150 years old, were reduced to rubble on the battlefield of Dutch Elm Disease. Two neighborhood elms ceased their parenting of our play. The poem below is my elegy to these trees.

Remembering the Elm
Ulmus americana

our days began
on elm-shaded steps
plenty of twigs to break
and flick until we were taken
by a breeze of purpose

if it was baseball
then to Berrian Park
where an elm played backstop
for errant pitches

provided oasis for canteen breaks
and baloney sandwiches

if hide and seek
then to back-alley elms
young enough to climb
or to the flanged old elms
with roots high enough
to lie between

if camp site
then to the meadow elm
with fire pit and sticks to burn
bark cavities to stash tools
plastic soldiers, geode diamonds

one summer we heard
"Dutch Elm Disease"
yellow crusted leaves
marched from elm to elm
leaving behind skeletal branches
the dead were sawed close to the ground
leaving spidery bases
as historical markers

I would walk now more
than Thoreau's eight miles
to greet an old elm
grandfather hands
lifting one hundred feet
holding more years
than my embrace
lifting one hundred feet

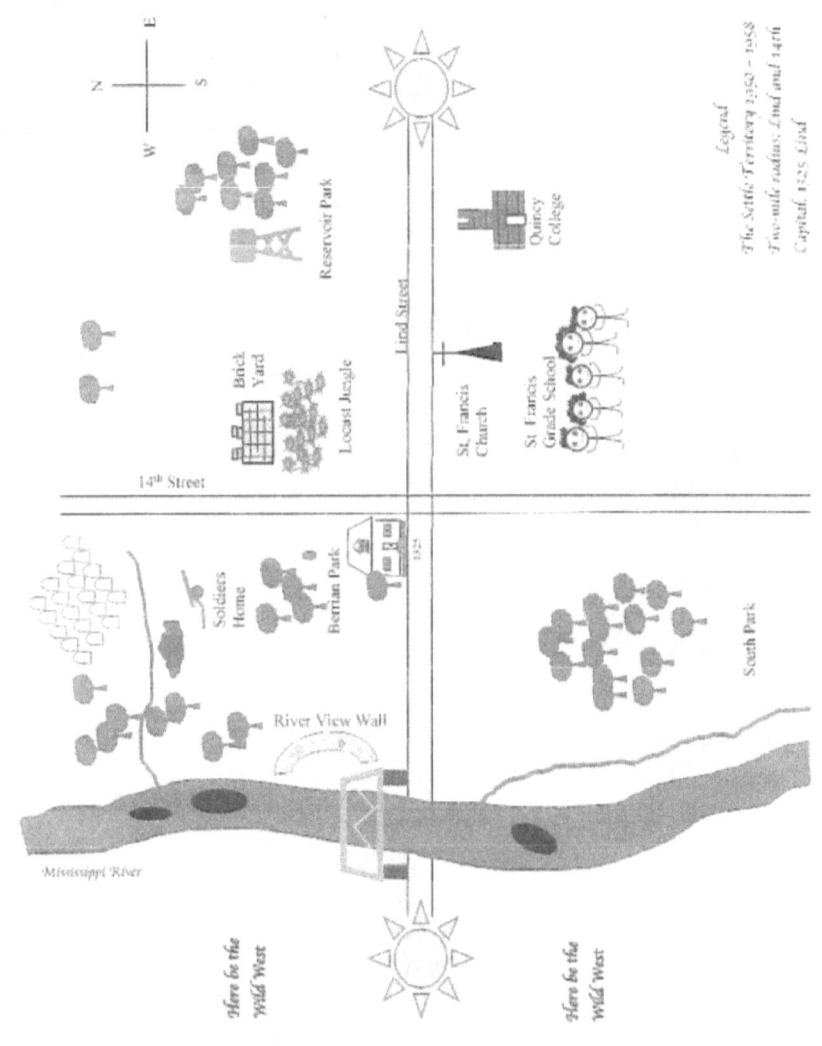

Map of our Play Territory

Backward Forward

Our generation was the first to be moving toward the "last children in the woods." If you compared what my father had done in his childhood with my own, you could tell that the post-WWII, rapacious industrialism and agri-business were beginning to pollute both the city and countryside. The empty lot next to the brickyard would soon be bulldozed for housing and commerce. The creeks became sudsy and filled with refuse. And the appearance of wildlife dwindled as creatures had to live a subsistence existence.

I have tried to capture the inroads of this break between the past and present in the following poem. It reflects not only physical pollution but the moral pollution that goes with it.

Cane Creek

as a boy my father stole watermelons
and hid them to cool
in deep currents of Cane Creek

naked in the sun
he would swim with friends
then find shade in hanging willows

on shores below the falls
the ritual of watermelon required
a piece of chert to split seams

hands to dig out flesh
lips and tongue
to spew the farthest seed

2

when my time came
I cycled to the creek with friends
we scoured the countryside for watermelons to steal

there were none
only acres of soybean and corn
a chain-link fence encircled the new plant

falls fell with detergent foam over
lime stones stippled with fossils
we knew we would not swim

looking for something that could be a story
among caches of rusted beer cans
we found a magazine curled in leaves

we peeled the decayed pages
to feast on the secrets of our bodies
what men do to women to swell their bellies

The actual name for the creek was Whipple Creek, but I changed the name to Cane Creek for poetic reasons. Pollution of land, body, and mind are inter-weaved. You cannot have one without the others.

As with most future developments, we as a people can change them if we don't like them. All we need have is the will. Children *can* be provided with the wherewithal to experience nature in an unfettered way. In order to do this, we would have to change a lot of liability laws. You can't play in nature without cuts, bruises, insect and snake bites, broken bones, and, perhaps, worse. Places with wildlife and unpolluted water could be made available to children, even in the city. And systems of unsupervised play could be developed that keep adults on the periphery and keep away any threats from pedophiles. There would be no smart phones in these oases; there would be tools provided, but no power tools. And there would be animals and plants making a living in these areas.

Of course, this approach would require risk. The question would be — is it worth the risk? I think to truly answer this question, parents would have to realize that over-protecting children is also a risk. What do we risk when we hover over our children to the point that their clothes never get dirty? We have found that children living in environments too sanitized develop allergies. They don't build up the immunities of children playing in dirt. Do children need to grow *down* as much as they need to grow *up*? Do they need to be balanced by sinking their roots into the natural world? What do we risk when we try to make children's lives totally safe? What do we lose if children's imaginations are shaped by monitors where fantasy heroes replace the complexity of living beings in nature? Those quest-ions are charged, and how you answer them attaches to what you think the future should be.

CHAPTER 3

STORIES TOLD FROM A KNEELER

"It is the test of a good religion whether you can joke about it."
—G.K. Chesterton

Beginning of Scenario

You are a policeman cruising the neighborhoods at five o'clock in the morning. It's winter and there's a blustering wind that is creating snowdrifts that smooth out bushes to cupcakes. Suddenly, you see a little figure bundled up like an Eskimo child with head down facing the elements as he trudges with rubber, buckled boots. The snow seeps over the top of his boots.

You turn on your flashing lights and stop the boy, thinking that he is a runaway and needs to be taken to a shelter. You get out of your car:

"Hey, little man, what are you doing out so early in the snow. Running away from home?"

"No, sir. I'm going to St. Francis Church. I'm serving Mass."

"Well, I'm not a Catholic, but isn't Mass on Sunday, and isn't it a little early?"

"All I know is that priests have to say mass every day, and we got a lot of priests at St. Francis. The early masses are called Duck Hunter masses."

"But ducks aren't in season."

"Doesn't matter. There are always five-thirty masses."

"How old are you, boy?"

"Ten, sir."

"How come your mom doesn't drive you? St. Francis is quite a trek in this weather."

"My mom never gets up for Duck Mass mornings. She just sets my alarm, and I sleep on the couch, so I don't disturb the rest of the family."

"Well, I hope you had a good breakfast at least."

"Can't. Got to fast because I'm going to communion. No food or drink from midnight till after Mass."

End of Scenario

What does the police officer do? Does the officer take the child home and talk to the parents? Does he go to St. Francis Church to see if, indeed, there is a Duck Hunters Mass? Does the officer turn over the child to Children and Family Services?

In the 1950s, I was this boy in the wee hours of morning making my way to serve early Mass. I was among many who did the same thing, and I was preceded by many of my relatives who went through the same ordeal. I say "ordeal," even though at the time I thought nothing of it. Neither my parents nor I thought it was unsafe for me to be walking the streets at 5 a.m. The police in our town would not have stopped me because I was out. And the idea of not having breakfast for a morning would impinge on my schoolwork or my energy in the playground didn't occur to my mother. Till this day I don't eat breakfast despite what all the pundits say.

St. Francis Solanus Church

Becoming an Angel Scout

Why would any child of ten *choose* to do this? I remember the beginning of sixth grade when the call went out for try-outs for altar boys. "Try-outs" — yes, try-outs. Volunteering was not enough and only a handful of those that wanted to be altar boys became altar boys. You went through a kind of basic training to earn your surplice (the outer white top of the altar boy).

This picture shows the common regalia of an altar boy.

If you think boys sought to be altar boys for religious reasons, you would be far off the mark. Most of us resisted holiness with a passion. No one wanted to be the pious boy-saint Dominic Savio, who was reputed to kneel in the snow in adoration of our Savior. No, our salvation had more to do with prestige. We wanted to be like the eighth-grade guys who were on the main altar with an angelic patina that appealed to teachers, parents, and girls. This status had to be earned through a series of obstacle courses.

Veni, Vidi, Vinci

The first major test of endurance eliminated a lot of the novices seeking to become eagle scouts of the altar. I'll give you a hint: "Ad Deum qui laetificat juventutem meam" (to God, Who gives joy to my youth). I don't believe those words gave any joy to me, but these were the first lines that an altar boy needed to recite. They are so ingrained in me that I'm sure I'll be able to recite them in a dementia ward, where the nurses will confirm that I am out of my mind because I'm mumbling nonsense.

Memorizing Latin for the Tridentine Mass (the Latin Eucharistic liturgy used by the Roman Catholic Church from 1570 to 1964) at the time was a process that took months. Of course, we had no idea of the meaning of the sounds we were memorizing nor were we even curious. We did, however, have a few phrases that we made into jokes, which helped along the memorization. For instance, the Pope's phone number was "et cum spiritu tuo" (2-2-0). And we did have prayers that had rhythmic repetition — *mea culpa, mea culpa, mea maxima culpa* (through my fault, through my fault, through my most grievous fault) — that made memorizing easier.

But in general, it was just raw rote drilling of meaningless syllables into your head. In order to support us in the process, we were assigned our own eighth grade drill sergeant instructor, altar boy, who had earned his stripes. Every day my drill sergeant moved me syllable by syllable toward a complete recitation of my Latin prayers, until I was ready for the next step of the obstacle course.

Brother Martin

"Pious" is a word that is seldom used today, and with good reason because there are few persons that could be described by this word. The word has gone out of fashion not because there is no such thing, but because no one sees it anymore to put a word with it. Of all the priests, nuns, and brothers who taught me about piety as I was being raised Catholic, not one incarnated this virtue except Brother Martin.

Most people who are not Catholic are familiar with priests and nuns, but most are unfamiliar with brothers. Brothers are like priests in that they are male, but unlike priests in that they do not say mass or disperse the sacraments. Brothers are the male counterparts of nuns, and they provide a variety of services — all the way from carpentry to teaching to janitor to household management.

Brother Martin was a Franciscan brother, who took care of all the liturgical needs of the altar, a kind of stage manager for the Mass. Into his purview came the training of altar boys. After we had learned our Latin prayers, the next part of our training had to do with the choreography that was the Mass. We needed to know where to move in synchrony with the priest, when to genuflect, when to bow, when to ring bells, and when to assist the priest with wine and water.

When I began my instruction in Mass choreography, there were six of us that met in the sacristy awaiting instruction. As you would expect from young primates, we were goofy and noisy. Then, Brother Martin walked in, or I should say limped in. He was pale and old with thinning white hair, wearing the brown Franciscan robe and the rope belt with three knots of chastity, poverty, and obedience. He had the most peaceful face that I had ever seen, like water that only reflected. When he spoke, he spoke barely above a whisper, and we all leaned in, concentrating on what he had to say. From that moment on, any notion of giddiness left us as he began revealing the mysteries of the dance of the Mass.

Brother Martin Lang

I have never been with a person who commanded so much purity of spirit. He never raised his voice to us, and he never pleaded for our attention. When we went out onto the main altar to practice, I suddenly felt immersed in sacredness — a feeling quite new to me despite all the rituals that I had participated in. It was Brother Martin's genuine piety that seemed caterpillar-like in its ability to cocoon you in his silky silence.

There was much more to learn in the dance between priest and altar boy than the untrained would expect. First of all, there were many kinds of Masses — low Mass, high Mass, Requiem Mass (for the dead), seasonal Masses, and Masses with Benediction — each with different setups and duties. There were many configurations of priest and altar boy all the way from one altar and one priest to multiple priests and altar boys. The fancier the service the more coordination was required of the movements of the votaries.

Besides movement, there were a host of skills that you needed to learn. Some ceremonies required a censer — a device on chains with hot coals to burn incense. The censer (also, known as the thurible) was swung like a pendulum side to side, and as it swished through the air, a scented smoke emerged. The smoke was symbolic of purification and of prayers ascending into the heavens. As far as I was concerned the scent and smoke made me want to sneeze and cough.

Candle lighting was another skill. You wouldn't think that lighting candles would be a skill, but it is if you light candles that go up to ten feet high on the high altar. To do this required a brass candle lighter five feet long. You would load the candle lighter with a waxed taper a couple of feet long that could be fed from the handle into the tip of the lighter. When lit, this device was raised above the candles. If you were lucky, the wick (which you couldn't see) stood erect within the candle's brass cap. If you were unlucky, the wick was lying on its side in the wax. In these situations, you had to give the lighter more taper, creating a rather large flame for the wick to catch on fire. If you were really unlucky, the wick wouldn't catch, and you became a source of entertainment for those attending mass, wondering how long your arms could hold out or if you were creating a big enough flame to burn down the church. At the end of the service, you would snuff out the candles with the empty brass bell on the other side of the lighter.

Once we finished our tutelage with Brother Martin, he was not entirely out of our lives. We often needed refresher courses in some of the more complicated liturgical events like Stations of the Cross and Processions. But, perhaps most lasting in our encounters with Brother Martin, we got to see him in our peripheral vision during the Masses. He would be kneeling with his crippled leg stretched out on a single kneeler in the sacristy. He was not visible to the congregation. Even with his damaged leg, he knelt during the entire service and kept one fist on his breast. There was a glow on his face that came from the dim light in the darkened sacristy, and his expression was one of total ecstasy. I always thought that one day I would glance over at him, and he would be levitating as God took him bodily into heaven.

The Father Cyrenus Test

Having passed all the tests up to this point, you were qualified to be a server for a priest at an actual Mass on a public altar. This was the final test, and it was subtly designed to be a test of your resolution to be an altar boy. The first priest that you would serve for would not be just any priest, and the Mass you served would not be just any Mass.

My first assignment as neophyte altar boy was a week's worth of the earliest Mass at 5:30 a.m. You had to show commitment to be able to get up at 5 a.m. with no food and make your way to the rectory in total darkness in all kinds of weather. But this would be a minor inconvenience to the second part of this assignment — you were to be paired with Father Cyrenus.

After I had donned my cassock and surplice on my first outing as a PA (priest's assistant), I went upstairs for the preliminary aid that a server gives a priest with his vestments. He had not yet arrived, so I waited in the dim light of the neo-gothic sacristy of dark-stained oak. I could hear my priest coming before I saw him. His gasping breath made its way in my direction through a blackened corridor; it sounded like something wounded. This gasping was accompanied by a muffled scraping sound reminiscent of a corpse being drug across a waxed floor.

When Father Cyrenus made his appearance, his face came out of the darkness like a chiaroscuro of Satan himself. I was paralyzed. His sallow skin, the color of the undead, had deep furrows that looked like they had been made by bear claws. He had gray/black eyebrows that projected an inch in brambly profusion as they perched above two beady, burning coal eyes. He was in a bedraggled housecoat and slippers, and the little hair he had stuck out in maniacal directions. The dragging sound had come from his faded purple slippers, which slid along the floor as he walked. He never acknowledged me as he shuffled by, which was good because I was frozen and speechless.

I took a deep breath to break the initial shock of this vision and began to do what I was trained to do. I placed myself behind him to assist him in the process of putting on his alb, amice, and chasuble. When it came time for me to hand him the cincture (a rope belt that went around the alb /cassock), two hideous hands came together behind his back — his fingers had swollen knobs and his yellowish fingernails were so long they curled. Maybe, I told myself warily, Father Cyrenus's freakish appearance had got the best of my imagination, and things were going to be just fine once we made our way to the altar.

Wrong conclusion. Thank god, we were on some little side altar that no one paid any attention to. All the signals that priests are supposed to give their servers to perform certain tasks were done away with by Father Cyrenus. They were replaced by phrases like, "Move the damn book, boy" or "Ring those goddamn bells" (Surely, I thought, you can't say "goddamn" on the altar). When it came time to pour water and wine into the chalice, Cyrenus reversed the usual proportions — most priests took a tad of wine with a lot of water; Cyrenus took *all* the wine with a couple drops of water. Finally, Father Cyrenus was not much on waiting for my Latin responses, which I had to go through at supersonic speed.

The next six days with Father C didn't relax our relationship an iota. He still cussed on the altar and demanded responses that he had not signaled for. We never talked, and he never changed his cantankerous approach to the Mass. Later it was explained to me the anomaly of a priest who was kept in the deep recesses of the rectory never to be seen in daylight or by the general public.

It seems Father Cyrenus was a chaplain on the front lines in WWI. It was there that he was exposed to a relentless pounding of artillery and exposed to mustard gas that scarred his face. When the war was over, he was diagnosed as having "shell shock," a term which today we call PTSD (posttraumatic stress disorder). It seems he never mentally recovered from his war experiences. Since he was a Franciscan, his order was his family, and they dutifully cared for him within the seclusion of the priests' living quarters.

Cyrenus was the last hurdle that I passed to become an altar server. It was an initiation and reminiscent of a hazing. Once I had finished a week with Father Cyrenus, I belonged to an exclusive club, and all the older boys could now put their arms around me and say, "I hear you passed the Cyrenus test." And then there would be an exchange of stories of terror and relief.

And so it came to pass, I had overcome all obstacles thrown in my way to earn my angel scout badge. I would now be free to serve Mass on the main altar and be available for school masses, Sunday Masses, funerals, weddings, and a variety of sundry rituals provided by the Catholic Church.

Of the Unleavened and Levity

Perks of the Trade

Once I became a bona fide altar boy, I could begin to take advantage of the perks of the profession. First of all, there was the gateway drug of altar wine. Most altar boys knew where the altar wine was kept and on occasion took a couple of swigs not so much out of a zest for alcohol but a desire to be naughty. I don't believe anyone got sloshed on altar wine; in fact, it tasted god awful. Certainly not something you would serve to guests at your house. Further, there just wasn't the taboo of drinking for Catholics as there was for other Christian sects. We had a German congregation who loved their beer, and beer was often a part of our church fundraisers, with the parish priests tipping a few. Therefore, taking a few swigs of altar wine never seemed to be very sinful.

Personally, as a perk, I liked to eat the communion wafers of our church. When the wafers got stale, I would ask Brother Martin to give them to me. Since they weren't consecrated, they were considered just plain ole' unleavened bread. Of course, they were rather dry and stuck to the roof of your mouth. One of the first things you learned when you went to communion was how to peel "Jesus" with your tongue back toward your throat and swallow— no one liked the idea of chewing on "Jesus" with their teeth. When I brought home the unconsecrated hosts, my brothers and I tried to make them palatable by putting peanut butter and jelly on them — a kind of Catholic hors d'oeuvre.

Another food available to altar boys was the chocolate milk and stale rolls we would receive after serving Mass at the Catholic hospital. If this doesn't sound savory to you, that's because you've never had Modern Dairy chocolate milk in small bottles chilled in an ice bucket and day-old pastries from the hospital cafeteria. The combination of the two plus the forced communal fasting was what I would call gourmet. Forget your French sauces and caviar. I would pay a hundred dollars for a reprisal of these flavors.

Speaking of Tongues

In the old days at St. Francis, there was quite a distance between the congregation and the altar. Being up close to the main altar allowed one to see the small display of martyr's bones that were inserted into the altar. These bones provided me with a diversion when I was bored with the service. From grade school on, I had a fascination with the skeletal remains of beast or human. Looking at these bones, I always tried to imagine the life and suffering of the saint they belonged to. Then I wondered how one went about saving martyred bones. Did they dig them up later or when persecutors were gone, or were they pieces of a body torn apart and thrown to the crowd? Were they the real deal or were they phony like pieces of the true cross? Maybe they were the bones of an unknown soldier found in an old battlefield. And did they possess miraculous powers if someone would touch them? Why weren't they liberated to be touched by the congregation on certain holy days? Maybe there would be a miracle.

Tongues were another advantageous view for the altar boy. I don't mean speaking in tongues but observing tongues. Few people in their lives get to see people display their tongues in such close proximity as an altar boy. We're talking about a diversity of tongues — young tongues, old tongues, male and female tongues, diseased tongues, wounded tongues, short and long tongues, wide and narrow tongues. The reason for this was the ritual of communion.

When those at church in the 50s (it's done differently today) wanted to receive communion, they approached the altar railing and knelt twenty abreast. The priest placed a consecrated host on the tongues of each of them. An altar boy accompanied the priest with a brass plate on a foot-long handle called the paten. The paten made sure that any dropped hosts or pieces of hosts or hosts spit out were caught and disposed of in a sacred manner by a priest. It was always considered a special day if you caught a crumb of "Christ" and kept it from falling on the floor. If Jesus saved me, I could say on multiple occasions I saved Jesus.

The revelation of tongues came when people kneeling to receive communion had to lean their heads back, close their eyes, open their mouths, and stick out their tongues. The priest would then lay a host on their tongues. As easy as that sounds, there were problems for priest, altar boy, and parishioner. Some people did not open their mouths very wide nor stick out their tongues very far. The dexterity of the priest was challenged at this point to get a host on the tongue without breaking it on the person's teeth. This situation always caused altar boys to be alert for breakage and to hold the paten with special care to make a catch.

Then there were those who could not seem to coordinate opening their mouths, sticking out their tongues, and closing their eyes at the same time — sort of like rubbing your stomach and patting your head at the same time. Their eyes fluttered and their tongues darted in and out like serpents. The priest had to be quick to get a host on the tongue during the fraction of a second the tongue exited. Again, the altar boy waited tensely like a spotter in gymnastics. For me, I had the additional problem of not bursting out into laughter at these absurd displays of facial contortions.

The tongues that came out of people's mouths always posed imaginary stories for me. An old man's cratered tongue with pieces missing out of it suggested the scarred body of a warrior who had survived many battles on the plains of supper tables. The sharpened tongues of some women darted out of their lipstick like tropical fish out of coral. Then there were these bulky, slimy tongues of blue/ black color like a Shar Pei's. They reminded me of snails emerging from their shells. Going up and down the communion railing was a smorgasbord of tongues, emanating tales and fantasies. The best tongues of all were the tongues of the girls that you liked in school. I always gave them particular attention as well as giving the girl a slight karate chop in the Adam's apple with the paten. Ah, the signals of love at age twelve.

Taking a Knee

One of the quaint aspects of being Catholic is kneeling and genuflecting. You can't be a "sissy" and be a Catholic. You can't be a Catholic and have bad knees. Catholics are the NFL of Christian faiths. You're constantly popping up and down during the service like you're participating in some kind of exercise class. Sometimes you're kneeling for long periods of time when the only option to alleviate the pain is to cheat and rest your buttocks on the pew seat. I suppose it's better than some other religions where posturing can even be more difficult: the lotus position of Buddhism or the jilsah of Islam.

I was born in a family that was not good at kneeling. I don't mean to say that we didn't like to humble ourselves, but we had a long history of knee problems. My knees were knobby, and they cracked every time I genuflected. It was bad enough being a participant of the Mass as a congregant, where padded kneelers were provided, but as an altar boy the altar steps meant kneeling on marble. My bony knees never could find comfort on stone, and the pain that I felt resulted in my most passionate if not loftiest prayers — "Please, dear God, hurry this priest up."

The most excruciating ceremonies of all were those that required acolytes, a form of altar boy that carried a lantern on a long stick. The time spent on marble steps during these rituals of pomp and circumstance felt like I had joined the ranks of those tortured during the Inquisition. The marble ate into bones until the only way I could stay kneeling was to hold onto my acolyte lantern like a sailor holding onto a mast in a stormy sea. I had no trouble believing that communities of monks wore grooves into stone steps on which they kneeled over the centuries. I wish I had known about kneepads.

Sprechen Sie Deutsch?

Besides serving Mass at our parish, we also were recruited by St. Mary's Hospital to assist in religious services. These Masses were even farther away than those at the parish and required that I take my bicycle in order to get there. The same conditions of weather and early hours held for services in the hospital chapel. While a few patients, visitors, and workers at St. Mary's attended these masses, the bulk of attendees were a community of nuns who ran the hospital.

The first time I served morning mass at the hospital chapel I had to find out how to get to the sacristy. There was no back entrance. You had to cut through the chapel in order to get to the sacristy. They kept the chapel very darkened and, as I was making my way through, my motion was suddenly arrested by a lone figure in a pew that was apparently having a vision. She was a nun with her arms outstretched like the crucified Christ. As far as I knew there were no etiquette books that included what to do if you interrupt someone having a vision. Do you tiptoe past? Do you wait until the person's finished? Maybe you were intended to join in? Luckily, she put her arms down, and I assumed she was through with Jesus or Mary or some saint. Only later did I find out that this was the usual posture of prayer for this order of nuns.

When I made it to the sacristy, it was pitch black except for the flickering of a few votive candles.

"Hello, hello. Is anybody here?" I said just above a whisper. I could detect some black motion breezing past the candles.

"I'm here from St. Francis to serve Mass. Hellooh."

"Ichen haben der stabben fillen," came out of the darkness. (At least that's what I thought I heard. I knew no German.)

"I'm sorry. What did you say?"

Emerging from the darkness was the smallest nun that I had ever seen. She was like a rotund bowling ball with legs and arms and her rosary beads clacked fiercely as she moved.

She repeated, "Ichen haben der stabben fillen," and then turned on the lights in a room filled with cassocks and surplices. I assumed that she wanted me to get dressed.

After I dressed and came out of the room, she quickly turned off the lights. Maybe she belonged to a nocturnal order of nuns, I thought.

"Liten gesundheit vasser einem, bitte." I hesitated to move and then she pointed to the candle lighter and the altar candles.

"You want me to light the candles?"

"Yah, bitte."

For some reason the candles were particularly high and difficult to light. I forced the taper out quite a ways, until I had a ball of flame hovering over the candles. I could see pieces of wick floating down like black snowflakes.

"Nichts! Nichts! Auchtung vahausen ich liebe dich!" Sister Katharina yelled from the side lines. I suddenly noticed a drapery nearby was smoking. So, I quickly backed off and pulled in the taper.

"Patience, Marty. Patience," I told myself. I eventually persisted and lit the candles without burning down the hospital and throwing Sister Butterball into a guttural attack.

When mass was concluded, Sister Katharina appeared like a black apparition out of a corridor. She was carrying a basket, and she signaled me to put my surplice in it. Then she handed me the basket.

"Gehen tag frischimmel satzen einen. Yah."

"Eh...Yah."

She began to waddle in front of me, and I followed, not having the foggiest idea what I was supposed to do or where I was going. Soon we arrived at a steep set of stairs. She pointed to the top of the stairs where there was a closed door and a small landing. Then she trundled off, leaving me holding the basket. Not knowing what she wanted, I climbed the stairs and left the basket like an offering in front of the door. I must have done this twenty times before one day I bumped open the door with the basket and found a woman behind it who washed and ironed the clothes. It was almost like Sleeping Beauty finding the woman with a spinning wheel.

Getting the Clapper

The last Mass that I ever served at St. Mary's hospital was a memorable one. The Mass was on Good Friday and was a special one just for the nuns at the hospital. I was joined by two of my friends because this service was one of high ceremony.

When the three of us gathered in the sacristy, we laid out our duties ahead of time. Mike Broeker was going to take the censer, Bill Bregach was going to do communion, and I was going to ring the bells. All very straight forward and, as far as we knew, problem free.

When I took my place on the altar, I encountered the first problem of the day, the crotalus. I had forgotten that during this Lenten service, we did away with bells to keep a more somber mood during the weekend of Christ's passion. The crotalus was basically a wood bell that clacked instead of making pleasant bell tones. I had never used "the clapper" before, as it was sometimes called, but I thought to myself how hard could it be? Hard.

My first attempt at using its muffled sound was suggestive of someone falling down a set of wooden stairs. My companions stifled their laughter to keep a modicum of decorum. My confidence had been broken, and I wondered how I was going to attempt the next series of rings with the clapper. Obviously, I needed a new approach. I decided to be more vigorous with the crotalus. Bad move.

When I rang the Sanctus, which required three rings, or should I say "claps," I could see the nuns who were praying in their crucifixion postures, open their eyes, startled by the disturbance. This time I had created sounds that matched an all-out bar fight. Again, I could see my companions squelching their laughter with every fiber of their being.

While this was going on, the censer needed to be taken care of. During a high Mass, the priest and altar boys always huddled up like football players to feed incense to the censer. On this occasion, the censer had a broken ceramic top and the metal beneath it was exposed. This meant the altar boy holding up the lid, if unaware, could burn off the first layers of his fingertips. Bill Bregach was unaware, and I could see him grimacing as he held the lid up, watching the priest leisurely scooping up incense and then breaking it up into smaller chunks. It was an act of martyrdom the likes of which I had not seen. He never cried out in pain or dropped the lid onto the priest's fingers while his own fingers were smoldering.

Once the censer was refilled, the incense for whatever the reason was exceptionally smoky. When I looked back at Mike Broeker swinging the censer back and forth on his knees, I could see huge puffs of smoke billowing out. Soon he disappeared entirely into an opaque cloud. After about five minutes of these conditions, I heard a *clank* and a *clunk*. The *clank* came from the censer hitting the floor, spewing hot coals everywhere; the *clunk* came from Mike's forehead hitting the marble altar steps. He had passed out in the airless realm of pure, incense smoke.

A shout came from the wings, "Heimlich auf wedersehen mein Gott in heiben!"

The irony of all this was that it occurred in a hospital with a congregation who were mostly nurses. It was the perfect place for this accident. Mike was gathered up, put on a gurney, and brought to the emergency room where he received stitches for the cut over his eye. While he was being attended to, Bill, the other altar boy, put Vaseline on his burnt fingers, and lastly the priest had time to show me how to use the clapper. Sister Katharina attended to the burning coals, with epithets not understandable.

Thus, it was that Good Friday became a Bad Friday. Eventually we finished the service without any further mishaps. The three of us told that story for years afterwards. If anyone thought we were exaggerating, we'd use as evidence the scar over Mike's right eye.

Backward Forward

From my altar boy days, many changes have occurred in the Catholic Church's liturgy. The requirements, I'm sure, are no longer as rigorous as they once were. There is no Latin to memorize and no complex choreography to learn. Congregants give themselves communion standing without the need for priest or paten. And there are no longer just altar *boys* but altar *girls/servers*.

Since I no longer keep track of such things, I have no idea if they still have servers of age ten walking the streets at 5:00 in the morning. I know there is no longer a need to fast before communion. Thereby, there is no longer any danger of altar servers going hungry.

Even though I am no longer a Catholic, I like to on occasion visit a Catholic Church nearby that has the old Tridentine Mass. I fluidly follow the Latin and motions of the altar servers. Once in a while, I am treated to some of the old hymns written by the great composers of the 17th and 18th centuries — Haydn, Bach, Mozart, and Beethoven. If I'm really, really lucky, I get to hear a Requiem Mass where the last hymn is the hauntingly beautiful "Dies Irae." As a choir boy for funerals, I could mostly ignore the sadness of those attending the service but, when the Gregorian chant of the "Dies Irae" began, I became immersed in waves of sadness that went off into eternity.

Do I believe that the old ways of the Catholic Church were better? Was Vatican II mistaken when they changed the liturgy? I can say, first of all, that these changes were not my reason for leaving my Catholicism behind. I can, also, say I liked the old ways better. I liked the idea of not understanding what I was saying but knowing that what I was saying had been passed down for over a thousand years. My wife is Jewish and doesn't understand Hebrew, but she feels its mystery and history when she recites it.

Latin provided me with those same feelings.

In the old days, I could meditate in a pew while the Mass continued before me and wouldn't worry that I would miss a response or body position. After all, I had seen the ceremony a thousand times. Although it was always the same film that I was seeing, in each viewing I could take time out and ponder on a number of themes or ideas. Personally, I like less communal participation and more internal emancipation.

I liked and continue to like darkness in my churches to surround the mystery of it all. Votive candles flickering in darkness are the brief candles of our lives. Darkened churches are the modern versions of our ancestors' religious rites in caves like Lascaux. They are wombs out of which we will emerge reborn, or the belly of the whale in which we are immersed and then spit on shore to begin a more noble existence. The modern architectural models for churches are too enlightened for me. Paradoxically, I must be in the darkness to understand the light.

I will leave this chapter in the way all Masses ended in my era. The priest would say as his last words:

"Ite, missa est." [Go, you are sent.]

The congregation would make its last response with:

"Deo gratias." [Thanks be to God.]

The humor of this last response is that it was often said with the intonation that meant, "My God, I'm glad this long Mass is over."

So, I say unto to thee, my dear reader, "Ite, missa est." Answer as thou choosest.

Chapter 4
CATHOLIC EDUCATION: LORD OF THE RINGS

"The vitality of religion is shown by the way in which the religious spirit has survived the ordeal of religious education."
—Alfred North Whitehead

I wish I could say that I survived Whitehead's ordeal of religious education. I have not. From the age of five through 21, I was immersed in Catholicism in grade school, high school, the monastery, and college. No one could say that I left the Catholic Church because of ignorance of its doctrines or lack of exposure to its rituals. I have school friends that have taken the same route as I have and not only survived but continue to thrive in their history and practice of Catholicism.

So as not to denigrate their faith and goodness, I will say that the observations that I will make about my Catholic education are strictly personal and hopefully without bile, even though I have good reasons in some instances to be bitter. The title to this chapter, of course, is taken from the fantasy writer J.R.R. Tolkien's (a devout Catholic) trilogy *Lord of the Rings*. I use it as an attention-getter, but actually it is a play on words. In addition to referencing Tolkien, I'll be alluding to Dante's rings of Hell, and the Lord, in this case will be Lord Jesus.

As I think about my journey into Catholicism, I see it as a descent into hell. Unlike Dante's concentric rings that contract, mine open up into expanded versions of hell. As I moved through my religious education, I moved from innocence to the blackest areas of my soul.

I only have six rings of hell while Dante had nine. I can only say I couldn't have stood any more.

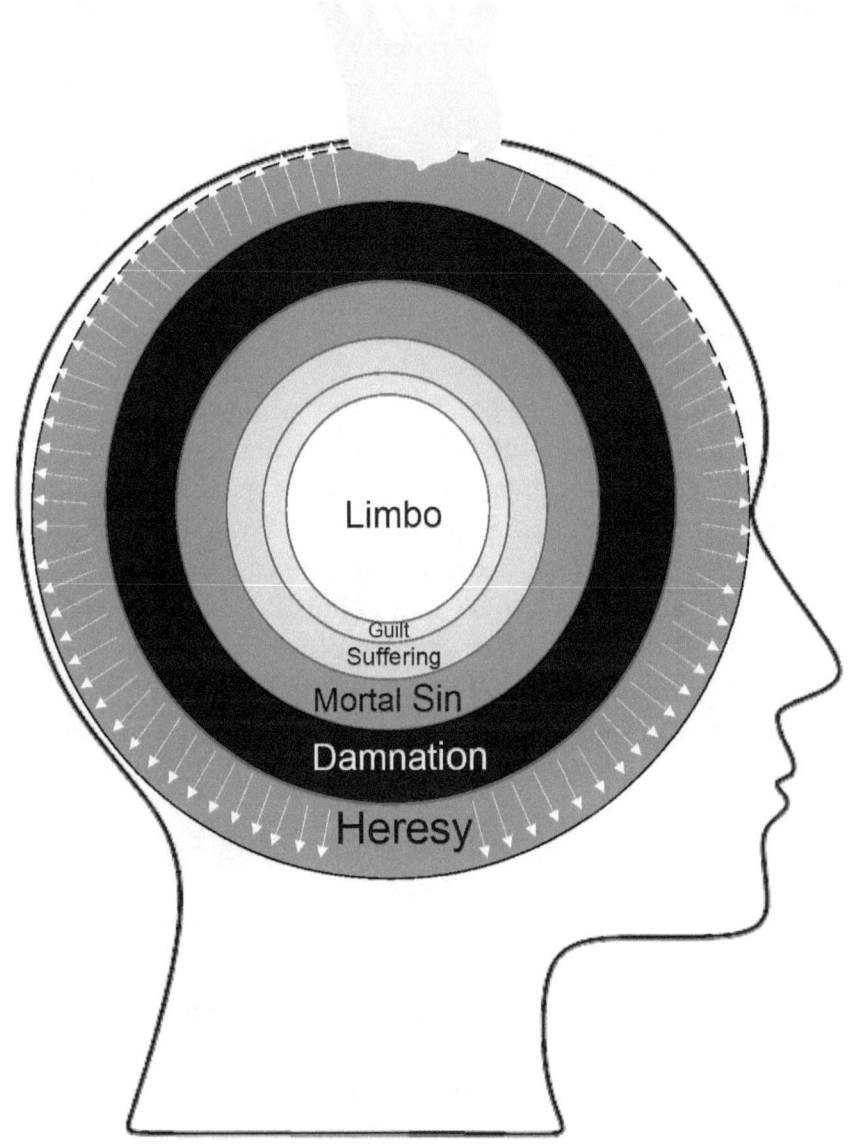

The Expanding Rings of Hell

First Ring: Limbo

For a long time, Catholic theologians divided up the possibilities of where one went after death. Most people were not perfect enough to go directly to heaven; they had to be purified in a place called Purgatory, which was just like hell only it wasn't for forever. You had to purge yourself in Purgatory, and then you could enter heaven for all eternity. Another place a person could go was Limbo (presently discredited by the Catholic Church). Those that went to Limbo were those that were totally innocent of conscious sin (babies that died at birth, for instance), or they were people of good will who were ignorant of Jesus Christ because they lived before his birth (Socrates, for instance), or they had never been introduced to the Gospel (like the great masses of people in China and India).

I always liked Limbo because it was supposedly a lot like earth, except you could never see the face of God or have the beatific vision. Heaven seemed so unfamiliar and boring when I looked at paintings of the saints gathered around the throne that Jesus sat on and staring at his radiance. I thought, *I'll take continued existence on plain ole' planet earth, thank you very much.*

My first five years of existence was a Limbolike existence. If there was anything that I was curious about and had reverence for outside of my family, it was animals. My mother would call me St. Francis because I was always coming home with stray dogs. God was not mentioned very often. Santa Claus and the Easter Bunny were the only beings of the word made flesh for me.

My parents were both Catholic, and we did say some prayers before we ate and before going to bed at night. It was in this Limbo I first experienced some subconscious serpent that all was not well in paradise. Our supper prayers started and ended with "the sign of the cross." We said the usual, "Bless us, oh Lord, and these, Thy gifts, which we are about to receive from Thy bounty through Christ, our Lord. Amen." But then we always added to this in a call/response way with one person (usually my father) saying, "Jesus, Mary, and Joseph," and the rest of us responding, "Assist us in our last agony." "Our last agony?" I wondered about that.

Then there were prayers on our knees before bedtime. "Now I lay me down to sleep and pray to the Lord my soul to keep. If I should die before I wake, I pray to the Lord my soul to take." "Die before I wake?" That phrase sneakily inserted fear into our sleep in much the same way the lullaby... "When the bough breaks/The cradle will fall/and down will come baby/Cradle and all." Again "the sign of the cross" beneath a large crucifix above our bed with the figure of the tortured Christ. ("Have a good night's sleep, children.")

Second Ring: Guilt

Leaving Limbo, I was enrolled in Catholic grade school at five years of age. Above the main entrance to St. Francis Solanus Grade School, there was a sculpture of an angel and a boy. The angel was pointing heavenward with one wing around the boy, and the boy was looking up very pious with his hands folded in prayer. On the lintel below their feet was chiseled the words GOD'S WILL, THE END OF MAN. I thought nothing of this before I could read, walking through this portal many times with an innocence as white as the statues themselves.

As my education with the nuns progressed and my reading skills began to improve, I began wondering about the meaning of those words with the statue. By the time I was seven, the Catholic Church and Catholic education thought I had reached the age of moral consciousness. It was time for me to enter the second ring of Hell. Thus, I was introduced to the concepts of sin, guilt, and retribution. It was during our second-grade year that the nuns prepared us to participate in two new sacraments that went hand in hand — confession and holy communion. In order to receive communion, your soul had to be pure; in order for your soul to be pure, you had to confess your sins to a priest to receive absolution and a penance.

And it came to pass that at the ripe old age of seven, I had begun to participate in the Catholic tradition of internalizing sin. I would now look up at the school's portico with a new interpretation of what I saw and read: The boy was terrified, pleading with the angel not to send him to Hell; the quote below confirmed God's disdain for the evil ways of MAN, who He was "hell bent" on destroying. My consciousness had expanded to help me understand I was bad and that humanity was bad.

Much of our preparation to be communicants came from studying and memorizing *The Baltimore Catechism*. This book was the standard school text and instruction manual for Catholic children from 1885 to the late 1960s — an everything-you-didn't-want-to-know-about God-and-were-afraid-to-ask text. The lessons were delivered in a numbered question and answer format. They started off simple. The first two questions and answers were:

1. Who made us?

God made us.

2. Who is God?

God is the Supreme Being, infinitely perfect, who made all things and keeps them in existence.

Then they continued for over three hundred numbered questions and answers. The material became increasingly complex and theological. You'll notice that even #2 above is quite a leap in abstraction from #1. By question #25 we were into the Trinity, which posed the idea that three can be one like the dog Cerberus that guarded Hades. But most devastating for me was the idea of Original Sin, which meant I was born guilty:

60. What are the chief punishments of Adam which we inherit through original sin?

The chief punishments of Adam which we inherit through original sin are: death, suffering, ignorance, and a strong inclination to sin.

Gee, nice to know. In general, *The Baltimore Catechism* part of my Catholic education represented an emphasis that is more Catholic than other Christian sects. The Catholic Church was more interested in theology than the Bible itself. During my time, it was more interested in doctrine than it was in the teachings of Christ, and it was more interested in the discipline required by sin rather than the joy of salvation. Maybe this was an ongoing result of the Counter-Reformation, where the Catholic hierarchy tried to take control back from Protestant movements. Theology and fear of damnation became their means of keeping congregations from straying.

Third Ring: Suffering

We had no lay teachers in St. Francis Grade School. All the teachers from first through eighth grade were nuns of the order of Sisters of Notre Dame. The principal was a nun. The nuns at this time wore their full regalia — wimple (the black and white hood that covered head, throat, and bosom), black shoes, a many-layered habit, and a large rosary that clacked when they walked. Their faces were extruded out of the wimple with no forehead and no hair exposed. The only other flesh that was revealed were hands and occasionally the forearms.

Because of their high voices and lack of facial hair, we knew they were female, but other than that there were no indications of the curves of a woman in their get-up. I could not imagine their lives as anything but school teachers. Once the school day ended, they entered the convent nearby never to emerge until the next morning.

What they did in the convent, I had no idea. They were not nearly as visible in the community as priests.

In the early years with nuns, I felt that I was in the arms of the Great Mother. There was comfort to be taken from their hugs and the divine smell of incense and worsted wool clothing. They were loving, fantasy creatures. And magical — if I needed a pen, pencil, Kleenex, or whatever, the sister would find it in the folds of her garb or her Batman belt. It was like pulling a rabbit from a hat, and we all marveled at their gear.

In the sisters' presence, there was an enthusiasm to learn and to be noticed. One could always hear walking down the hallways a sibilant sound coming from the lower grades, a stormy beach. Students would vie to answer a question with hands waving like seaweed and whispering "Stir! Stir! Stir!" "Stir," which was our contraction of "Sister."

This didn't mean that the nuns didn't run a tight ship. We were obliged to eat in silence in the cafeteria, and sisters patrolled our long tables like prison guards. They also demanded that you clean your plate, and they waited by the disposal barrels to inspect.

This was a great dilemma for me because in our school of German origins we had sauerkraut once a week. I couldn't face one strand of sauerkraut without a vomiting reflex. "Just don't ask for sauerkraut," you might say. One rule that you learned very early in the food line is that our volunteer cooks were not a jovial crew. They were older, no make-up, no-nonsense women with breasts large enough to hold a food tray. They filled your plate as you walked down the line, and any requests about smaller portions or no portion was rewarded with a double portion. I always got plenty of napkins when we had sauerkraut, and then scraped the kraut into them so as to appear having cleaned my plate.

But this loving sense of nuns all changed in the fourth grade with our introduction to Sister Nicolas. By nature, Sister Nicolas was a sadist who should have been born during a time that the Catholic Church could better have used her services — the Inquisition, for instance. She had pale skin with a grayish luster, and she stared with lifeless eyes reminiscent of a shark. Her sense of what caused pain and her creative methods of torture would certainly have weeded out many heretics in the past — or at least provided many confessions. For us, she was the beginning of a new kind of nun who belonged to the religious order of Our Lady of Perpetual Pain.

Need I say that Catholic education in general and nuns specifically have a long history of severe discipline? Only in the last twenty-five years have some of the most grizzled stories of child abuse and even murder at Catholic institutions come to light. Nothing happened on this scale at St. Francis, but that doesn't mean we were spared the rod of God.

We had spankings, switchings, paddlings, slappings, draggings, and torturing. Many parents wanted this kind of hardcore corporal punishment. Even non-Catholics sent their children to Catholic schools to be more sternly disciplined — something unavailable in public schools. Then, too, this was an era where parents told their children that if you get a "whipping" at school, don't come home and complain because you'll get a second whipping to reinforce the first. So, it really did no good to complain about the methods of St. Nicolas. We realized silence was the best approach to take about the punishments that went on in school; further, parents would always take a nun's word over ours.

Sister Nicolas performed with gusto the usual whacking hands with a ruler, but her ruler was especially hefty, and she went for your knuckles on the back of your hand rather than your palms. Also, she enjoyed having you stand next to your desk with your arms in the crucifixion position. If you happened to look into one of her classes, you might think there was a re-enactment of Calvary. There was an incentive not to drop your arms before the proscribed time, lest Czar Nicolas decided on a more creative punishment. It behooved you to grit it out.

Creative punishments included drawing a circle on the blackboard, taking one or two steps backward, and then placing your nose in the circle. In this leaning position, you could not use your hands and, if you did, you received a nice whack on the buttocks with the wooden pointer. Another specialty of Sister Nicolas and by far the most painful of her assortment of tortures was to have you kneel beside your desk on your knuckles. The floors were wooden, so there was no nice cushioning of a rug. This was pure agony with many students falling forward on their heads, which only meant more time added to your ordeal and more embarrassment.

Sister Nicolas found boys particularly irksome and deserving of purification. The boys had to be much more careful about infractions than girls. One of the restrictions that we boys found particularly odd was that she would not allow boys to put their hands in their pockets. If she caught a boy in her class or anywhere in the school — class, playground, or cafeteria — with his hands in his pockets, he was summarily punished. We had no idea what this was about, but only that it was forbidden. Only later did we figure out that she was afraid of us playing "pocket pool." Such a sexual obsession with these imagined sexual proclivities of boys in fourth grade was another indication of her psychopathology.

The ring of Hell that I entered in fourth grade was reinforced by the many images that we were exposed to at St. Frances. Images and statuary of the martyred saints filled the church next door where we went to daily Mass. Sometimes the martyred saint was portrayed holding the instrument of his or her torture — an ax, a toothed-wheel, a clutch of arrows, etc. Holy cards were given to us as prizes by the nuns. They often depicted saints in the throes of agony, my favorite being St. Sebastian tied to a tree with arrows coming out of him like a pin cushion. We had few images of the risen, triumphant Christ; only crucifixes proliferated every class and every rosary. As students, we were immersed in the tortures of the committed Christian, and I often wondered how long I could have held out if someone tried to torture me until I rejected Jesus. This thought coupled with my experiences at the dentist was not encouraging.

Sister Nicolas did her job in preparing us for pain and eventual martyrdom. No more fantasies about a benevolent figure like St. Nicolas (Santa Claus), but only the raw reality of suffering and offering it up to God, who may just for the fun of it, give you another whack.

Fourth Ring: Mortal Sin

Mortal sin was the phrenology of Catholic theology. From it

sprung a legalistic thinking that characterized much religious education from the sixth grade on. I can still picture the images on the blackboard. There were three circles: one filled with a white chalk patina, the second speckled with dark dots, and the third empty and black. These represented respectively the soul full of grace, the soul with venial sins, and the soul in mortal sin.

If you died with your soul in mortal sin, there was no begging God for mercy — you went directly to Hell and did not "pass go." If you died in venial sin, you went to the fires of Purgatory, but you had a "get out of jail" card. None of us cared much about going to Purgatory but going to Hell did get our attention. Thankfully, we had the sacrament of confession to return our souls to a pristine state so that we could sleep well on white, bleached pillowcases and not worry about "if I should die before I wake…"

Most of us understood why some sins could be punished by damnation. Murder, for instance, or husbands and wives cheating on their spouses. But there were many minor infractions that were labeled as mortally sinful that we had problems with — eating meat on Friday or not going to church on Sunday. These didn't seem to be on equal footing with, say, stealing from the poor.

Thus was born the jurisprudence kind of theology that Catholics were famous for at the time. Someone in class would always propose a hypothetical case for us to go over:

"So, if Al Capone received the last sacraments (extreme unction, as it was called) on his death bed, his soul would be pure, and he would go straight to heaven. Is that right, Stir?"

"True, Bobby. The sacrament would erase all his bad deeds, and he would join the saints in heaven for all eternity."

Bobby had just begun. "Then he would receive no punishment for a life of killing people and stealing their money. All this would be forgiven? That doesn't seem right."

"All sins are forgiven through God's grace and the sacrament of confession. He probably won't get as high a place in heaven as those that lived their entire lives being good." (To us, getting to heaven was the point. Whether it was a higher or lower place meant nothing.)

"Doesn't matter if you're Adolph Hitler," added Sister Gabriel.

"If you receive Extreme Unction on your death bed, you go straight to heaven." (The monster of the century could go to heaven!)

"Well what if a little old lady who has spent her whole life doing good deeds and going to church is killed by a car on the one day she slips and eats meat on Friday. Is she going to hell while Hitler's going to heaven if he had extreme unction?"

"That's the problem with mortal sin, Bobby. You never want to stay in the state of mortal sin because as the Gospels say, 'Therefore keep watch, because you do not know the day on which your Lord will come.' The old woman made a big mistake, and she will suffer all eternity in Hell for it." (She may as well have said, "God is a quirky one, and you really can't count on him to be just or merciful or rational all the time.")

These kinds of slicing and dicing arguments were very common in the classroom as we tried to get the lay of the abstract land of theology. They became increasingly acute when problems of a sexual nature were added to the mix. Nuns were particularly inadequate to the task of explaining the theological ins and outs of sex (no pun intended). My sixth-grade teacher Sister Mariam tried her best to distract us from questions surrounding our sexual awakenings:

Sister Mariam and the Legendary Hohner Marine Band Harmonica

Sixth grade was the season
of sexual awakening
I was puzzled at the water fountain
how I drank in Cheryl Volm's legs
an unfamiliar thirst
directing me like a divining rod

Sister Mariam seemed to detect
the change in her students
she offered us lessons
with harmonicas that gleamed
in blue and red boxes
something for our lips to do

we sighed in and out
scales from the blues
thinking only of parties

with spinning bottles
and tentative chords of kissing

soon we abandoned
our 10-holed Hohners
in favor of more complicated strains
leaving Sister Mariam to a black and white world
where we were told
God's breath was enough

The idea of mortal sin was timed to coincide with the period of our sexual awakening. This was done so that you would control your sexual urges for fear of damnation.

Once we became interested in "making out," "necking," and "petting," the theological discussions became focused on how far we could go. It was evident that sins of a sexual nature were many, and most were mortal sins. Therefore, we wanted to know that *exact* point when we passed from venial sin into mortal sin. This was very much like trying to keep the temperature just high enough so that water wouldn't boil. No one minded going to Purgatory for sins of the flesh of a venial nature, but we were concerned about mortal sin and the embarrassment of confessing such sins.

Questions of great moment were: How long could a kiss be? Was a French kiss a mortal sin? How close could we dance? Could we move our hands over the clothing of the other? Being concerned about mortal sin, of course, spoiled a lot of the pleasure of our early sexual explorations. Watching the secondhand of your wristwatch while kissing *does* detract from the pure enjoyment.

Mortal sin created a mindset for many kids called "the scruples," a neurotic obsession to confess every little sinful thought or action for fear it might be mortally sinful. Thankfully, some priests in the confessional would tell us to calm down and not to worry about confessing every little thing. Consciousness of mortal sin brought about a lot of these psychological ticks in the fourth ring of hell.

Fifth Ring: Damnation

Up to the point I entered high school, I had survived fairly well the slings and arrows of outrageous Catholic education. But high school had a special ring of hell reserved for me from which I would never entirely recover — damnation.

As an agnostic today, I have many Christian friends worrying about my eventual demise in the eternal fires. "Don't you believe in Hell?" they ask me. I always reply, "Oh, yes, I believe in Hell because I've been there." And I'm not kidding.

The Catholic high school that I attended was an all-boys school run by a religious order called the Christian Brothers (yes, the ones that make the brandy). They were a hard-nosed group that kept us rowdy, adolescent boys in check. Corporal punishment abounded in this atmosphere with the brothers not thinking twice about disciplining with knuckles to the head, slaps, punches, and slams against the lockers.

On the other hand, academically they were very sound and frank. I liked the way they required intellectual rigor — something that I have kept with me all my life. I have often been grateful that I was not raised in a Christian tradition that had problems with Evolution, for instance. There was not even a pause or apology for teaching Darwin in biology classes or religious studies. The Bible in many instances was not to be taken literally, and figurative interpretations had their own beauty and truth.

Unlike the nuns, the Brothers were frank about sex. As a freshman, I remember Brother Timothy, the school principal, coming into class early in our freshman year and writing "FUCK" on the board. That definitely got our attention in 1960, when the F-word had the taboo that the N-word carries today. Brother Timothy followed this up with the actual pronunciation of this word in class — "Today we're going to talk about 'fuck.'" If your parents hadn't already given you the sex talk, you got it that day.

As frank as the talk was, it was still cloaked in the current Catholic theology. And while we learned about sex acts and devices (birth control), we found that almost all of them were mortally sinful, unless you were married. Parodying Paul Simon, we found out that there must be a least 50 ways to go to Hell.

Out of all the new possibilities of damnation for us, one sexual sin received particular emphasis and that was masturbation a.k.a. self-abuse. While most of the sexual acts were unavailable to us, especially in an all-boys school (there was absolutely no reference to same-sex acts), masturbation was a temptation that we had access to and a vice that we could develop if we were not careful.

Looking back to these days, one has to wonder why our religious instructors were so obsessed with this sexual act. Today, we would view masturbation as quite normal for budding teens as a way to release some of their new sexual energy. In fact, it might be recommended as a way to keep from sexual activity that might have more dangerous consequences. However, within the Catholic Church at the time (and many other institutions and medical professions as well), masturbation was a kind of onanism that perverted the use of sperm for procreation. Some contemporary psychologists were concerned about its debilitating effects on the psyche as well as the body. Pimples, shyness, urinary diseases, finger biting, nervous ticks, etc. were all related to self-abuse.

Occasionally, we were reminded of this "evil" act in high school when we had religious retreats, where the confessional lines grew with young men getting up their courage to cleanse their souls of secret sin. One of the "hired guns" who was brought in to talk to us about masturbation was a priest who worked for the bishop's office. His specialty was plain talk about pleasuring oneself. In retrospect, he gave a presentation that could have only been done today by Monty Python. But he was taken seriously by everyone and even reverenced for his self-effacement in talking about his own masturbatory life.

The good Father made the core of his presentation a mathematical attempt to calculate the number of times he had masturbated in his life — an algorithm for emissions (reminiscent of the scene in *Silicon Valley*, where they try to calculate "mean jerk time"). He had dates and places. Apparently, he at one time was so much in the grip of self-abuse that he had masturbated on the altar. The resultant calculations of his sinful sexual history indicated a very busy man when it came to "boxing the Jesuit" as he called it, and I would not have been surprised if he had calluses on his "Jesuit." I suppose he could have gone further in his mathematical approach by having us figure out the volume of sperm this represented and what kind of container would be needed to store it. As comic as this sounds and as light-hearted, there was no diminishment of the fact that masturbation in our lives needed to be eliminated; it was a mortally sinful behavior that could send us to Hell.

To my misfortune, I took this all very seriously, and it seeped into my mind as a metastasizing, black cancer. It controlled my mind as I became fixated on this secret sin. I had no idea that this was normal behavior. All I knew was that I was an "addict" and that I must fight this abasement of my body. But all my efforts and plans for a more rigid approach to my sexual appetites always failed and always left me more helpless and despairing.

The burden of secret sin was laid out to me quite clearly in my English classes when we studied Nathaniel Hawthorne. The gloom of his stories reflected my gloom, and the hidden sins of the tortured souls in his stories — *The Scarlet Letter*, "The Minister's Black Veil", "Young Goodman Brown," and *The House of the Seven Gables* — represented the hair shirt of my tortured soul. My fellow students noticed that I had changed from the carefree individual that I had been in grade school. I had become serious and more withdrawn. I kept diaries in which I would chastise myself and make future plans for a more chaste life. Someday I planned to use these diaries to write my book. The book would be entitled *The Great Masturbator* after Salvador Dali's surreal painting of the same name. Like the Rev. Dimmesdale on the scaffold in *The Scarlet Letter*, I would reveal my life as a sinner and, perhaps, expiate my sins.

In all manner of ways, I attempted to sublimate my evil impulses into behaviors that were redemptive. I became a super student, pouring my seed into my studies. I was at the top of my class academically, not because of my intelligence, but because of a relentless work ethic. In the same way, I had a rigid approach to physically working out — I wanted to be pure in mind and body, if not soul. Finally, I became increasingly religious and pious, hoping that someday my devotion to Jesus would open me up to Salvation. Of course, none of this obsessive behavior cured me, as I became increasingly morose in a moribund system of psychology. My condition in modern psychological terms would be that I was a victim of The White Bear Effect.

Impure Thoughts and the White Bear

Psychologists who have studied thought suppression have found that there is an odd phenomenon called the White Bear Effect. Dr. Daniel Wegner, a psychology professor at Harvard University and the founding father of thought suppression research, performed several experiments where he asked his subjects to *not* to think of a white bear while they verbally described what was going on in their minds for five minutes. He performed this experiment with many variations and control groups. But the bottom line of Dr. Wegner's studies is: deliberate attempts to suppress certain thoughts makes them much more likely to occur. People that were asked not to think of white bears were thinking about them all the time.

Of course, the relevance of such a study can be seen when put in terms of mortal sin and impure thoughts. The more I tried to suppress my sexual thoughts, the more they arose in my mind. When this cycle is in your mind, there is no place to hide. Since there was no exit, I suffered greatly and unnecessarily. It was natural to think about sex as a sexually budding teenager and, if I hadn't viewed them as mortally sinful, I would have given them no special attention. Giving them the special attention of damnation led to obsessive behaviors.

There is a strain in Catholicism which leads to a kind of mind control that keeps one close to Mother Church and the confessional door. Perhaps, one of the most absurd things Jesus ever said is reported in Matthew 5:28: "But I say to you that everyone who looks at a woman with lustful intent has already committed adultery with her in his heart." Really. Is it possible to have the kind of mind control that Jesus calls for here? All I can say here is that it does not stack up with my experiences with heterosexual married men. I think my brother Larry expressed it best on this subject: "If I can't covet, shove it."

The only role models that the Catholic Church had to offer to free me from my psychological loop were quite austere. I could be like St. Francis of Assisi and roll in the snow to ward off bad thoughts. Or throw myself into a thorn bush like St. Benedict. Finally, I could take St. Bernard's route and take a plunge into an icy pool. Besides leading to my eventual incarceration in a mental institution, none of these methods had any real appeal for me.

So, the white bear of my soul gnawed at me from the inside. I knew Hell in the way that Mephistopheles of *Doctor Faustus*:

Hell hath no limits, nor is circumscribed
In one self place, but where we are is hell,
And where hell is, there must we ever be.

Hell is not a place, but a state of mind. It is not a *where* but a *within*. It is within you no matter where you are or go. By the time I graduated, I decided to take my Hell to the monastery in the hopes that I could in that environment expiate my soul. I would reach at-one-ment by serving Jesus as Brother Edmond Giles, the name I took during my time at the seminary.

Sixth Ring: Heresy

I never finished my first year in the monastery. Despite all the counseling that I received about the devil trying to give me reasons to leave the order, I left the cloistered life in the foothills of the Ozarks, despondent because I could not raise myself above my guilt. My options had run out. What was I going to do — kill myself, become a recluse, take drugs, do mindless kinds of work, curl up like a fetus?

My parents compassionately realized that I had been damaged by my experiences at the monastery, and they swaddled me in a protective cocoon that put aside pressures for future plans. And they gave me the perfect task to fill my days — refinishing an old dining room table.

I became like Dr. Manette in *The Tale of Two Cities*, who mindlessly cobbles shoes to alleviate his mental stress. The table was a large oak table that had been handed down in the family. It made a great Thanksgiving table that could be expanded to accommodate a dozen people. Each day my raison d'être was to hand sand every crevice and cranny of the table down to the bare wood. The repetitive motion and the abrasive hiss of the sandpaper was like an ocean's surf. It ground the edges of my damaged brain into a smooth, seashell surface.

As the days passed, my hands became callused, and so did the blisters on my brain. After a couple of months, I was able to face the world again. I enrolled into the local Catholic college (Quincy College), which was across the street from my grade school and run by the same Franciscan order. I hadn't gone very far in life.

I went to college with no idea about obtaining a degree but just to be with former classmates and to learn about the many academic areas in which I was interested. Despite the fact that this was a Catholic college, it was quite secular in most ways. There were students and professors that were not Catholic, and there were no requirements to take classes about Catholicism or participate in Catholic ritual. This was a comfort since I needed to get away from much of Catholic thought.

Ironically, at a Catholic college, I found an exit from Catholicism. When you are entrapped by a seemingly unending wall, if you feel your way around the periphery long enough, you can find a door. My door was made up of many elements — young women, philosophy, literature, and the hippie movement. The times they were a changin'.

Separation from the opposite sex had not been good for me. An all-boys school had made me into a social misfit around girls. They were so other-worldly to me that it was difficult to just sit next to them in class. But the friends who I had made in high school and now hung around with in college helped me break through this shyness. Being promoted in our family restaurant to the level of bartender (there were no restrictions on age for a bartender if your family owned the bar), also opened me up to the behaviors of men and women. Slowly and steadily, I began to be comfortable in the presence of young women and to have a kind of fun I never knew was possible.

On the theological side, mortal sin and sexual restrictions were being eroded. The society in general was beginning to open up to pre-marital sex and looser views of what was sexually acceptable.

The priests at Quincy College were very liberal, and some had affairs with students. As one of my friends commented, "The priests are getting more pussy in college than we are."

My studies were taking me along new pathways of thought that had nothing to do with Christianity. I immersed myself in the Beat writers — Kerouac, Ginsberg, and Ferlinghetti. The songs of Bob Dylan and his lyrics of outrage spoke to me in exciting ways the Bible never had. Then there was the architect, philosopher, anticipatory designer Buckminster Fuller. I was a Fuller votary in deeper ways than I ever had been for Jesus Christ. The satire of Kurt Vonnegut appealed to the inhumanity that I saw all around me, and Rachel Carson sounded an apocalyptic note that rang more true than *Revelations*. I did not get my new consciousness, however, through drugs. With my mental instability, I was very afraid of what further damage a bad trip could mean for me.

These answers that were blowin' in the wind are what in the past the Catholic Church would have called *heresy*. I had become at Quincy College a heretic. And I performed eventually the act of all heretics — to accept damnation for new beliefs. Like Huckleberry Finn's acceptance of hell rather than turn in Jim, I consciously decided that I no longer believed in Jesus Christ, which meant that I could not be saved. It was not a decision that I took lightly and, along the way, I struggled mightily to make some kind of compromise with Christianity, but I could not.

Once made, the decision to consent to eternal judgment opened up large rents in what I had thought were the inescapable walls of Catholic education. As in one of Lawrence Ferlinghetti's poems, I found there was "...a wide vent in the battlements/where even elephants/waltz through." Where there were once the cold shadows of gray stone, there shone sunny horizons beckoning me to spiritual quests of another kind.

Backward Forward

That my personality had been damaged irreparably by my Catholic education, there can be no doubt. The wound of an idee' fixe like masturbation and mortal sin never totally heals. To this day, I must fight obsessive-compulsive behaviors that are the result of holes burnt into the synapses of my brain.

Yet I do not hate, and I do forgive — Father, they do not know what they are doing. Most of the priests, brothers, and nuns in my life were people of good intention and passed on to me things that they thought were solid ideas and practices. And, indeed, for many, these ideas were good. Not everyone reacted to Catholic teachings like I did, and many of my school friends are sustained to this day by their Catholic education and Catholicism.

I really don't know if what I have become today was the result of destiny, mistaken decisions, or of a struggle to carve out a life from a crippling start. All I know is that when I reached out in the most despairing parts of my life, the mythologies of Christianity did not save me. The worlds of literature and ideas saved me as did friendships and family love. So, I am like the tree that has been nibbled on by deer in the early years — my growth has been stunted but my branches are thick and full. The internalization that was my early lot in life has turned me into a writer. And I feel full in this present moment as I now finish this sentence.

CHAPTER 5
DEATH OF A ROMANTIC

"The sparrow is sorry for the peacock at the burden of his tail."

—Rabindranath Tagore

John Schutte, Student Council; Pipe and Derby Club; *Pet Peeve:* Having to share my bathtub with elephants; *Ambition:* To be a professional underwater polo player; *Hobby:* Roasting marshmallows.

Romantics have huge, hungry hearts. They are ever called to the next horizon. Life twinkles, glimmers, shimmers. They hear the mermaids singing. The glass is not half full nor half empty; it's a cornucopia.

John Schutte (ironically pronounced "should-he") was a romantic down to his core, which means he was constantly replacing his disillusionment with life to the next call to adventure. I first met him in high school. John was a country boy with brown, coarse hair combed over like wheat ready to harvest. His clothes were mended and plain and his bearing was rugged but not intimidating. It was his blue eyes that were his striking feature. They were wild and untamable. You could look into those eyes and realize right away this person was up for anything.

Close Encounters of the Weird Kind

Because we were often seated alphabetically in high school, I always had the good fortune (or misfortune) of sitting next to John Schutte in double desks. Watching him peripherally during a class was a distraction. He'd be messing with paper folding or a deck of cards or a crossword puzzle or who knows what — anything but follow what was going on in class.

Let this not lead to a false conclusion that John was unintelligent. Actually, he was very smart, but he was easily bored by much of what went on in the classroom. He could've easily been an honor roll student, but grades never motivated him — only things that appealed to his immediate, insatiable curiosity moved him.

My first encounter with the essential Schutte was during a freshman class where we were supposed to be following along in our textbook as Mr. Christian, our history teacher, was pointing out important passages for a test. I glanced over at John and, as was his custom, he had another book tucked into his textbook. Now the books that he would furtively read were not adolescent schlock. They were books like *The Communist Manifesto*, *The Stranger*, and *Madame Bovary*. In this case, he was reading *Gone with the Wind*.

Feeling a bit punitive for his constantly distracting me in class, I leaned over to him and whispered, "Let me tell you the ending." He had only 20 or fewer pages left to go of a rather hefty novel, and he looked back at me with an expression of horror. Could anyone be so cruel as to deprive him the ecstasy of arriving with Margaret Mitchell to her book's poignant ending? He had spent many an illicit hour in class totally engrossed in this story, and he couldn't believe that I might ruin the last mile of a marathon. Little did he know that I had no idea how the book ended since I hadn't read the book. But his alarmed expression was enough to goad me on.

"Don't fuck with me, Settle."

"The ending's really cool. What happens is..."

At this point (and this is pure Schutte), he put his hands over his ears and began rocking back and forth like a mental patient. He accompanied this rocking with a loud "Ah-ah, Ah-ah, Ah-ah."

As you would expect, Mr. Christian looked up and said, "Mr. Schutte, have you gone mad?"

John quickly pointed out, "Settle was going to tell me the ending to *Gone with the Wind*. Look how long it is! I couldn't let him spoil it, could I?" The class was amused at this outrageous defense.

"Well first of all, Mr. Schutte, you shouldn't have been reading this book while class was going on. Secondly, you have thoroughly disrupted my class. Both you and Mr. Settle need to go and have a little talk with Principal Timothy."

"Wha...wha...but, Mr. Christian, I didn't...I wasn't the one who disrupted class."

"You got him all riled up, Mr. Settle. So, get your butt down to Timothy's."

While we waited in Timothy's office, John calmly finished the novel, while I pondered my downfall from grace. It was the first time I had gotten into trouble in high school, and the one and only time that I had ever been to the principal's office. *Damn, John Schutte!* I thought.

These were the dangers if you hung with John Schutte, the romantic. He was unpredictable and not really intimidated by authority. This meant you could get yourself into trouble, not criminal trouble, but trouble with parents, teachers, minsters, and adults of all kinds. He always put his pleasures and curiosity before the daily grind. His formula for life made for an unstable compound.

The Once and Future King

As the years passed in high school, it became clear that John Schutte was liked by everyone. This was because he really didn't see fellow students as rich or poor, popular or unpopular, handsome or plain, shy or gregarious, smart or dumb. He could move from group to group in high school as seamlessly as type O-negative blood. John had no sense of decorum or social exclusivity.

Those of us that spent time with him would rag him mercilessly about his projects and ideas. But he would take it, willing to laugh at himself and not altogether defenseless in getting us back. One of the things we liked to razz him about was his car. In a day of drag racing and hot cars, John had a junker that should have been taken off the road. To ride with John just to the grocery store could mean that you would never come back.

First of all, there was a substantial hole in the passenger's floorboard. You could stick your foot through it to the street below. If you wanted to, you could help stop the car by dragging a foot, which at times seemed necessary because his brakes were never that good, and he often had to resort to the emergency brake. Finally, you needed to be prepared for rain, which could pour through the floorboard hole at higher car speeds in fountain proportions. Anything you were wearing could get soaked and spotted with street debris.

He *did* have belts in this car, but they were not safety belts. These were the days before safety belts. Instead John had leather belts to keep the passenger door closed. He had to get into the driver's side first and unbuckle a belt to let you in the passenger side. Then you could either ride holding the door shut by hand or buckle it to a bar beneath the front seat. Going around sharp curves gave one a giddy sense of the possibility of suddenly being spewed out onto the road.

In addition to the previous dangers, Schutte's car had bald tires with no hub caps, no workable radio, and a profoundly rusted body. Not exactly a car to pick up "chicks" with, unless they were immensely tolerant, had expansive senses of humor, or were downright desperate for a date. We never went cruising in John's car. It was strictly a male vehicle.

On one occasion, I remember going on one of John's bizarre "short" errands. John, I, and a fellow classmate Jim were going to pick up some tools to build a set for an upcoming dance. Jim was a meticulously neat and well-coiffed individual. His family had money, and he always dressed in button down shirts made of the finest material as well as expensive sweaters, pants, and shoes.

Jim had never had the "privilege" of traveling in Schutte's leper-mobile, and he looked a little uncomfortable as John unbuckled the door for him to get in. But one thing you could say for Jim, he was nice to the core, and you never got a sense from him that he was anything but egalitarian.

The place we were heading for was the Holtschlag farm. Leroy Holtschlag was another classmate, and he was going to lend us a few of his father's tools. Leroy was one of the older brothers in a family of 17 children (this was a Catholic area and many families counted more than ten). The brothers and sisters looked alike — short, stout, and strong. They had unruly hair reminiscent of yellowing corn shucks. And they played rough out there on the farm like a group of wild burros. I had been to the farm before playing tackle football in their fields, and the younger boys were capable of taking you out with spearheaded tackles.

So, I was on the alert when we arrived. You never knew if you would suddenly be drawn into some rough play from Holtschlag boys. We pulled into the gravel driveway and saw no one as we parked the car. Jim unbuckled and swung the door open and stood up. He was immediately hit in the head with a dirt clod. He stood there stunned with blood trickling down his forehead. John and I both knew what was happening. We crouched down, using our car doors as shields. "Jim, get down! Get down!" But he stood there in disbelief that someone could hurt him so intentionally. After a second blow to the head, Jim decided that humans intentionally giving pain to others could be part of the human condition. He ducked behind the passenger door.

"We need to make our way to that tree over there," shouted Schutte. "There's ammunition and protection."

The clods were coming in like mortar rounds, bouncing off windshield, tires, and doors. We could see figures dropping out of the hayloft and moving in from behind the barn. We had to crawl on our bellies like soldiers exposed to machine gun fire. Jim was suddenly aware that this was a real fight, so he didn't hesitate hitting the dirt in his fine clothes and crawling like a wounded gator to the large tree that sat atop a ravine. It was here that we broke off chunks of dried dirt. We could now fire back, and after being hit in the head twice, Jim the Benign became Jim the Destroyer. He was firing back his artillery with a zeal I had never seen in him before.

Soon, because they outnumbered us, they began to outflank us and close in. In response, we piled a heap of ammunition and made a dash for the house, firing back as we were running. The boys came out of their hiding places, running and whooping full speed after us. When we made it through the back door and closed it, a series of thumps tattooed off the wooden door.

"My god, we made it," I gasped. Schutte was laughing with the greatest pleasure. And Jim was ready to go out and kill the Hun "bastards." It was a baptism of violence for him.

When we left with the tools, I thought we might have to go through this again. But the Holtschlag boys had moved onto something else (maybe killing feral cats to make hats with their fur) and were nowhere to be found. We went forth unmolested, although I could see that Jim was carrying chunks of soil just in case.

Schutte had a way of taking the common and turning it into a story. By the time our senior year rolled around, each of us had our favorite Schutte stories. He was beloved by all. Thus, it was not the quarterback nor the most handsome guy in class nor the guy who that belonged to the popular clique who became homecoming king — it was John Schutte, who probably didn't have a suit and had to buy one for the occasion.

Jane Rupp (Queen) and John Schutte (King)

With What I Most Enjoy, Contented Least

Imagine you had a golden lab with all its good-natured sense of fun and propensity for retrieving sticks. Your dog has never been to a body of water before, and then one day you take him to a dock on a lake and throw a stick. What do you imagine will happen? Will the dog dive? Will it retrieve the stick in an element it is unfamiliar with? You know the answer: not only will it dive, but it will thrive in this new environment. After all, it was bred for such things.

Now imagine John Schutte after we graduated in 1964, heading into the new freedoms of college and the incipient freedoms of the hippie era. Yes, he dove off that dock, and he took his time returning. Unorganized time and questioning authority were the staples of his life. I remember John reciting a quote by e.e. cummings that he lived by: "Follow no paths. All paths lead to where. Truth is here."

Many of my high school classmates went to Quincy College, our local college. We knew very little about college since we were mostly first-generation college students. The only reason I went to college was for the "lofty" reason that my friends were going. Perhaps, that was John's reason for going, too. In addition, it would be a new experience for him and that was his raison d'etre.

As you might expect, John's first year of college was a roller coaster affair. Even the fairly loose structure of college became *somebody else's* path. He had either A's or F's for his classes, depending on his interest in the class. Cutting classes went from occasional to habitual. The school cafeteria became a place for his studies as well as his new favorite pastime, bridge. Eventually, he became a master bridge player.

After a year at Quincy College, all of us had lined up summer jobs because we were not among those privileged few that did not worry about paying for the college experience. Even though Schutte was constantly and forever in need of money, he had managed to save up fifty dollars and was going to have an "on the road" summer experience like Jack Kerouac. His quote for the occasion was from Walt Whitman:

> *...light-hearted I take to the open road,*
> *Healthy, free, the world before me,*
> *The long brown path before me leading wherever I choose.*
>
> *Henceforth I ask not good-fortune, I myself am good-fortune,*
> *Henceforth I whimper no more, postpone no more, need nothing,*
> *Done with indoor complaints, libraries, querulous criticisms,*
> *Strong and content I travel the open road.*

I have already described the car that he was going to make this spontaneous road trip in. And, as you could surely predict, it broke down irreparably on a highway going through Oklahoma. Most of us would have called it quits right there. Most of us would have called a parent or friend to rescue us. Not John. He pushed the junker to the side of the road and continued on, hitchhiking with just of few bucks in his pocket.

John's parents, the long-suffering souls that they were, received a call from the Oklahoma State Police — John's car had been found and impounded, but no John. Of course, Mom and Dad had no idea where he was. They questioned us, and we had no idea where he was. All they could do was wait and worry. But we just continued working and shrugged our shoulders and said, "Well, that's Schutte."

He came back a few months later a little lean, but all tanned and healthy. He had hitched his way into Mexico and wandered from village to village, doing farm work and drinking tequila with the locals — a reversal of the usual Mexican migration of coming to the States to pick crops. We glommed around him at The High Hat, our local tavern hangout that served us even though we were minors (very common in a German town with family taverns). He told us about warm nights under the stars in the Mexican fields. Of wild dancing in the village plazas and the dark-eyed, young woman who took a shine to him. We envied his utter abandon to seek adventure with no money and his courage to face starvation in a land where he didn't even speak the language.

Since now he had no car, he began working in a filling station and saved up enough money to buy — what else? — a motorcycle. I remember him roaring to my house after he bought the cycle to take me for a spin. My parents knew John and really liked him, but they begged me not to get on his bike. They knew that John for all his sense of fun was not of the right temperament to handle 250 cc's of power.

But I got on, ignoring my parents' pleas. John's first ominous words were "Let me show you what she can do." My protests were drowned out by a blast from the exhaust pipe and a wheelie out of the driveway. We went through town in record time, weaving in and out of traffic. Soon we were on a two-lane highway (which was the only kind we had in Quincy) where he could open "her" up. The 100 mph on the speedometer was not decorative. My screams of "Slow down for god's sake" only brought out sadistic laughter from Schutte. When I got back, I hugged my parents as if I'd been gone for ten years and admitted that I was not too old for their advice.

I never road with John again. Nor did any of my friends once they had been initiated as passengers. There were no atheists that rode with John Schutte.

Schutte started his second year of college with less enthusiasm than his first. I could see the signs of restlessness in him as he reluctantly participated in the sophomore curriculum. One evening, he came into The High Hat Tavern after he had finished his shift at the filling station. He cashed his check and brought a pitcher of beer over to our table.

"School is bullshit," he said, pouring himself a glass of brew. "Lot of dead ideas from a lot of dead men. I need to get outta here. Experience the world." This was not new material from him.

"Where would you go, John?" one of us said. "How would you live?"

"Somewhere in the Northwest. I've never been to the Northwest. I'd be a firewatcher for the forestry service or maybe a lumberjack."

"Well, good luck with that, Kerouac."

We moved on to our usual topics, none of which were intellectual in the least — girls, parties, and short cuts to passing our courses. But as Schutte drank, he became more morose and began denigrating our college aspirations as futile and a waste of time. Well, we didn't mind him complaining about his own education, but when he began chastising us as a mindless bunch of lemmings, we took umbrage.

"Okay, John, we get it. We're unenlightened morons. But you're here with us, Man-With-No-Balls. At least we're not phonies and don't claim to be dissatisfied with our lot in life. But you...you talk and talk and talk. We're getting tired of it. Shut up or put up. Easy to talk, not so easy for us having to listen to your sniveling."

This seemed to arouse him from a drunken stupor. "By god, I will!" he said, slapping his hand on the table. "Give me a ride to the train station."

"Now? It's almost midnight, John."

"I'm leaving town tonight. No more '*indoor complaints, libraries, querulous criticisms.*'"

"John, you crazy bastard. Think it over. Wait until tomorrow. You're drunk and don't know what you're saying."

"*Healthy, free, the world before me, the long brown path before me leading wherever I choose,*" he burbled on.

"What in the hell are you talking about?"

"I'm not a man without balls. Take me to-the-FUCKIN' train depot!"

Suddenly we all had the same epiphany — what fun this could be! Why not take him to the train station. This had all the makings of another Schutte adventure. We all piled into a car and drove to the depot, which was on the other side of the Mississippi in Missouri. For the entire trip, we goaded him on, and insincerely supported his decision to leave town and follow his bliss. We all came in from the darkness into the yellow cast of the depot's fluorescent lights. The woman, nodding behind the ticket window, jerked to attention. We were so noisy she had no idea if we were there to buy a ticket or to take over the depot. John took out a wad of cash from his pocket and plunked it on the counter."

"Where will thish take me?"

"Well where would you like to go?"

"Any...any (hic) where in the Northwest."

"Well, let's see. For a few dollars more, you could go to Portland."

We immediately threw in a few more dollars.

"Done," Schutte pronounced.

We stayed with him until his train arrived, continuing to drink from a six-pack someone had brought along. Then we helped him stagger onto the train; he was almost asleep by now. I can still remember seeing his nodding head in a hoody as we waved goodbye as the train pulled out of the station. "Wow!" we smiled to ourselves, "this is the greatest prank we'd ever played. Wait till he wakes up few hundred miles from here, heh-heh. Maybe in Kansas City. He'll have to hitch back or get his sister to get him. Probably one of us will have to get him."

As it turned out no one had to get him. The joke was on us because we didn't see him again for two years.

Return of the Native

I had almost forgotten about John when a couple of years later, I answered my phone to a resonant baritone voice I didn't recognize.

"Hey, I'm back in town. Let's go get a drink."

"Who's back in town?"

"John. Your ole bud."

"Oh, *John.*" My mind was working frantically through storage bins of Johns. It was quite a popular name.

"Yeah, John Schutte of silver streak zephyr fame."

"Jesus, John! Where in the fuck have you been?"

When we met, he looked as cleaned up as I'd ever seen him — no jeans, no t-shirt, no sneakers, no wild hair. In addition, he had a different way of speaking. At first, I wondered if this was some kind of simulacrum. Maybe aliens in the Northwest had taken over his body.

I got down to business immediately. "What happened to you after we put you on the train? We thought you'd be back in a couple of days. Then...nothing. You scared the shit out of us!"

His story was a combination of resourcefulness, hutzpah, and luck. When he arrived in Portland, he got off the train without a penny in his pocket nor anything he could barter for dough. But he did notice that the hippies in the area had begun to ask for "spare change" from passersby. In that way, he managed to get enough money for coffee and food.

His first night in Portland was spent in an all-night laundromat, pretending to be washing clothes. There were newspapers spread around the laundromat where he found the HELP WANTED section of the newspaper. He decided to spend the next day looking for work because it was not very comfortable sleeping sitting up in an orange plastic chair.

After some begging in the morning and purchasing a city map, he began locating businesses that were hiring. For the next three days he pounded the pavement looking for work, asking for spare change, and returning to the laundromat to sleep. One night he had to strip down naked and hide in the lavatory while he actually did wash his clothes. It's hard to get a job when you smell like decaying cheese.

Finally, a small radio station hired him on as a janitor. The guys that ran the station were young and hip. When they heard about John's dilemma, they advanced him a few bucks and let him sleep in the janitor's room. In a few months, he accumulated enough money to rent a small apartment.

The announcers at the radio station recognized that they had a character in John, and he fit in with the outrageous bantering and fresh spirit of a new radio station. One fateful day, as John was mopping the floor while a phone-in talk show was going on, the announcer spontaneously said, "Well let's ask the janitor about that." Without hesitation, John sat down and poured out his opinions, which were both cogent and funny. The audience liked him. Liked him so much, that he became a segment on the show, "Let's Ask the Janitor." His popularity rose until the radio station finally hired a new janitor and gave John his own show.

Let me summarize the absurdity of this Schutte pathway. He was shanghaied on a train, then homeless on the streets of Portland, then a janitor that slept with mops, then a janitor interviewed on a radio show, and then a radio talk show host. I think you would agree that this is not your usual pathway to becoming a radio announcer. Yet this improbability became the reality. Certainly, most people that go into radio announcing go to school and through long internships before they get their own show. However, even though this new career was not his goal, John Schutte had become a radio announcer with his own show within a year. If there's anything that I learned from John, it is that luck is not blind; if you have the right spirit, doors shed their locks.

Suddenly I realized why Schutte's voice sounded so different. He had picked up the cadences and the deeper tones of radio announcers.

"So, John, you're taking a vacation from your job in Portland."

"No, I quit. I was getting tired of the daily grind."

I should've known that the fantastic opportunity that was handed to him could not hold him. Opportunity could knock, even come in and sit for a spell, but it couldn't stay.

Say Watts

John had come home, but he wasn't destined to stay for long. The magnetic lines of force from California were pulling on him. Every kind of social experiment, radical movement, new drug, and new idea was coming from the West. This should have been no surprise if you considered the history of our country as it expanded from the East Coast. The cutting edge of Manifest Destiny and new ways of living moved ever westward until it got jammed up in California against the ocean. The most radical and adventurous became condensed along the coastline with nowhere else to expand.

During the next couple of years, I kept a loose contact with John mainly through letters. He had tried LSD, he had discovered Richard Brautigan, he began writing short stories, he began experimenting with making large collages, he had flopped in the apartments and vans of a thousand different people, he had lived on the streets, hung with the homeless and the elite, and spent days at a time in libraries and museums reading literature and learning about art.

In the early 70s, I decided I wanted some adventures of my own. I bought a van that I could sleep in and began traveling across the western part of the U.S. When I arrived in LA, I gave Schutte a call. He was now back in school at USC (University of Southern California), studying film. He gave me a place on campus where we were to rendezvous.

His first words to me when we reunited were, "Let's go to my place so I can get rid of these books, and then we'll go give blood."

Blood? All my Schutte feelers suddenly came to life. Some time had passed since I had last seen him, and for a moment I was lulled by the thought that somehow he might have changed. But "blood" was a quick reminder of whom I was dealing with.

We casually chatted about school on the way to his dorm building. Then, without so much as a pause in the conversation, I found myself going up the fire escape and entering his room through a window. I paused the conversation.

"Is there any reason we took this route to your domicile?"

"Oh, yeah. I'm a little behind on paying my fees. They've tried to lock me out. If anyone knocks while you're here, don't answer."

I gave a sigh of contentment. On my trip, I had experienced the "shock of the new." It was satisfying to know that some things or people don't change.

"Okay now for the lobster and steak dinner, Settle."

"Can't we eat in the cafeteria or are you banned there, too. I'm a little tapped for cash, my man."

"That's why we're giving blood. They pay twenty-five dollars for a pint at a place I know. Let's get going. The blood center is not a safe place to be after dark." Again, those casual phrases, where you take pause — "not a safe place to be after dark."

The place was in Watts, which bordered the university. It was a dangerous area for Black people, let alone white people. They used murders in Watts as fillers in the LA newspapers. The blood center was on a street that looked like a bombed-out neighborhood in London after WWII. Some buildings were still scarred by the Watts riots in 1965 of "Burn, Baby, burn" fame.

When we entered the *center* (a word too lofty for this operation), we took our seats among winos, heroin addicts, and the homeless. The center reeked from a combination of sweat, urine, vomit, and Lysol. We were the only people there that were white (we were probably the only people that were white in a ten-mile radius). John struck up a conversation with the guy next to him, who was bent over and shaking fiercely with three layers of clothing on, despite the temperature outside being 90 degrees Fahrenheit.

I have to say that when they called our names to give blood, I was relieved to find out that the medical area was neat and clean, and the nurses seemed to be trained and knowledgeable about what they were doing. After our experiences in the waiting room, I was expecting something more like a back-alley abortion setting.

With twenty-five dollars apiece in our pockets from our blood donations, Schutte guided me to a place famous for its surf-n-turf. We wined and dined first class. With the little money we had left after this splurge, we bought a magnum of rot-gut champagne and weaved our way back up the fire escape and through the window. Here we listened to the latest Joni Mitchell album. It wasn't long before I passed out, but I kept waking up during the night seeing John still sucking on the champagne, reading and writing poetry. He never did go to sleep that night. You can always separate true romantics from the rest by the few hours they need to sleep.

The Tipping Point

If I were to pick a time in John Schutte's life where he really had the opportunity to put aside his youthful dreams for a more sobering and restrained existence, I would say it would be his marriage to Annie Bartholomew in 1973. When John started dating Annie (he had returned to Quincy again), I thought at the time, *Here is a person that can center John and curb his restless ways.* Annie was a sweet, intelligent person and had a no-frills approach to life. She didn't require lots of money or a fancy home. She knew most of the people that John knew because she was raised in Quincy and was a member of John's Class of '64. Her family was salt of the earth citizens in town.

When John proposed to Annie, I think he really was making his best effort to become a "normal" person and to "put the ways of childhood behind him" (Corinthians 13:11). After a down-home wedding, I expected that John was ready to embark on the journey that led to the stability of spouse and family. They started off with a plan and moved to Los Angeles where Annie had obtained a high school teaching job. She would provide most of the finances, while John went to film school at the University of Southern California.

To me, this was an adventurous launch for a couple. Together they would be facing a difficult enterprise that would bring them closer together. Neither of them knew anyone in LA, so they would be depending upon each other a great deal to make their way in a new life, but soon it became apparent to Annie that she would be in this alone. John's erratic behavior, whether being out all night or immersed in his projects, were never shared. John Schutte would never be a good life companion. In this isolation, they separated and divorced after a mere eight months.

John had carried his bride over the threshold, sat her down, and then left her. It was as far as he could go along the path more traveled by. It was his last chance, I think, for happiness. From this point on, I watched his life steadily decline as the fire of his youth could not kindle the more substantial logs of middle age. Oh, he had his moments where he was the old Schutte. He didn't go into a complete downward spiral. However, it was getting harder and harder for him as the years rolled by to capture those hours of splendor in the grass.

My last encounter with John Schutte years later was when he came to Quincy over the holidays. It was very much like the movie *My Dinner with Andre*, where two people discussed their lives — one person who had devoted his life to bizarre, new experiences; the other who had become staid. I was the staid one. I had taught high school for 15 years and my path had become fairly predictable. John, on the other hand, whose life was a series of pursuing the impossible dream, had stories and experiences that were becoming a bit more disturbing. The older a romantic becomes, the more self-destructive his quest becomes.

Unfortunately, Schutte had discovered cocaine. If there were one drug that could be John's kryptonite, it would be cocaine. It was the one drug that gave him the feelings of euphoria that he had sought all his life. But there is a great deal of difference of euphoria earned and euphoria in powdered form. As I talked with him, I could see the cocaine was having a profound effect on his mind. He talked morosely instead of joyfully of pushing himself to life's extremes. He had become infatuated with death and the life force within everything as it stubbornly struggled against extermination. When we departed for the last time, I was glad to quickly get away from him. He was descending into some murky waters that led to the dark night of the soul.

His dark night of the soul came on May 12, 1988. And he didn't pass through it. The story of what happened that night is still unclear. What is clear is that John was stabbed in the chest thirty-five times. As you would expect, Schutte's family preferred to believe that he was stabbed by an intruder. After all, can anyone stab themselves in the chest 35 times? Because of my last meeting with John, I was convinced it was an act of suicide. Even the police investigators said because of the angle of the wounds that they were self-inflicted. I believed that if you are high enough and despairing enough, you can stab yourself multiple times and feel little pain. Thus, the expansive heart of John Schutte stopped beating.

Backward Forward

"Though nothing can bring back the hour / Of splendor in the grass, of glory in the flower; / We will grieve not; rather find / Strength in what remains behind."
—William Wordsworth,
"Odes on Intimations of Immortality"

I think about these lines when I think about John Schutte and my own life at 73. I would have loved to share my aging with my old friend, laughing at our youthful foolishness and our misguidedness while at the same time acknowledging that our idealism led to something real and necessary in the world. I, too, throughout my life have had a romantic strain that has and continues to be nourished by the life of John Schutte. If he were around today, I'm not so sure I'd be as settled as I am. Perhaps, I'd hear the "Song of the Open Road" again and wiggle out of my Barcalounger.

What remains behind for me is not the image of John Schutte stabbing himself multiple times. The mention of his name brings back to me only the call of the highway and living more with your heart and less with your head. It brings back to me the deepest kinds of regrets one can have in old age — the regrets of what I could have done in my youth and did not do because I was afraid.

It would be easy to denigrate John's life because he did not temper it more with reason. Yet how many of us are ready to denigrate our own lives because we did not follow our bliss. This latter state of unfulfillment can be just as deadly to the spirit and can lead as well to suicide. I cannot say I'm on the brink of suicide, but I will say I often wince when I think of the opportunities I let go by because I wanted to play it safe. I'd give myself a C+ in life, almost but not quite making the honor role. I've learned to endure these failures, and I have forgiven myself for most of these mistakes.

I have not entirely forgiven myself for what I could have been for John Schutte. I was one among many that fed on his enthusiasm as if it were a cornucopia and cost John nothing. I was one among many willing to goad him on so that I could vicariously live his adventures without any investment of my own. I should have shown him more concern. As I look back, he had the makings of a good writer or artist, but because he was so far ahead of my art sensibilities, I dismissed most of what he wrote or created, not understanding what he was trying to do. I could have been the encouragement and audience that he needed for his creations. In his last years, I virtually abandoned him as he went through his crisis of faith in romanticism. John was not the old John as he arrived down at the bottom of a well that had gone dry.

As Horace Walpole once stated, "The world is a comedy to those that think; a tragedy to those that feel." John Schutte's life was a tragedy, but he is still a shining star for me — remote yet inspirational. "Sorry, John. You were smarter, more creative, and more courageous than I ever could be. You lived more deeply than I ever could allow myself. I did not have the courage to understand or to follow your path. I did not have the strength to save you."

CHAPTER 6
THE PRIDE OF LIONS

"A friend awakens your life in order to free the wild possibilities within you."

—John O'Donohue

Sadly, I was not going to write this chapter in 2020. It would have been a significant omission in my early life story in Quincy, but after writing about John Schutte's tragic story in the preceding chapter, I thought I couldn't bear revisiting a second tragedy in my life — Emily Dickinson's "My life closed twice before its close." Yet redemption was around the corner, and it came as the result of another tragedy.

Despite its pandemic proportions, Covid 19 had some unexpected upsides. For instance, people drove less back and forth to work and, thus, the air quality in cities became better. People who hadn't had time to read a good book suddenly were found on the couch in the afternoon with a page-turner. Book sales went up. Some families benefited by being brought closer together because of more time spent out in nature, eating together, playing games together, and surprise of surprises, *talking* together. Many of the things that people had put off, they decided to do once they were working from home. For me it was making a long, overdue phone call.

When I say overdue, I'm talking in terms of a half century. Bill Bregach (pronounced bree-gotch) was another romantic in my life like John Schutte. While John Schutte was a good friend, Bill Bregach was my very best friend through high school, college and, thereafter, for a few short years. Sometimes people just grow apart over time, which can be a very natural process — marriage, children, job, and relocations can become so salient in their lives that they put away past friendships like tattered, old photo albums in the attic. But sometimes a breakup can be dated to the year and day. My break-up with Bill Bregach was the latter. So, when I tentatively decided to call him one afternoon in the summer of 2020, I had no idea if the ties that once bound us had become so frayed as to be nonexistent — Marty who? But before I go into the details of that call, permit me to recall.

Elementary School: Get Thee to a Nunnery

I knew Bill Bregach fairly well before we became inextricably entwined in high school. In fact, I knew everyone fairly well who I went to grade school with. How could you not in a small Catholic elementary school with the parish as the school boundary. Living in a square mile area, most of us would have run into each other whether we went to the Catholic school or not. As you would expect, there would be no bussing and very few children were driven to school — we walked, picking others up along the way like a stream picks up tributaries.

What I recall about Bill Bregach in grade school was that he was a physically diminutive fellow. In some ways this had to do with having a birthday in December, which made him the youngest of his classmates. Along with his size, he was cute and well-mannered. He seemed to be the ideal, dimpled student with neatly combed over black hair and respectful brown eyes that the nuns were looking for. This often saved him from being blamed for drinking altar wine or going up to the church bell tower to eat his lunch during recess. "Why little Billy wouldn't do that!" Oh, yeah.

And David Slew Goliath

None of his fellow classmates made that mistake, however. We remembered him as the David that slayed Goliath in 6th grade. The Goliath was John Shoop. Who knows how many grades that John

Shoop had been held back? He was at least 6 ft. of muscle at the time, and everybody stayed out of his way, including the 8ᵗʰ graders. John was the classic "hood" at the time with motorcycle boots and jacket and the DA (Duck's Ass) haircut. Shoop's face, however, was deceptive; he didn't look the part of a thug. He was strikingly handsome with auburn hair and piercing blue eyes. But behind those blue eyes, unfortunately, there shone no light of understanding — a dog's kind of eyes that seemed on the verge of language.

I had made my peace with Shoop. The sisters usually arranged our seating alphabetically in class. Therefore, John *Shoop* was always placed behind Marty *Settle*, where he could cheat off me unremittingly. I allowed — even encouraged — him to do so, because he was my safe passage past the bullies of our school — "You mess with me, you mess with my gorilla, John Shoop." John felt a need to protect his cash cow so that he could graduate from grade school before, let's say, he got married.

Bill had made the mistake one day of not giving up his place in the water fountain line to Shoop. We all made way when the beast wanted to drink. The result was Bill being tossed along the well-waxed corridor like a bowling ball. This scene only reinforced our commitment to not cross Shoop in his time of thirst. John got his drink, wiped his mouth with his leather jacket, careful to avoid the zippers, and didn't even look at Bregach sprawled on the floor. We thought that was the end of it. But as John Shoop paused above a set of stairs, he was suddenly propelled over the brink by a mouse-like creature behind him.

He took quite a spill, landing up against the bars of the steam radiator below. Blood was flowing from a cut over Shoop's eye, and he took his finger and looked at it as if he had never seen blood before — at least not his own blood. Then he got to his feet. He was steady and seemed to be fine. We invoked Jesus, Mary, and Joseph to save Bill's ass. Bill stood frozen staring down at John at the bottom of the stairs. But Shoop laughed. "That was pretty good," he said to Bill. "You got balls, Bregach." After that they were friends. None of us, however, were going to use this strategy later to befriend Shoop.

A dimple on the wimple

On another occasion, Bill and John Kolodziej (I always thought his last name should be a line on an eye chart) were throwing snow-balls after school — one of the delights if you're born in a climate with snow. Even more delightful is when the snow piles up on the streets and cars go back and forth over it like rolling pins, changing it into slush. Slush allows you to make an *ice ball*, which is quite different from your common *snowball* — the difference let's say be-tween being hit by a BB and an M16 slug. Ice balls were deadly and could knock you out.

As Kolodziej and Bregach were having their afterschool war games, they noticed Sister Mariam Francis walking on the side-walk heading toward the convent. Bill decided to give her a scare and packed an ice ball, because she was getting out of range (You could throw an ice ball farther because it was heavier). Lining her up and taking into account windage and the Sister's speed, Bill released the ice ball, which was intended to land in front of her. Whether Bill's aim was bad or Sister Mariam sped up, Bregach could see that his projectile was drifting toward her head. Then he heard *Wham, ubble, ubble!* — the sound of impact on Mari-am's wimple (the starched headdress that nuns at our school wore). She staggered but didn't go down. Mariam Francis was one tough nun.

Both John and Bill dove under a car so as not to be detected. As was often the case, the slush under the car was melting; it had melted to the point where they had to lay still in puddles of freezing water. No amount of pain or suffering, however, would have coaxed them from under the car until they were convinced the coast was clear. If they were caught hitting a nun in the head with a slush ball, they knew they would receive the fury of justice from every quarter — nuns, priests, members of the parish, parents, relatives, and even classmates, who enjoyed shenanigans, but not at this level. They froze for about a half an hour before they emerged, cautious as field mice with hawks overhead.

Fortunately, nothing was mentioned about this incident the next day of school, and Bill and John felt unburdened from the thought that their days might be numbered.

High School: Pride Goeth before the Lions

As I mentioned in Chapter 4 on Catholic Education, high school was not a particularly happy time for me. When people tell me that they would like to return to their good ole' high school years, I always shudder at the thought. However, there was one light that burned bright in that night sky of high school and that was the development of a fast friendship with Bill Bregach.

I remember once seeing a *National Geographic* documentary on lions. It seems the young, male lions are kicked out of the pride by the alpha male. They are then forced to roam the plains alone or to bond with other males in the same situation. The bond that develops between these males become lifelong, even after they separate as adults with their own pride. I found my adolescent years on the sexless savannahs of Quincy similar to that; Bill Bregach was to be the young lion that I romped with. We roamed — every nook and cranny in the city and outside the city; day or night; winter, spring, summer, or fall.

Nature amused us greatly. We were always stuffing a backpack with food, filling a canteen, and going on a day's hike. There were plenty of places to explore — Soldiers Home's outlying wilderness, the railroads tracks, river parks, and river bottoms. We threw rocks, stuck knives, chopped down small trees, explored abandoned houses, shot pellet guns, and built fires — all with concomitant stories.

We saw ourselves as Daniel Boone/Davy Crocket types, although our fierceness and temperaments could sometimes be called into question. I remember when I got a new pellet pistol for Christmas. It was designed to look like a .45 pistol, which thrilled my sense of its deadliness. It was capable of shooting either pellets or BB's. I couldn't wait for Bill and me to take it out for a spin. When we did, we decided to walk down the railroad tracks, shooting everything in sight — old bottles, beer cans, and rusted tin. When Bill spotted a bird on a telephone wire, he shot at it like a cowboy from the hip. The bird dropped without a flap as if it had a heart attack. "What a shot!" I said, but there was no joy in Mudville for Bill. He didn't think he could *really* kill something. As I said previously, we were questionable pioneers.

Encountering creatures was another part of the fun of exploring Quincy's outer limits. The bottomlands on the river were full of creatures of all sorts, some a little scary. On one outing on the bottom lands, we were hopping around an area identifiable because it contained a Sulphur spring, which put out a smell like rotten eggs. The bottomlands were full of tributaries and marshes, and we were forced to jump from island to island to keep from sloshing in some swampy areas. As I was ready to make a leap across a small stream, I turned to look to see if Bill was following close behind. He was, but he had an expression on his face of abject horror. When I turned to see what he was afraid of, there was a cottonmouth reared up with his fangs exposed. I could see the white interior of its mouth. Not only did we exit with alacrity, not taking time to worry about getting our feet wet, but we ran at top speed for about a half mile before, bent over panting, we decided it was safe. I don't know what Daniel Boone would have done, but I'm sure we would have outrun him.

We were into physicality of all sorts. Besides the great outdoors, we played a host of sports with one another — basketball, football, baseball, soccer, and even gymnastics. Often, we would go to the local YMCA to work out with their weights. There was nothing we would have liked more than bulging biceps — the Holy Grail of a chiseled body. Bill achieved this goal more than I. No matter what kind of shape I got into or how much I worked out, my body never coughed up the gift of showy biceps. Sigh.

Bill Bregach's Bulging Bicep   *Marty Settle's Lesser Bicep*

I Like Poetry, Long Walks on the Beach, and Poking Dead Things With a Stick

While all this sounds quite normal for *Happy Days* teens, Bill and I had a few specialties uniquely our own. An example would be cutting off the heads of dead animals. Yes, you read that correctly. That does sound ominous, like the history of children who would grow up to be serial killers. But in our case, it was unabashed interest in biology, a subject both of us excelled in in high school. The decapitated animal's head would be taken home and boiled to get rid of most of the fur and flesh. Then we would soak the skull in borax to rid it of any remailing tissue, followed by bleaching it in the sun to get the degree of whiteness that we wanted. Bill was the mounter of heads, and his bedroom proudly displayed our work.

What was even odder about this activity was that it was not an assignment; it was motivated by pure curiosity. Secondly, as Bill's unflappable mother was driving us around, she would point out dead animals on the side of the road and pull over so that we could cut off their heads and put them in her trunk. She wasn't the squeamish type and, apparently, she wasn't worried about us becoming serial killers.

December Sky

One of the joys of adolescence is roaming in the night. It is a clear breakaway from one's cozy, family hearth to be a nocturnal creature. Unfettered, Bregach and I combed the neighborhoods, observing the scenes of activities available through open curtains or silhouetted on closed blinds. We sniffed around the downtown, where I shoplifted for my one and only time. We played Putt-Putt under the bright lights, and we stopped in the Maid Rite for pinball and a burger. Again, normal enough. But then our imaginations never rested, and there was that deadly question that started off with, "Wouldn't it be cool if ...?"

"Wouldn't it be cool if ...we had a Fourth of July celebration on an early December night?" Our imaginations put together quickly all the ingredients — we had fireworks left over from the Fourth of July, we had a bow, we had arrows, we had electric tape, and we had a cigarette lighter. Most importantly, we had questions that we wanted to get answered through the scientific method of experiment.

How high could we shoot an arrow laden with M80s into the night sky? Would the fuses on these fireworks be put out by the speed of the arrow? Would sparklers work? Would electric tape be good enough to hold M80s on the arrow? Would anyone be concerned about this activity on such cold nights?

When we assembled everything on a clear night, we went to Berrian Park where there was an open field ideal for such a launch. We were both as giddy as Homer Hickam of *October Sky*. The bow was powerful, and we had great hope that our missiles would reach significant heights. Bill notched the first arrow and bent the bow; I lit the fuses with a cigarette lighter. *Woosh!*

The reality was better than the dream with the arrow reaching church steeple heights. Then *wham, wham, wham* with sparks spraying everywhere. My god, what had we wrought! We were emboldened and began firing arrows at a rapid pace. Sparklers worked better than Roman candles with after images floating across the sky. Soon another set of lights entered our area at ground level — the flashing blue lights of a police car. We got one of our questions answered — residents near the park were not amused.

The police, of course, had no chance of catching us on our home turf in the dark. We knew every nook and cranny of the park and could have easily eluded them blindfolded. We bathed in the glow of experimental success. All our questions were answered. However, you may have noticed that we failed to ask one important question — what happens to the arrow. Risk analysis was not our strong suit. That the arrows could land on someone's roof and cause a fire, or worse yet, that they could land on someone causing injury had never entered our calculations. As with much that we did, we were lucky.

The Two-headed alien in your window

Another night activity that was a specialty of ours had to do with the fact that I was good at gymnastics and Bill Bregach was extremely strong. We spent many afternoons under a silver maple in my front yard doing gymnastic-doubles stunts. Bill would be the holder as we progressed from my doing balancing stunts on him in a prone position with his knees up to the more complex position that required that he stand and swing me up into a handstand on his shoulders. (See below.)

Bill Bregach (bottom) and Marty Settle (top)

As you might expect, we were show-offs in displaying our gymnastic skills. Enter another "Wouldn't it be cool if...?" The epiphany came one night as we were walking past a friend's house. It was one of those brick, shotgun cottages, which Quincy is full of, with long windows on the sides. We could see our buddy inside. That's when we decided to do our handstand-on-shoulders routine in front of his window. When the friend looked up, I could hear him say, "What the fuck!" before he realized it was us. This turned out to be a great laugh, which in turn primed the pump for more reprisals.

I don't how many windows we eventually stood in front of with this balancing stunt — surprising, stunning, and scaring the bejesus out of people who had settled in for the night. I never got to see the householders' reactions since I was upside down. But Bill did, and he reported the degrees of facial changes from initial puzzlement to the realization of the unlikely vision appearing in their window. I'm sure some thought they were hallucinating or had been visited by an elongated alien with heads on top of one another. Before viewers had a chance to take any actions, we were gone in seconds, leaving them with a sense of mystery that inherently inhabits the night.

Late Bloomer

In his junior and senior year in high school, Bill Bregach went through a transformation both physically and socially. As I said previously, Bill was rather diminutive in grade school, but late high school he grew about four inches and put on twenty pounds of muscle. No longer was he cute little Billy, but he was handsome and rugged Bill.

With his new body, he went out for football and gained a new respect from his fellow classmates as a hardnosed defensive back. Further, he became a starter on our soccer team. It was a little disconcerting for me to watch Bill's late blooming. I had always looked down on Bill from my 5'9" perch. Now I had to get used to looking up to his 5'11". I hadn't filled out either, wrestling in high school at the 112 lb. to 120 lb. weight category. Bill was a stout cudgel; I was a willow switch. Was I a bit envious? *Damn right*. But despite all, we still matched well in athletic abilities.

Concomitant to Bill Bregach's physical growth was a social growth. His new manliness was attractive to many in school. He was included in activities with new groups of people, and it wasn't long before he established himself as a central figure in these groups. As a leader, he was a natural because he knew what it was like not to be among the popular, so he was inclusive in all his dealings. Also, he had an irrepressible sense of mischief and fun. His sense of humor could be self-deprecating as he related the more awkward years of his life. I've always believed people love you more for revealing your weaknesses than your perfections. Was I envious of his new social success? *Hell no.* Bill was my entre into circles that I had never been in before. Our bond was strong, and there was no way he was leaving me behind.

College: The Local Yokels

It has always seemed to me somewhat facile when people seem to all agree that it is best for a student to go away to college. That was not true for me when I decided to go to Quincy College (QC), a college just across the street from my elementary school and parish church. The Franciscans of our parish and elementary school would be the same religious order that would run the college. If nothing else, there was a strong continuity in my Catholic education.

I've never regretted my failure to make the leap to college in another location rather than just walk across the street. My friends in college were for the most part all locals who I had gone to school with through grade school and high school. You would think that I had had enough of them. Not true.

In the new freedoms that we had obtained in college, the bonds of these earlier relationships went from rope to forged chains. Even though we still had the presence of parents to subdue our wilder enthusiasms toward adulthood, we often had fewer restrictions than those from out of town, living in the dorms. We had no curfews and few party restrictions. We had our own local tavern that allowed us to drink underage, and we studied better in our homes without the distractions that commonly occur in the dorms.

For me as a person who had just come back from the monastery after high school, I was dazzled by what I could now do at QC. The contrast between the discipline of the monastery life where I had to wake up every morning at four to feed the chickens before matins and the college life where I didn't have a class to attend until ten in the morning was so overwhelming that I froze at first to inaction. Lucky for me, I had the ever-faithful Bill Bregach and other long-time friends to nourish me to social health.

I Once Was Blind But Now I Ski

I went to the Christian Brothers' monastery to learn faith and failed. But Bill Bregach taught me faith in the most visceral of ways. It was not an epiphany like that of St. Paul, but it took a certain amount of blindness, nonetheless.

Being a local in college had its advantages in knowing the terrain and participating in its pleasures. For us river rats, living on the river meant water skiing. In college, this activity would take on a whole new meaning. We knew people with ski boats, we knew the sandbars and islands, and we knew where we could party without interference by the authorities — something the out-of-towners couldn't do.

Bill was a consummate water skier; I, on the other hand, was a land lubber. When I got back to Quincy, Bill took me out with some guys who loved the river, water skiing, and partying. At first, I would just enjoy the rides in the boat and campfires and picnics on Hogback Island. But the day for my baptism came as Bill was being pulled out of the water from a dazzling display of slaloming over wakes at high speeds. He said to me, "Put on this life jacket and get in."

"Whoa, whoa," I said, "you know I can't swim."

"You don't have to. You just have to have faith in me and your lifejacket." (Everyone wore a lifejacket skiing on the Mississippi in case you were hit by a submerged log and knocked out.) Before I had time to say "Titanic," I was bobbing in Old Man River, flailing away, trying to get the skies on my feet. Bill threw me the tow rope.

"We will gradually get you started. Don't try to get up. Just bend your knees slightly and lean back. Let the boat do the work.

It will pop you out of the water. Then keep your balance, lean back, and enjoy."

Sure enough, I popped out of the water on the first try and, after a few clumsy steps, I glided with giddiness. Unlike St. Peter, I had enough faith to walk on water. That was the beginning of many skiing afternoons on the Mississippi, and a new physical exhaustion that made partying on the sandbars that much better (nothing like a cold beer after wrestling with the river). My faith was blind, but not so blind that I didn't learn to swim in the near future. When I think of my college days with Bill Bregach, a river always runs through it.

I Get A Kick Out Of You

Soccer was another college experience that Bill Bregach brought me to. As I stated previously, we had a soccer team at our high school. In fact, Catholic schools in general were into soccer long before soccer took hold in the public schools. One of the reasons for this is that Catholic schools in the U.S. often had students from other countries where soccer prevailed as the most popular sport. Secondly, soccer was inexpensive in comparison to football; thus, soccer could replace football as a fall sport, or it could be easily added to the school's sports program.

Since Bregach played soccer for Christian Brothers High School, he joined the soccer program at Quincy College, which was one of those schools that could not afford football. The competition was a couple levels above what Bill had experienced in high school. QC had a very good soccer team because it was the destination of many Catholic students from the St. Louis area, which had developed soccer leagues that spanned from grade school through high school. If Bill was going to play for QC, he was going to have to up his game.

In a small way, I helped with this, which turned out to be a benefit to both of us. Unlike many of the soccer players on the team, Bill didn't have a group of guys to play soccer with when they went home for the summer. He only had me and, at first, I wasn't particularly interested in soccer. But, what at first was just my putting Bill through his paces, I began to enjoy parts of the work out, especially dribbling. That's when he convinced me to go out for the team.

Of course, there was no way I could be a starter for the team or even a reliable substitute, but I was good enough to be part of the practice squad. I played against some soccer players who eventually turned pro when the North American Soccer League was established in 1968. From the bench, I watched and learned about soccer, a sport few people knew about at the time. Bill was a starter, playing Outside Left (I guess today that would be a Wide Left Midfielder); he was a solid player among teammates with far more experience than he and, since I played his position in practices, I watched him carefully to learn other subtleties of the game besides dribbling.

In the end, Bill Bregach was an important element of Quincy College Hawk history, because this team won the national championship in 1966. The entire team was later honored by becoming part of QC's sports Hall of Fame. What is amusing (and even laughable) is that I can claim to be a part of a National Championship soccer team, and I am included in this Hall of Fame. The practical benefit to this experience came years later in life when I had a daughter who played soccer. Guess who was the ideal parent to coach her teams? Mwah. I knew ten times more about soccer than any of the other parents, who were not raised with soccer.

ENTERING QUINCY UNIVERSITY HALL OF FAME 9/23/06
1966 Quincy College Soccer Team:1966 NAIA National Soccer Champions (13-0-0)

Bill Bregach, second row, second from right;
Marty Settle, first row, second from right

On the Fields of Troy

Another sport that Bill and I picked up along the way in college was handball. Since we had often gone to the YMCA to weight lift and do gymnastics, we came across people who played handball and, as we observed the game, we decided to give it a shot. We loved it.

At first, when we were learning the rules and strategies of handball, we played civilly and without keeping score. But this was short-lived, being replaced with games and matches that rivalled Olympic elks competing for mates. These battles on the fields of Troy filled the echoing chambers of a handball court with screams and shouts and unrelenting profanities. Once we were asked to leave because our language offended the values of the Young Men's Christian Association.

Handball was an ideal sport in many ways for the both of us. It required only two people and little equipment — handball gloves and a ball. Previous to handball, physical activities that we had practiced were more cooperative in nature, but handball was mano e' mano in both the sense of "hand to hand" and the mistranslation of "man to man." It challenged all our physical abilities in direct conflict against the other — endurance, agility, quickness, strength, and cunning. There was no clear winner in years of playing handball. But when we were finished with a session, we went out to get a large pizza with plenty of Coke. Not a smidgin of animosity remained in our systems.

One incident that is worth recounting that had to do with handball was when instead of getting a pizza after handball, we went over to Bill's house for a Thanksgiving dinner. They had some guests and assigned seats. We arrived a little before the family prayer, which in Bill's family would have been done very reverently. As I bowed my head and listened to the prayer, I made the mistake of putting my legs under my chair. Sometimes I cramped up after our handball workouts. If you've ever had your hamstring muscle cramp, you do not wait to attend to it a few minutes later. I straightened my legs out at the speed of light, rattling the china on the table. Then, I came out with "Jesus Christ." All heads popped up puzzled, when Bill came to the rescue with, "He gets like that when he's moved by the Spirit." Everyone seemed to accept that I was extremely vocal about my love of the Lord and bowed their heads to finish the prayer.

The Road of Excess

One of the most important reasons for going to college besides the academics is partying. When I say "partying," I am not saying "debauchery." If partying turns into debauchery with people passed out everywhere and women being sexually abused, then the partying loses its legitimate value.

And partying *does* have legitimate value. When students arrive at college, they are in an environment with freedoms never used or tested. Even as locals at QC living at home, we found our parents granting us a certain permissiveness not granted in high school. The philosophy was — don't ask; don't tell. Curfews were gone. No questions were asked by parents after listening to repeated flushing of toilets in the middle of the nights. It was assumed that it was better to assume that little Johnny or Jane was peaked in the morning because they were suffering from the flu. (Yeah, right. The Budweiser beer virus.)

Partying allowed us to try on personalities that we had never tried on before. Liquor was just an excuse to be funny, to be flirtatious, and to be excessive. Often people were not as drunk as they pretended when they tried on new masks of behavior. In this partying milieu, I found out that I was funny, really funny; that I was a good dancer; and that I could attract females. But I could not carry a party on the strength of my personality. I was merely a spoke; Bill Bregach was the hub.

The Synonym for Party

If for Ursula Le Guin "The word for world is forest," for college students the word for adventure is party. The locals would go to great lengths to create a party that would be worthwhile talking about the next day and, perhaps, years to come. Academic adventure was not enough for us; we wanted our own mythology. We had two means to do this: 1. build a party around a new venue or experience; 2. invite Bill Bregach to the party. As locals, we had knowledge and access to places that those from out of town did not have. As locals, we had Bill Bregach, who could carry a party by the strength of his personality. Bill could drink, tell stories, get giddy, play the ukulele, and befriend both men and women. When you had all of these ingredients, your chances for adventure were high, indeed.

For example, John Schutte and I organized a party that would occur in a cavern near the river. No one but the locals would know about this place. Beforehand we had set up a roaring bonfire and had pillows and blankets strewn everywhere. There were coolers with beer and soda iced up, and guitars were laid out awaiting their musicians. We had even decorated the walls of the cavern with petroglyphs.

This party was billed to our dates as a mysterious experience. If they wanted to come, they had to be blindfolded, so they could never reveal our secret location. As cars arrived at the site, the girls were led around in circles until they could hear and feel the bonfire. Blindfolds removed, they could see this pleasure dome under the starry skies. I remember Bill playing his ukulele and encouraging singing around the fire. Bill played Dylan and drank far into the night, indefatigable, as the stars winked out along with the embers. It was an event talked about for years to come.

Do Not Hump

Parties could be just a masculine affair. As you would expect when the drinking group was just men, the character of a party changed greatly. There can be no doubt in my mind that the presence of women civilizes men. When the party was just my buds, the behaviors took on a cruder tone in both word and deed. We really didn't need to impress one another, so we farted, cussed, drank, and talked about women without inhibition.

One particular all-male affair took place in the Ozarks. Bill Bregach, John Lammers, John Wachtel, Mike Hutmacher, John Schutte, and I decided at the end of the summer to have a bash before school started. All of us had had enough of our summer jobs

(Mike Hutmacher and I had worked at tedious, dirty jobs at Quincy Compressor), and we were ready to cut loose.

Camping out has its virtues for rowdy males. You can be vigorous with chopping wood, hiking, and swimming in the lake. You can drink with impunity. And with no women around, you can keep your mind in the gutter. Passing out is fine, puking is fine, keeping the same clothes on for days is fine. Here's a picture of such males in the Ozark Mountains:

Bill Bregach, Mike Hutmacher, and John Wachtel

You'll notice nothing but slabs of meat will do for mountain men; we may not have even used silverware. Even before the Men's Movement, Bill found it a requirement for us to dance around the campfire, proclaiming our ferocity and friendship. We were warrior brothers of a sort. The "Do Not Hump" sign was a trophy that we stole from a railroad car (Humping was a process used by the railroad to connect cars; cars with delicate loads were not to be "humped."). It does not mean safe sex, but we, of course, gave it its sexual connotations. We kept that sign for years to come as a talisman of our tribal unity.

You wouldn't think so, but this kind of partying led to deep philosophical speculation around a campfire. Staring into flames and watching the sparks go up into the Milky Way creates the conditions for asking the fundamental Gauguin questions: *Where do we come from? What are we? Where are we going?* This was deadly serious talk about the mystery of existence. Like in the ancient Greek symposiums (Latin for "drinking party"), we dropped off to sleep one-by-one with our Socrates, Bill Bregach the last to go.

Tribal Members: John Wachtel, John Schutte, Bill Bregach, and Me

Beam me up, Scottie; beam me down

If there is one facet of life missing in this memoir of my early years in Quincy, Illinois, it is romance. Mine was a purely masculine experience until around age nineteen. I was raised in a family with two brothers and in a neighborhood where no one had daughters near my age. I went to an all-boys high school and made friends exclusively with males. Then I went to an all-male religious order. To say that girls were mysterious to me would be an understatement; they were aliens.

For me, there would need to be a lot of handholding by both men and women to move me along the road of courtship. Parties were great for this because it would have been impossible for me to muster up the courage to ask a girl out on a date one-on-one. I needed a group activity where I could be relaxed enough to carry on trivial conservations with young women and to learn from friends how to behave with women.

Bill Bregach was my main resource in the dating game. Bill was not just a man's man; he was a woman's man. Ruggedly handsome while at the same time humorous and charming was a deadly combination for attracting women. We often worked in tandem entertaining at a party, and this association brought me to the attention of some young women. With encouragement and instruction from the master, I made my way into the soft light of romance.

As you might expect from a high school recluse and college monk, I had never fallen in love. But once I got on the path most traveled by, it was bound to happen that I would find a girlfriend. It was an e.e. cummings kind of love — impossible and glorious. Those first kisses of discovery of our love would never be reproduced in my life for their innocence and ability to open every faucet in my body. They flowed deeper and faster than the nearby Mississippi where they occurred.

Her name was Diane Scott, aka Scotty. During the same period, Bill Bregach had found his own love, Kathy Merriman. What a crescendo we made double dating, a consummation devoutly to be wished in our friendship and a strengthening of the bond between us. Now we could play on a new level, attending to two females. We picnicked, drank, regaled these women with stories from our past, performed our gymnastics, and played our guitars. And like the song, we drove Bill's chevy to the levee and made out on beach blankets until our lips were raw.

Kathy and Scotty

As inevitable as it was that I would find a first love, it was just as inevitable that we would break up. I was ill equipped to know what to do once I had found a girlfriend for the first time — I knew little about handling jealousy, sex, smothering a person, etc. In the same way, I didn't know the impact that breaking up would have on me — I was depressed for quite some time and refused to believe that I could not win Scotty back — no one could "ever dissever my soul from the soul" of Scotty. Bill, on the other, had much more experience in these matters. He did provide me with comfort and insight but, as far as Kathy was concerned, he eventually married her. I often thought it would have been mythical had we had a double ceremony.

Lucy in the Sky with Diamonds

As alluded to in the introduction to this chapter, I can name the day and year when our friendship broke up. The year was 1973 and the day was June 23. Bill and Kathy had moved to Boulder, Colorado, and I went to visit them in my Dodge van, which I was living in at the time. In most ways, I had bought into the hippie way of life — on the road looking for adventure.

Bill and Kathy lived in a "pad," the word at the time for an apartment with batik curtains, mattresses on the floor, and orange crate furniture. As usual, Bill was always industrious and energetic about earning a living. He worked for a company that made silver spurs. In addition, he began making stained glass mirrors, an enterprise that later turned into business called Orpheus Mirrors. Boulder, Colorado, was a haven for the craftsman hippie who wanted to enjoy nature and work with his/her hands. I loved crafts myself, so I was interested in what Bill was doing with stained glass. On the surface, it might appear that we were surfing the same wave and that all would be well. All was well, except for one insurmountable difference — drugs.

I was a hippie in all things, except drugs. Mentally, I did not trust what any drug would do to my unstable psyche (I had bouts with depression). Bill, Kathy, and their friends had given themselves over to the new consciousness that LSD brought. They took it frequently; they chose a pathway of enlightenment which I could not follow for I feared what would happen to me if I dropped acid. Buckminster Fuller was my steadier and gradual pathway to enlightenment. When I left Bill and Kathy, I went to San Clemente, California, to follow my dream of building geodesic domes out of fiberglass. But more sadly, I knew on the day that I left, I wouldn't be seeing Bill for some time to come (a half century as it turned out). Our different approaches to experience would drive a wedge into our friendship.

Backward Forward

If I've learned anything about the lives of John Schutte and Bill Bregach, it is about the nitroglycerin mixture of courage and risk in romantics. Both believed in the strength of their own minds and their ability to be indomitable when encountering the shock of the new. Both eventually came up against an experience that they could not master — cocaine.

I have already written about John Schutte's dark night of despair. But Bill had a similar three o'clock in the morning dark night of the soul experience. But instead of suicide, he called out, "Jesus, Jesus, save me." The next morning, miraculously, he was done with cocaine. To this day, he is an ardent believer in Jesus Christ, truly his savior.

Now I'm not a believer in Jesus, but certainly Bill's story indicates some sort of miracle occurred. However you want to frame this experience, I was grateful that Bill Bregach was still alive when I tried to reunite with him so many years later — my own little miracle. Our first conversation on the phone was a lovefest — two dogs rolling on the ground in ecstasy at returning home. What was amazing was how fast we caught up and how fast we began sharing our lives again. He has become an abstract artist, and I have become a writer and an assemblage artist. We fit again hand in glove, reaching for the higher things. If it weren't for Covid, we would have physically embraced by now in joy.

There are so many senseless chapters in a person's life. If you don't have these, I must wonder if you have ever really lived. Of the many regrets that I have in my life, I would have to say that not re-establishing my relationship to Bill Bregach much sooner ranks high on my list. Some would say better late than never and, while this is too facile, it will have to do. It makes me think of Tennyson's poem "Ulysses," where Ulysses has grown old and wants to return to his quests on the seas. Pure foolishness. Bill and I will never be two young lions again. Yet I am at times roused by Bill to youth no longer reflected by my body, and I am ready like Ulysses to go on a young man's quest:

> *Tho' much is taken, much abides; and tho'*
> *We are not now that strength which in old days*
> *Moved earth and heaven, that which we are, we are;*
> *One equal temper of heroic hearts,*
> *Made weak by time and fate, but strong in will*
> *To strive, to seek, to find, and not to yield.*

REUNION AND HOMECOMING: AN ELEGIAC

Besides John Schutte, many of the people that I have gone to high school have died — all candles burning in a sacred grotto in my heart. I wrote the following poem for the occasion of the fiftieth reunion of the Christian Brothers and Notre Dame High School Class of 1964 in Quincy, Illinois. If you do not know Quincy, it is built above the limestone bluffs of the Mississippi River, which is an important element at the end of the poem. If you do not know Catholicism in the 1950s and early 60s, you do not know that we often had outdoor processions, where we would chant in a responsorial fashion, the names of the saints. This would be done in Latin. An example would be:

Priests: Sancte Ioseph [St. Joseph]

Congregational response: Ora pro nobis [pray for us]

Priests: Sancte Ioannes et Iacobe [St. John and St. James]

Congregational response: Orate pro nobis [pray for us]

I used this responsorial system in my poem where I made the saints into classmates who had passed away since our graduation in 1964. The only change I made in this rendition is that I did not include the long list of deceased classmates, but only included a few who have passed to give the reader an idea of how a responsorial poem could work.

Finally, I do not think that the specific references to place and people destroy the universality of poem. There is nothing like the passing of 70 years to bring us all together under the inexorable unifier of aging: birth, marriage, reproduction, and death.

Reunion and Homecoming

Written for the occasion of the fiftieth reunion of the Christian Brothers and Notre Dame High School Class of 1964 in Quincy, Illinois, on the banks of Mississippi.

half century of exile
enough to know there is no cheating
I should have danced with the girl in the corner
stood up to the bully
skipped school in cloud absolution
should have wandered to hidden chapels
should have trusted blindfolds
should have stood closer to the fire
should have

I summon today that whistling boy
in numerology of 1325 Lind –
you too are with him –
down the street, up the alley
in the park with ball glove, bike
in Putt Putt nights
near the house where I kissed Phyllis

I return by the sunset gate
where I first was called away,
embrace that boy,
tell him I have lost and gained faith
lost and gained a wife
lost parents became a parent
crawled out of holes of disillusionment
celebrated on crests
he tells me that he and I are one
that he has never left me
always at my back
in cut grass vapors
in burning leaves
shooting baskets in twilight
always there
quick behind my eyes in the mirror

I summon you
who have walked with me
in many processions
to open-mouth schools
to communion rails of tongues

to ceremonies of robes
our names being called one at a time
down sacramental aisles with white-laced spouses
down gold-handled paths to tombs
always thinking whose turn next

I summon those who have gone before
through the darkest door –

in the name of Bill Abel
mythological boy first slain   *ora pro nobis*

of John Schutte
restless romantic doomed to early death   *ora pro nobis*

of Larry Waterkotte, the loving bear
of Leo Vogel, tragic Huck Finn   *orate pro nobis*

of all the saints of my school days   *orate pro nobis*

blesséd be their sanctity
blesséd be the unceasing river
blesséd be our bodies that wrinkle in the wind
blesséd be the torches of old teachers
blesséd be the divine aroma of nuns
blesséd be the waxed-floor corridors, locker doors slamming
blesséd be the quarterback, the nerd, the clown
blesséd be the stuttering, the shy, the bold, the polio embraced
blesséd be the male and female body, the courtship syrup
blesséd be our children and children's children
blesséd be the dead that cease to breathe but not inspire
blesséd be the burden of youth that was ours

my companions,
have you failed enough to forgive?
have you betrayed enough to withhold judgment?
have you lived long enough to be condemned and redeemed?

you have been in my dreams
dust dancing in curtain light
once I thought I knew what was best for me
once I thought I was lighter than my losses
I would speak now for consolation
in the buoyancy of shared sorrow
in the consecration of your faces

tinted on the horizon
reflected in the river

ahead I see
the layered limestone bluffs weep tears
the floods cycling, the silt settling
forgiven, forgotten
in new generations of bottomland corn
And I see once more the statue
of angel and child above the grade school door
and read, as when I first could read,
that double-edged message
"GOD'S WILL, THE END OF MAN"

beyond that vision
I only have hope
for a homecoming where the ancestors wait
with time enough to tell all the stories
until we see each other for the first time
in a merciless light that allows mercy
burning away all earthly crust
until we stand purified
pillars of flame

River Route of Jim and Huck in Huckleberry Finn

Dotted line shows they did not cross the river into Quincy, even though it was in a free state. Too many slavery sympathizers.

CHAPTER 7
MINORITY REPORT

"We must mend what has been torn apart, make justice imaginable again in a world so obviously unjust, give happiness a meaning once more."

—Albert Camus

The End of the World That Wasn't

As a sixth-grader reading *Huckleberry Finn* in Quincy, just 15 miles north of Hannibal, Missouri, it puzzled me why the slave Jim just didn't cross the Mississippi River into Illinois, a free state. When I looked on a map (See above), the route Huck and Jim chose to freedom seemed extremely circuitous, going all the way to Cairo and then trying to make their way up the Ohio River to Cincinnati and then to Canada. It was like trying reach a mountain top by spiraling around it when a short, straight, smooth path was available. But I had not yet received all my history lessons of racism in Quincy.

The Mississippi River provided an east-west boundary between Illinois (a free state) and Missouri (a slave state). You could even tell linguistically the difference between the two. For instance, when I would go to Missouri, I would hear "y'all," which I never heard in Quincy. Missouri had a more deeply Southern culture than Illinois and, I would say, in general, was more deeply racist. Only in Missouri did I see before entering some small towns, signs that said, "Don't Let the Sun Set on You N-----." I never saw such signs in Illinois.

However, Quincy back in the middle 1800s was far from an abolitionist bastion. Posses from Missouri hunting down runaway slaves were a regular occurrence that received little opposition from the city. To our credit, we did have an Underground Railroad that tried to funnel slaves to Chicago and Canada, but they represented a small minority of residents. To give you an idea of the general population's viewpoint about abolition, you need only look at the history of Quincy's most heroic abolitionist, Dr. Richard Eells.

Dr. Eells was a respected physician in Quincy and the leader of the local and county Abolitionist Party. Secretly, he also was responsible for taking in hundreds of runaway slaves and starting them on their journey on the Underground Railroad. In 1842, Dr. Eells was caught transporting a slave named Charley. Here is what *The Quincy Herald Whig*, the local newspaper, had to say about the incident the next day, Aug. 27, 1842:

> *"The second day after the occurrences alluded to above – which was Tuesday last – a warrant was issued for the apprehension of Dr. Richard Eells – an old and respectable physician of this city, a well-known abolitionist; in fact, **one of the principal head men of this misguided sect in this county** [bold is mine]..."*

"Misguided sect" does give you an idea of what the majority opinion was in Quincy. Of course, the situation was even worse by the time Huck and Jim decided to escape because The Fugitive Slave Act of 1850 had passed. There were heavy penalties for anyone aiding and abetting a runaway slave.

While many would love to dismiss history and claim that the past has little to do with the present, I still found remnants of this history replayed in my town. Because I was only a child when I was introduced to established forms of discrimination, it took me a while to break out of these early assumptions about African Americans. When I looked out from the back seat window of our family car as we were driving through the Frederick Ball Projects, the Black people who lived there did seem different from "us." The way they lived seemed slovenly and lazy in comparison to the neighborhoods I lived in. Our neighborhoods (lower middle class) had green lawns, painted houses, and no trash or litter strewn around. The projects didn't have yards, but dirt patches littered with trash. What was a child supposed to conclude? I had no historical perspective; just what appeared in the present.

I had no Black models that I could turn to contradict the idea of a basic inferiority of Black people. I encountered no teachers, priests, doctors, dentists, etc. who were African Americans. My father had hired a Black janitor named Maryland Pearl to clean our tavern, but he was no model because he was not dependable, often not showing up because he went on a drinking binge. Again, more evidence that the general opinion of whites about Blacks in Quincy was true. Finally, I didn't get to know any African Americans as customers at our family businesses because Black people were not served. They would not be kicked out if they came in to one of our taverns or restaurants; they would just be ignored.

Then, too, we as white children were surrounded by many uses of the N-word. We never hesitated to use the N-word in songs or jokes. We thought Al Jolson and blackface was entertaining. And Black jockey boys were ubiquitous in the city. Further, we were always told never to put our mouths on public water fountains because some N-word might have drunk there and contaminated it. We facilely called Brazilian nuts "N-word toes."

On the most fundamental level, and I wish I did not have to say it, my parents were prejudiced, especially my father. I had no guidance from them to wend my way through the appearances of self-fulfilling prophecy. In some ways, it is surprising that my father was as racist as he was. His childhood home abutted the projects, and he had many Black playmates in his early years. I remember one day when we were taking a walk, he went right through the projects without hesitation — something most white folks wouldn't do because the projects could be rough. However, as we were walking, I began to hear voices from the stoops, "Hello, Jack," "Jack, how's your sister Dolly?", "Jack, you still think you can whip me?" and more. *What the hell!* I thought. I had no idea that he knew so many people in the hood.

But as he told me later, a real split occurred between him and the Black community when he went to high school. They went their separate ways when the socialization process of peer groups, dating groups, religious groups, and career groups kicked in. But despite his early years, my father still used the N-word when talking about Black people and fervently believed they were an inferior race.

My mother was not nearly as overtly racist as was my father. Maybe it was because she was a child of Italian immigrants who lived in a little ghetto in Hershey, Pennsylvania, and she had been on the receiving end of prejudices from the local population. She never used the N-word because she may have remembered the sting of "Wop." Her prejudices had more to do with a basic, gut reaction to the African American physiognomy. The idea of a Black man kissing a white woman was more than she could bear. Once she told me that there were two things that she would disown me for: 1. dropping my Catholic faith; and 2. marrying a "colored" woman. Neither of these seemed even remotely possible at the time. So, I continued on blissful in my ignorance of Black people: their historical roots, their capabilities, their injustices, and their beauty.

Going to Catholic grade school, I encountered no Black students. This absence made it impossible for the intimacies and friendships that develop in the early years to occur. Even in our Catholic parish, which included at least a thousand people, there were no Black members of the congregation. Later, when our family was assigned to another parish, my brother Kirby befriended the one Black child in his new grade school. Without hesitation, he brought his new friend home after school. Everyone was polite while Henry was there, but once he left, Kirby got a taste of the adamantine rules of race relations. My father said that under no circumstances was he ever to bring a "*colored* person into our home." And that was that.

All these lessons about race relations, both overt and covert, I took for granted and never questioned the status quo until I went to Catholic high school. Christian Brothers High School was an entirely different beast from grade school. The religious order that ran the school, while being no-nonsense disciplinarians, were also no-nonsense intellectuals who took a very liberal approach to social issues. The nuns of my grade school were too meek by comparison to stand up and fight for justice like the Christian Brothers. As I progressed from my freshman year to my senior year, the turmoil of the Civil Rights Movement entered into our classrooms. And even though we didn't have one African American student in our school, the Brothers preached equality, supported Martin Luther King, and encouraged protesting for racial justice.

In my sophomore year, Christian Brothers High School put its money where its convictions were by hiring the first African American teacher in our city, Essic Robinson. The move shouldn't have surprised me because the Catholic religious orders in Quincy had a history of being in the forefront of social change. In the 1870s, Augustus Tolton, who as a child was born into slavery, came from Missouri with his newly freed family to Quincy, Illinois. He was taken under wing by Father Peter McGirr, who sponsored his enrollment into St. Peter's parochial school. As you might expect, this was not a very popular decision by Father Peter, but he persisted, and Tolton received his early education.

As time went by, the Franciscans took Augustus Tolton into their Catholic college, St. Francis Solanus College (it eventually became what it is today Quincy University). Here Tolton was nurtured to the point that he wanted to enter the priesthood, and in 1886, he was ordained and became the first Black Roman Catholic priest in the U.S. Thus, a Catholic high school hiring the first Black teacher in Quincy was part of a long tradition.

Father Tolton — On June 11, 2019, he received the title "Venerable," which brought him a step closer toward sainthood

Mr. Robinson was a man who commanded respect in my all-boys high school. He was a physically imposing figure of six-foot-five with an athletic build. He had been a starting basketball player at the local college, Quincy College. I remember when he had us break up into basketball teams during P.E. He had a basketball palmed in each hand as he pointed to the group that each person was to join. All of us were amazed at how he held the basketballs like softballs. None of us could image saying something of a racial nature to him.

But besides his physical stature, no one could imagine saying anything of a racial nature to him because he had such a warm and caring disposition. In his history class, I began to not only understand intellectually the plight of the Black man in the U.S. but also to feel it. The commentary that he added as the nation struggled with Civil Rights became the way I put a face with an issue. I wanted for him, his lovely wife, and his adorable daughter the same opportunities in society that all of us in our school had.

One day Mr. Robinson approached me with a request. He wanted me to represent our school on a civil rights panel. The panel would meet at our local public high school and include high school students from around the region. The reason he approached me was because I had a reputation for being a good public speaker. I had won an all-school speaking contest my freshman year. Hesitantly, I said, "Yes," feeling inadequate to the task.

Essic Robinson center, Left Brother Bernard, Mr. Bocke; Right Brother Jerome

But, as is often the case, the rewards of stretching oneself outweigh the pain. As a panelist and speaker at the symposium, I became involved with both Black and white students passionate about the injustices of racism. Their fire ignited mine and, while in the past I supported the Civil Rights movement in a rather silent way, I left the symposium with tongue aflame ready to speak out.

The first place that I spoke out was, perhaps, the most difficult — our supper table. The family dinner in my time was still around the kitchen table, and the conversations ranged over many topics of the time. When I came out defiantly against my father's and mother's racial values, our dinner table became quite a lively setting for heated debate.

"What kind of trash are they teaching you at that school! I'm not sending you to a school so that you can defend 'n-----s.'"

"First of all, Dad, don't use the word 'n-----.' It's offensive. If you must, use *colored* or *Negro*."

Thankfully as my father was trying to digest this along with the fried chicken, my mother chimed in, "Jack, I have to say I agree with Marty. I never liked that word."

Begrudgingly my father said, "Okay, *colored people*, then. But no matter what you call them, they're not like us, and they will never be accepted as one of us. Look at how they live. Look at how they talk. They're stupid. They even smell different from us."

From this point, I began to give my father and mother a history lesson about Black people and why they had been unable to achieve assimilation like my Italian mother had. I talked psychology and sociology. I talked with fervor. However, most ashamedly, I talked down to my parents, who for the first time seemed uneducated to me.

More than a lesson for them about racism, it was a lesson for me in how not to win an argument. No one will ever listen to you if you talk down to them. My new knowledge about race was a heady experience that made me feel superior to those ignorant souls who could not see the truth. I felt like with a few minutes of instruction that I could change a bigot into a believer in equality. Such was my limited knowledge of how to change people's minds. The process of changing my parents' minds was going to take more than a few sessions at the supper table.

Over time, my brothers also began chiming in at the supper table. Occasionally, my father enjoyed trying to sneak in the N-word to see if we'd relented a bit, but we swarmed him like starved mosquitos. I don't believe we ever changed my father's mind about race, but we did make him aware that in these times, he needed to keep his racism to himself. My mother was less outspoken and more accepting of the changes that were occurring, although she would always be an advocate of miscegenation.

Besides the shoe of his own family, the other shoe of society dropped hard on my father. With the passage of the Civil Rights Act in 1964, our restaurant was forced to begin serving African Americans. For my father, his place of work was always his bastion of segregation. With no Black people allowed, he could tell racist jokes laced with an accent reminiscent of Amos and Andy. He could make negative comments about Black people that would be accepted and applauded by his customers. When he realized he would be unable to wriggle out of the new law, he awaited the coming days like a possible diagnosis of cancer.

We all awaited the descent of hordes of Black people upon our restaurant. And come they did in large numbers — for about a month. Most came just to show themselves that they could. Once they realized that they could, the numbers dwindled considerably to what common sense would dictate, considering the Black population of our town. Soon we had our Black regulars, and soon they became as endearing and financially supportive as any of any of our white customers. Whatever discomfort existed in the beginning was soon displaced by using each other's names and being able to exchange the kind of social pleasantries that we shared with all our customers.

Thus, all the tumult and shouting, all the fear and hatred dissipated in about 30 days as integration became the business of normal routine. It was quite a life lesson for me about social change. Were all the fire department water hoses, attack dogs, beatings, and murders necessary so that a person could ride in the front of a bus or eat at a diner? The eyeglasses of prejudice are thick and highly magnified. Under their gaze, a worm looks like an anaconda. For my father, doomsday never came to our restaurant. What he predicted would be a hurricane turned out to be a cleansing breeze.

I do not want to leave the impression in this minority report that racial problems in Quincy were solved after the Civil Rights Act. As in the entire nation, Quincy would remain scarred and damaged by its racist past. The fight is not over by any means as we view the current *Black Lives Matter* movement. However, looking at the successes of the past should keep us from despair. I have seen significant changes in racial issues, and I have an unswerving faith in continued progress, albeit it will require more protesting and more old, bigoted whites dying off.

When Gay Meant Happy

Same sex relationships were not only invisible to me as I was growing up, but they were also beyond my imagination. It was worse than non-persons in Communist Russian history. No indications in the society I was growing up in and in which I was immersed pointed to groups of people with different sexual identities. There was no vocabulary, no movies, no actors, no television shows, no athletes, no... nothing that hinted that there was anything but heterosexuality.

You would think going to Catholic schools that there would be some mention of homosexual "sin." If there was any topic that the nuns and brothers relished in talking about as well as the students discussing, it was sins of a sexual nature. Yet not a peep about what the Bible and the Church would consider an "abomination." In my last years in grade school (7th and 8th grades), I began picking up some words from my peers that had a teeny sense of sexuality — *fruit* and *fairy*. We used these epithets to describe more effeminate male classmates, but in my mind, the basic meaning of the word was "sissy." No images appeared in my mind of males being romantically involved with males. Moreover, these words did not apply to females at all.

In high school, the word *faggot* entered my vocabulary. Also, rumors circulated of societies of men that lived in the big cities and performed homosexual rituals. They were always portrayed as quasi-satanic and living in the darkest regions of the city like criminals in *Batman*. One of the rituals described was called the "fairy ring," where a group of men masturbated in a circle. These topics were never brought up by the Christian Brothers who ran the school, but through peers who had the skimpiest notions about homosexuality (Hell! In Catholic school we had the skimpiest notions about heterosexuality!). So, I went *gayly* on my way to college thinking that if there really were such people as male homosexuals with fairy ring rituals, then they were without a doubt perverse and deserved to be prosecuted to the fullest by the law.

Ironically, what I did not realize was that one of those supposed denizens of the underworld lived in my house. A denizen I had shared a bed with, showered with, played with, ate with, and loved — my youngest brother Kirby. I think all of us in the family saw Kirby as a bit odd. As the youngest child, he was always given greater leeway than my brother Larry and I. He was not an athlete nor interested in athletics as were my father, Larry, and I. By the time he was in sixth grade, he had his own bedroom, which he stayed in for long periods of time. Often, he was seen with a cup of tea in his housecoat and slippers coming and going from his sanctuary. He lived like an old man at the age of 12.

My father allowed him to drop out of Catholic High School to attend the public school, which was something that I found astounding. But despite all his eccentric behaviors and reclusiveness, we would just tell ourselves, "Well, that's just Kirby." The family integrated his behaviors without question, and there was never any thought of sending him to a psychologist.

Of course, looking back on this, I realized he was suffering a great deal. It saddens me to this day to realize what he had to go through in order to understand and accept his sexuality. He concluded that he was mentally ill when he realized as he was budding into his sexuality at around 6th grade (the same grade that I had budded into my sexuality) that he was attracted to males. As I have said previously, there was no vocabulary, models, references, etc. that he could latch onto. He thought that he was the only person on earth like himself. How tortuously awful! No wonder he was a recluse. No wonder that he was eccentric and secretive. No wonder many gay boys in his generation committed suicide. And, indeed, he did attempt suicide once, lying on his bed and waiting for the pills he had taken to relieve him permanently from his pain. Thank God he ended up vomiting instead.

I was a sophomore in college when Kirby came to me in a state of frothy anger. Dad had done something to him that put him in a rage. He and my father were always nitro and glycerin, and it didn't take long in each other's presence for an explosion to occur. He wanted revenge in the worst way this time, and he told me that he was going to tell Dad that he was a homosexual and that he didn't care if that became public. By this time in life, Kirby was a sophomore in high school and realized that there were others like himself. In fact, he had friends who were gay, so that some of the pressures of being isolated had faded away.

More than worrying about what he would say to Dad, I remember saying to him, "You're a homosexual? A homosexual?" I couldn't have been more shocked or confused than if he had said, "Marty, I'm actually an extraterrestrial being from the planet Throntar." But he didn't seem interested in explaining himself to me; he just wanted to destroy our father. So, I focused on the problem at hand and tried to convince him not to come out to our father. I told him to cool down before he did anything rash. What was it going to accomplish to hurt Dad with the possibility of hurting Mom, too? I knew that hurting Mom was something that he couldn't countenance. He loved her more deeply than anyone on earth. Kirby backed off then.

In some ways, I regret that I tried to talk Kirby out of this big revelation. In retrospect, I have come to believe it's always better for a family to bring things out in the open rather to be composted individually in the secretive recesses of our minds. Who knows how much more damage was done to the family by not confronting Kirby's sexual identity early on and head on? To excuse myself partially, I was flummoxed by the whole situation and had few opinions to base any decisions upon.

From that point on, at least, I could discuss and learn about homosexuality from my brother. What was once a non-category started filling up with data. What was once an invisible area in my life suddenly jumped to the foreground. I was like a bee that could see color patterns on flowers that I couldn't perceive before. I learned that The Continental Night Club was a meeting place for many gays in town. I became aware that my doctor A. A. Kuna was one of these denizens of the gay world, despite the fact that he was married and had three children. Some of the movers and shakers in the city were gay. Kirby pointed out customers at our bar who were gay. Suddenly my aunt, who had never married, became more understandable as a lesbian. As I took my literature classes in college, I first found that Walt Whitman was gay and then a host of other authors and artists were gay.

In order to understand what went into the "making" of a homosexual, I took psychology classes to get explanations for what was still considered a mental illness and was as puzzling to me as Relativity. The leading theory at the time was that dominant mothers "made" their sons gay. That certainly didn't fit into our family where my father was definitely the dominant figure, although Kirby seemed to be more closely attached to Mom than either Larry or I. Further, it wasn't just the causes of homosexuality that became a pursuit, but sexuality in general. Was there a plasticity to sex, which would mean that I may not be as heterosexual as I thought? Could one choose his or her sexuality? Was everyone bi-sexual? And what morally should I make of all this? The answers to these questions became a lifelong quest, and while I have satisfactorily answered most questions, I still have much to learn.

Having a gay brother was not without its advantages. It brought me into some refined, rich, and gay circles. For instance, Kirby's good friend was George Irwin, who was called the "godfather of Quincy arts." As a benevolent aristocrat, George Irwin endowed, preserved, and established more art projects in Quincy than can be imagined. First of all, and most marvelously of all, he established the first community arts council not only in Quincy, but in the entire United States. He supported the local symphony as well as being its conductor for years. He purchased countless historical buildings to preserve some of Quincy's best architecture. Quincy's Little Theater was revived and has survived all because of George Irwin. George was also a philanthropist and connoisseur of the visual arts. To go into his house on Main Street with my brother was to go into an art museum. Hanging on the walls were Salvador Dali, O'Keefe, Picasso, Leger, Burchfield, Calder, Nevelson, and more. The grounds around his home had sculptures by Richard Hunt. Being around George Irwin through brother Kirby was my introduction to a refinement and dedication that I never knew. Hopefully, one day George will be more directly recognized for all that he did for Quincy behind the scenes. I'll put my vote in now for his statue at Washington Square.

Besides the lofty realm of the arts, there was another more carnal advantage of my association with gay friends. The first gay person I knew besides my brother was my brother's friend Curt Pilatz. Curt was the stereotype of a gay person in these times. His gestures, dyed blond hair, and vocal intonations separated him out quite quickly from the straight crowd. He was gay and didn't give a damn who knew about it. My brother was another matter, and it would be difficult to know just what his sexuality was. However, I liked Curt. He had a wonderfully sarcastic sense of humor, and Curt liked me.

In my college days, I would often go to a last stop night club in town called The Barn to dance in the wee hours. Curt sometimes would be there with a group of female hair dressers (Curt had become a hair dresser). We would have a beer together, and he would point out the women hair dressers who were available to be hustled. But he would always end this litany with, "But if you don't find anyone tonight to take home, there's always me." And I would always respond, "Sorry Curt, but this place doesn't have enough beer to make that happen." At one time in life, I could imagine punching someone in the teeth for this kind of proposition, but I was becoming comfortable with men who identified themselves as gay. And after all, I made exactly the same kind of moves on women.

Curt Pilatz was not only the first gay person I knew outside of

Kirby, but also, he was the first gay person I knew who died of AIDS. There was always a tragic sense that surrounded Curt. I knew his father Myron, who was a customer at our restaurant. No one had to tell me that Myron was an anus sphincter, but Kirby filled me in on the abuse that Curt had received at Myron's hands. Much, I think, of Curt Pilatz's life was an attempt to be loved like he never was as a child. When Curt died, he and my brother both were living in the plague-ridden city of San Francisco, where the first devastating results of AIDS were felt. I dedicated the following poem to Curt Pilatz. This poem is an allegory for the biblical Last Supper. The dinner that I refer to was an actual dinner that my brother Kirby attended, where everyone at the table had been diagnosed with HIV, except him.

Fading Photograph of the Last Supper
for Curt Pilatz (1948-88)

in memory of you

I do

drinking a glass of wine
I hold an old photograph
and remember your revelation

with head on shoulder
you whispered in my ear
all here were infected with mystery

save me

death a palpable presence
Phillip's ebullience, denial
Thomas's eyes distant on doubtful years
Jude's active fingers belying calm on his face
James drawing on cigarettes with seething anger

all betrayed

"It's in my body. It's in my blood.

Let this virus pass from me."
I drank until I could barely stand

we drove to the park above the city
I sobered in night air
lights streamed in arteries below
I held your hand
while you recited final things

you'd return

home to the father
tell him you were gay
tell him you had AIDS
that you loved him
that you forgave him
that he could be redeemed

before I could comfort you
flashlights scorched our faces
cops had us step out of the car
I swung at one and caught him in the ear
that's when you stepped in front
to take the crushing blow meant

for me

I awoke alone in a cell
calling your name
my shirt and pants blood splattered
no one answered
charges were dropped when I denied

witnessing

I ran to your home
everyone gathered
they told me you were dead
a single sentence in the papers
to record your passing

by miracle I am the only one
left in this fading photograph
Jude committed suicide
James's and Andrew's ashes remain on my mantel

the rest abandoned to the dead to bury

the dead

the old places hold no ghosts
a generation martyred
a world without our past
sometimes I begin to doubt
you existed at all

only when I sleep
do you come to me across the waters
revived in those weekends on our boat
when you'd bend the mast to fill the sails
and together in spray

we'd ascend

Curt Pilatz — Requiescat in Pace

When Kirby graduated from high school, unlike his two older brothers, he couldn't get out of Quincy fast enough. Quincy with its established, secretive community of gays was not a place for a young gay man to try out his wings. He went to live in Edwardsville, Illinois, and attended school at a campus of Southern Illinois University. It was near St. Louis, and the large city enabled him to expand into younger and more numerous gay circles. How wonderful it must have felt for him to go from being the only gay person in the world to being in a world of gays!

Backward Forward

"We are getting beyond some of the old asininities — all of us, Catholics, Protestants, Jews, alike: We can't hold the world any longer to the old weights and measures." I write this quote by Walt Whitman as we celebrated his bicentenary on May 31, 2019. To me, Whitman was one of the first to open new perceptions about all groups of people and to do it in a loving way. This work of acceptance has been ongoing since Whitman's time, but it reached a peak during my time.

The Sixties were not only a magma period of U.S. society's reconfiguring attitudes, values, and perceptions of minority groups, but it became the meaningful work of many baby boomers for the rest of their lives. There were so many movements that occurred during those ten years — Civil Rights with Martin Luther King, Jr., gay rights with Stonewall, Feminism with seminal works by Betty Friedan and Simone de Beauvoir and the formation of NOW (National Organization for Women), and the environmental movement with the bombshell publication of Rachel Carson's *Silent Spring*.

Those movements at first scared the bejesus out of me. The new ideas challenged everything I had been taught and undermined my faith in trusted elders. But this shock of the new soon changed into elation and provided me with meaningful purpose. Once I had begun breaking out of these categorical restrictions, I acquired an appetite for fixing myself and fixing the unjust situations I saw all around me. These problems have not gone away, but they have progressed with blood, sweat, and years, which gives me hope that someday they will be mostly eliminated.

I could have included many more minorities in this chapter — women, Jews, Native Americans — but it would be belaboring a point about my early life in Quincy. Once one begins to see people not in black and white, once one begins to see differences among people as the rich, composite colors of the rainbow, then one begins to be suspect that all categories of people are but cultural constructs that often have little to do with reality.

This much we do know at this present moment: Race is an artificial construct and has no biological basis. Gay persons are born gay and do not *choose* to be gay. It is **normal** to be gay. Because you have a vagina doesn't mean that you can't be athletic, can't do mathematics, or can't serve in the armed forces. Just because you have a penis doesn't mean you can't nurture, can't be emotional, or can't solve problems without fists. Many of us know that if we go back a few generations, we are the immigrants coming to a new land, language, and life.

People often complain today about the PC environment, as if it's a horrifying thing to be sensitive to other groups of people. I always tell people I lived in pre-PC and in PC America, and I'll take the excesses of PC any day. If there can't be compassion for every group of people, then I'll take courtesy as the semblance of a culture moving minimally in the right direction.

There has been not only an expanding awareness of diversity in my social life, but a tradition in my family that I find deeply American and of which I am proud. I am labeled "white," but I'm glad to be a mongrel American with many nationalities in my background — French, Italian, German, English, and Romanian. My father's father was a Baptist who married a Catholic and became Catholic. My father did not marry the girl next door, but an Italian woman who lived in an Italian ghetto and who never learned English until she went to public school. And I followed this tradition by being a Catholic, who married a Jewish woman and decided to raise our child Jewish. I'm hoping my daughter continues this American tradition when she marries, so that over generations we won't be able to hate anyone — they'll be members of the family.

DON'T BE AN IDIOM

What's fascinating about idioms is that they change over time, go in and out of fashion, and lose their references to become incomprehensible in the present. I used to have an old Missouri farmer come into our bar and I'd always say to him, "Joe, how's it going?" And he'd always reply, "Draggin' a hook." What this meant I could only guess. In my mind, I could always see a carefree person fishing without bait, because he didn't want to concern himself with even catching a fish.

Many of the idioms that I grew up with have gone the way of dusty death or at least on their way to extinction. As you will see, many are related to a time when farming was still a dominant occupation and preoccupation in Quincy. Most people, while not farmers themselves, had backgrounds and relatives who were only a generation from farm life. It's a quality of idioms to come from the technologies of the time; for instance, a drunken sailor was "three sheets to the wind." In a more scientific society like our own, we have idioms that would have been incomprehensible to the past: "light years ahead," "on the same wavelength," and "not rocket science."

The following are a few of the idioms of yesteryear in Quincy. Some are easy to figure out, some are not so nice, and some are hard to envision. Hope you enjoy them. As for me, I'll be draggin' a hook.

Staggered around like a blind dog in a meat house.
I suppose we're not familiar with meat houses today, but we are familiar with drunks weaving around.

Could talk a hungry dog off a meat wagon.

Meat wagons are another extinction from the past. A person who could talk a dog off a meat wagon was a talker, indeed.

Uglier than a mud fence.

Certainly not a nice but a graphic description of an unattractive person.

He or she could eat corn through a picket fence.

Another nasty description of someone who had "buck" or protruding teeth. No dental braces in these days.

Never can tell the depth of the well by the length of the handle on the pump.

Either a way of saying "You can't judge a book by its cover" or two items don't necessarily correlate.

He/she has more [money, junk, acquaintances, etc.] than Carter's got Little Liver Pills.

Even when I heard this (and I heard it often), I hadn't encountered any of these pills. They had been around since the 1880s, and at one time there were obviously well known and plentiful. In 1959, they were forced to change their name to Carter's Little Pills, since they had nothing to do with the liver's health.

He or she was running around like a chicken with its head cut off.

Many of you probably cannot visualize this, but I could because I had been around a number of chicken beheadings, which are spooky because the headless chickens just don't flop over and die. They run erratically propelled by just by their nervous systems before they keel over twitching.

Madder than a wet hen.

Chickens have a kind of angry look anyway, but one with wet feathers and a wet, red comb seems consumed with anger.

Shit like a goose.

One of the drawbacks of raising geese is that they can contaminate an area like no other bird. If a person came to our bar with diarrhea or "shitting like a goose," we gave them our cure, which is a shot of blackberry brandy. As my father claimed, "Blackberry Brandy can stop a mudslide."

Better close your barn door or your horse will get out.

A way to tell a male that his pants were unzipped. Using *horse*, however, was a bit of male hyperbole.

Tougher than Kiefer's meat.

No one outside of Quincy would know what this idiom meant. It's a very local saying that referred to a grocery store in Quincy that sold the cheapest and worst cuts of meat. Anyone "tougher than Kiefer's meat" was a grizzled and rough hombre.

Ain't worth a hill of beans.

I wouldn't think the selling price of a hill of beans would be much, unless they were the magic beans sold to Jack.

Can't squeeze blood out of a turnip.

We had people who owed us money at our restaurant, but we gave up trying to collect because they didn't have any money — you couldn't squeeze blood out of a turnip.

Scarce as hen's teeth.

Since chickens don't have teeth, whatever is scarce is non-existent.

Living in high cotton.

Literally the cotton plants are healthy, and the crop will bring in a lot of money. Figuratively this translates to meaning that one feels successful.

Living high on the hog.
Another idiom than means one is prosperous. If you can afford the best cuts on a hog (pork chops and hams), you're eating the meat high on the back legs of a pig.

Fair to middlin'.
Unlike above, if you feel "fair to middlin'," you just feel okay.

Scarcer than horseshit in the garage.
That's pretty rare.

Raining like a cow pissin' on a flat rock.
A competitor for "It's raining cats and dogs."

Hankerin' and Gumption.
Two down-home words that I miss. Hankerin' means to crave something; gumption is like the Yiddish *chutzpah*, which means being audacious in your behavior.

Beating around the bush and *Pussyfooting around.*
Going around a subject and not coming to the main point.

Beating a dead horse.
Doesn't do you any good.

About as useful as tits on a boar.
Nipples on a man are pretty useless, too.

Cattywampus
Discombobulated and confused. I like the word's sound value.

Slower than molasses.
We never ate molasses when I was growing up; instead we'd use maple syrup and Karo (corn) syrup. But molasses is thick and doesn't pour fast. So, if you're as slow as molasses, you're pretty darn slow.

Rode hard and put away wet.

A horseback riding term. It means a person whose appearance either indicates they've lived a hard life, or they have been abused and neglected.

There's a pair to draw to.

Referring to two people as "a pair to draw to" means that they don't have much value like a low pair in poker. Mostly it was used in a kidding way to refer to a couple.

CHAPTER 8
GREAT UNCLE DOC AS PATRIARCH

"Why should the devil get all the good tunes?"
—apocryphal, Martin Luther

Scene:

A cold, winter day in January in the 1920s. The ice is so solidly frozen on the Mississippi River that horses and wagons can drive on it to cut blocks of ice. The blocks will be stored in limestone caves nearby in a bedding of hay. The ice will last all summer and into the next year. It will be sold to people who literally need it for their **ice** boxes.

The unusual part of the scene is that a group of men are gathered around one of the ice holes. Two of them are in a sitting position around the hole with one of their legs dangling in the water. The men are all from a speakeasy facing the river where a bet was made. The bet had to do with who could withstand the most pain. This would be determined by which man could leave his leg the longest in the frozen waters of the Mississippi.

End of Scene

One of the men with his leg in the water was Henry Estis Settle, my great uncle. No one, however, ever called him "Henry" — he was known as "Doc." He was probably known as Doc because he ran the speakeasy nearby, which provided illegal "pharmaceuticals" during Prohibition.

Doc defeated his opponent in the bet, who was a stranger passing through town. The bet was a set-up, which all his regular customers were in on. For, although Doc moved with the grace of a cat and was one of the best dancers in town, he had a wooden leg. Thus, the result of the contest was a foregone conclusion, even though Doc declared that he almost lost because he was freezing his ass off.

This scene above illustrates a lot about my family history. If I were to choose the Abraham of our family, it wouldn't be my grandfather. My grandfather was a boilermaker, who worked with and understood tools and toil. But none of his children — six boys and one girl — had anything to do with blue collar work. It was Grandpa Settle's brother Doc who set their course as proprietors of taverns, bars, and restaurants. Six out of seven of them at one time or another ran their own liquor or eating establishments, making the name Settle in Quincy synonymous with food and alcohol.

That Doc chose to run a speakeasy was understandable. He had lost a leg working for the railroad. As the story goes, he had been sitting on the cattle catcher of a train riding home from work. When the train had hit a break in the track, he had been thrown under it. Luckily for him that he only lost his leg. But it was a traumatic experience for him and one that continued to plague him because he suffered from phantom limb syndrome. Under these new conditions in his life, he decided to make his living through the use of his wits — a one-legger-bootlegger.

Picture of my Great Grandparents George Thomas Settle and Leora Adelia (Parrott) Settle and their children. My grandfather looms in the back row. "Doc" Settle is the first left in the front row.

Working with whiskey required not so much muscle as savvy. There were people to pay off and a persona to maintain of a man that was tough and not to be fooled with. Doc carried a gun, and the people who he dealt with knew he was not afraid to use it. In addition, there were other ways to make a living within the illegal liquor trade. Gambling, for instance. We have already seen the introductory story about the bet on the Mississippi River. Doc was also as good a card player as any Mississippi riverboat gambler and just as "honest." He was reported as having said, "These farmers, who come into my place to gamble, can shoot an eye out of a squirrel at 100 ft., but they can't see me switch a card right under their noses."

There used to be some marathon games at Doc's speakeasy with some rather odd rules. Players were not allowed to leave the table once the game started, unless they ran out of money. You were required to stay until there was one winner or that you peed. Peed? If you had to leave the table to pee, you forfeited your money. This was difficult to do since everyone was required to have a shot of whiskey every half hour. As unseemly as it sounds, every so often the players checked each other to make sure no one surreptitiously peed in their pants, which meant they lost their stake. In these games, because the players were so good, Doc could not cheat, but he could increase his odds through a regimen of bladder training. Doc would train like an Olympian for these games by clocking himself between pees and trying to increase his times between peeing. Over time he had attained a bladder muscle control comparable to a hibernating bear. Many marathon card games he won because of his opponent's urination forfeiture.

The love between Port Settle, my grandfather, and Doc Settle was fiercely affectionate. God help the person who did harm to one of them because the other brother would be seeking him out with a vengeance that no morality would restrain. Both brothers had done hard labor growing up as sons of a sawyer, which meant they spent their youths chopping and trimming trees and then snaking them out of the forest with a team of mules. That they were tough would be an understatement; that they would beat you into a bloody pulp would not.

It didn't matter to my grandfather that his brother was part of the crime underground of Quincy. It didn't matter that his children played in a speakeasy and learned some of the more disreputable aspects of life. My Uncle Merle learned how to fight at Doc's place. He and his friends would put on fighting performances for the customers and make some nickels and dimes for spending money. After his training with Doc, as a teen, Merle began fighting full grown men for money. He was like Jack Dempsey in his early years, where his appearance (young and skinny) belied the fact that he moved like a mongoose and hit like 100 proof whiskey. Quite a few bullying men bit the dust in the back lot of the tavern, surprised by the buzz saw they encountered. When Uncle Merle later road the rails during the Depression looking for work, he found his first job in Texas as a bouncer.

Other brothers, including my father, learned gambling skills, doggerel poems, and jokes. My father could play cards or dice with the best of them, not because he cheated, but because he never forgot a card played or the odds of any dice game. My aunt learned the give and take of a woman with the toughest kind of men. It was amazing to me how she could have these tigers turn into kittens around her. If you wanted to break up a fight, you wouldn't call in another man; you'd call in Aunt Dolly, who would have them purring and eating out of her hand in a matter of minutes.

They all learned the profitability of liquor (legal in this case) and the methods one needed to use in order to run a profitable, safe, and entertaining bar. The mark-up on liquor is considerable; something around five hundred percent. If you were frugal and watched your shot glass pours, you could make quite a bit on one quart of whiskey: a five-dollar bottle of wholesale whiskey had 32 ounces; with 2 ounces of spillage, you're talking 30 shots; at a dollar a shot that bottle of whisky sold for thirty dollars. Nice profit.

The Settles all ran liquor establishments where both men and women could relax and not worry about loud-mouthed drunks or over-aggressive men. If you wanted to have an intimate relationship with the pavement outside, just try to start a fight or be foul-mouthed to the women at one of our bars. If you were lucky, you might receive a warning, but your luck would run out for warning number two. Then you could leave peaceably or the Uncle Doc's air-borne way.

Of course, this island of safety created an atmosphere of relaxation and entertainment. In the footsteps of wooden-legged Doc, you could be counted on for the latest joke, some doggerel, or some trick or prank. People laughed a lot at a Settle's bar, and you could leave your day's burden at the door when you entered and took a seat. There you could sip your whiskey unbothered to watch or listen to the antics surrounding you; or you could participate with your own stories and opinions. The Settles were not butler bartenders who gave you your drink and then stood invisibly in the background polishing a glass. They were engaged with their clientele and ever ready to raise the level of a good time.

Since my grandfather Port's children (Doc was married but had no children) were a playful and gregarious lot, they took to Doc's lifestyle. None of them wanted the doldrums of the blue-collar trades that their father represented. They wanted to be around the easy money and the action. Coming home and spending an hour getting the grease off their hands had absolutely no appeal to them. Further, there was an odd pride about my uncles and aunt. They had a sense of superiority that saw themselves as too good to stoop to menial labor. Like Doc, they felt that they could outsmart the general public, who sweated and toiled only to die prematurely. Theirs was a cult of personality that kept people coming back to their bars just to be around them. They wanted life to be a party with them being the life of the party. My father once said, "If you give me a board and a few chairs, I can make a living."

Doc Settle's notorious life was not a long one. He died on November 2, 1931, at 45 years of age. As the account in *The Herald-Whig*, the local newspaper, indicates, there were strange circumstances surrounding his death. Once you read the report below, I think I can add a few points that the reporters did not know.

Monday, November 2, 1931
WOUND IS FATAL
TO "DOC" SETTLE
SHOT OCTOBER 26

Henry E. (Doc) Settle died Sunday afternoon at 12:40 o'clock at St. Mary hospital. Death was caused by pneumonia that resulted from a gun shot wound in the abdomen. Settle was shot at 4 o'clock on the morning of Monday, October 26, while in his room at 840 Jersey Street.

The death of Settle following a shooting, naturally arouses interest in the circumstances of the firing of the shot that proved to be fatal. Settle was the best known of Quincy underworld characters. He has usually been known as the leader cause of his ability and many experiences. He was interested in the George Rains-Slats Williams feud that sent Rains to the penitentiary for the shooting of Williams. He was arrested in the investigation of the attack on Thomas Baldwin. The most serious "rap" he took recently, however, was a house correction sentence of six months.

Settle insisted to the very end that he himself held the gun as it fired the shot into his body. He told this to the surgeons who dressed the wound and who expressed to him their doubt of his story. He told it also to his brother, "swearing by our dead mother." The only person present when the officers arrived at the room was Settle's wife.

Circumstances Are Strange

In spite of Settle's repeated statements, there are peculiar circumstances. The bullet went into his clothing, tearing a jagged hole just above the watch pocket on the right side. It entered the body just above the prominence of the hip bone and ranged backward and downward, lodging against the spine, lifting the peritoneum but not puncturing any vital organ. While it is not utterly impossible for a person to hold a gun so that the wound might be inflicted on his body in this manner, the position would be exceedingly awkward.

Settle said that he was cleaning the gun, although it was 4 o'clock in the morning. He said he was going hunting, although the only gun he was cleaning was a revolver.

Loyal to the Code?

The question naturally arises whether Settle was loyal to the code of the gunman to the end, or whether he actually was shot while the gun was in his own hands. The surgeons, police, and all others who have some knowledge of the shooting, will give their testimony at the inquest at the Haneen funeral chapel on South Eighth Street, Monday afternoon...

Indeed, the details of Doc's testimony of how he was shot were peculiar. I would go further and say they were outright lies. Who cleans his .38 revolver at 4:00 in the morning? Who cleans a .38 revolver in preparation to going hunting, as he testified? Nobody hunts with a .38! That the police would assume it was a crime-related shooting was understandable. But Grandpa Settle had an entirely different take on the matter.

Grandpa Port believed Doc's wife Dora had done the deed. This seems to be a far better theory than the police's. Doc's marriage had always been a rocky one with Doc being under the constant scrutiny of the law, landing in prison, and hanging around with a lot of unsavory characters. Further, Doc was a womanizer and had a stable of affairs. Coming home at 4:00 on that fateful morning could have been the last straw for Dora Settle. They would argue about his affairs, and she would shoot him.

Doc Settle would not have turned in his wife for two reasons, and they would both have to do with the code of the family. First, he did honor his wife's motives for shooting him, and he realized that he was guilty of breaking trust with her. Second, and perhaps most important, is that he did not want his brother to go to jail. The code of the family would have required my Grandpa Port to kill Dora. Port begged Doc to just give him a nod if it were Dora, because he was ready to end her life. Doc knew this, and he knew that if his brother killed his wife, he would go to prison, leaving his wife and six children without a provider. So, Doc never changed his story and went to his grave without divulging the mystery murderer.

Backward Forward

Doc was the Abraham of my father's generation and succeeding generations. He was not like his brother, my grandfather, who I would call *good*. Doc was not good, but then from my point of view neither was Abraham, who tried to murder both of his sons.

I would say that most of the Settles I knew growing up were not *good*. They were not interested in going to heaven, which sounded pretty damn dull to them. They weren't interested in charity, chastity, or obedience. They liked living on the periphery of the law, which enabled them at times to make a couple extra bucks.

My childhood friends had fathers who were church-goers and volunteers for hundreds of worthy causes. They were the salt of the earth, while my relatives were often salt in a wound. Their fathers took their children fishing and camping; while I learned cards, dice, mixing drinks, entertaining, and lewd stories.

Superficially, it would appear that I was little influenced by the patriarchy of great Uncle Doc. As an English teacher of both high school and college, my career path would seem miles away from the uneducated and raucous behavior at a smoky bar. But I took Mark Twain's quip to heart: "Never let your schooling get in the way of your education." While I was getting my BA in college, I was getting my "bar" degree at our restaurant. I would tell my father that I learned more bartending with him than I did during my first four years of college.

How was I an ancestor in the tradition of Doc Settle? First of all, I love lies. My father would say of many of the people he knew, "If he told the truth, he'd lie out of it." It is not a great jump to go from lies to literature. What is fiction anyway but lies? Early on both at my father's bars and in the local mythology of Mark Twain, I learned the value of the tall tale and the artful telling of it. I sat at the feet of the masters in recitation of doggerel and jokes. In *Huckleberry Finn*, I found a soul mate that used lying to get him out of trouble and into adventure. Often, I was not sorry for the Duke's and King's *marks*, who were so naïve they *deserved* to be taken advantage of.

In the classroom, I felt very at home promoting the lies of literature and the truths we may learn from them. I was at ease with my students as surrogates for the entertainment that I provided for customers at our bars. From being a great memorizer of bar doggerel, I transitioned to being a great memorizer of Frost, Eliot, e. e. cummings, Gwendolyn Brooks, Emily Dickinson, etc. And not only an excellent memorizer, but a dramatic presenter of a Shakespearean soliloquy.

My teaching career, in addition, followed in the Settle grand tradition of making a living by your wits in a job of relative ease that allowed you to have fun. I have always felt that I was a kind of con man, making money as an English teacher: You mean people are going to pay me for all the reading that I love to do and all the enjoyment that I get in talking about this reading and then give me three months off in the summer. Suckers!

So beware when you read my memoir. After all, I am descended from a family who cultivates deception. Some literary critics would say today that there are no such genres as memoir or autobiography; they've changed the name to *creative nonfiction*. I'll let you decide whether I'm a factual autobiographer or the name my relatives preferred to use — "bull-shitter."

CHAPTER 9
BUILT ON BLUFFS

"No moral argument, since the world began, ever prevailed over 25% profit."
    —Harriet Beecher Stowe in The Minister's Wooing

Quincy, Illinois, is a city built on the bluffs of the Mississippi River. These bluffs were a lucky geographical feature that protected the city in two ways — 1. they put most of the city high above the flood plain; 2. they kept the city from being exposed like other cities on the Great Plains from tornados. But there were other *bluffs* that protected our city because of its geographic location. These had to do with a peculiar relationship between the law in general and gambling in particular.

The towns and cities that popped up in Illinois along the Mississippi river because of the commerce during the riverboat era became more lawless the farther south you went until you arrived at Cairo. Even when I was growing up, we were warned about being the stranger in one of these towns, which did things their own way. For instance, hunting and fishing had no season downstate. If you were a game warden, you might find yourself tied to a tree in a forest if you tried to enforce the game laws, which was the case for a zealous warden near Cairo. These places during Prohibition went right on drinking, either making their own brew with stills or bootlegging.

In one category of lawlessness, Quincy was the capital — gambling. As I've written earlier, my great Uncle Doc was the proprietor of a speakeasy on the Mississippi and made his money bootlegging and *bluffing* his customers in games of chance. Much of what Doc did until his death in 1931 was helped along by people in the local government, whom he paid off. Thankfully (from Doc's point of view), he was not around to see Prohibition repealed in 1933, which would have signaled the end of his liquor enterprises.

But another bootlegger, Leo Monckton, who was on the scene at the time of legalization of alcohol and who was a friend of the Settle family, was faced with this predicament.

Leo Monckton

The Monckton Illegacy

I have heard people say that it was *rumored* that Leo Monckton made his money in illegal activities, that he was Quincy's Mob boss during the 1930s through 1950s, and that he at one time had Al Capone as a visitor to his home. Let me assure you: these are no rumors; Leo lived up to all these things. He made his money with a variety of illegal activities: slot machines, gambling rooms, and prostitution. He was a mob boss who would do violent things to keep his territory. Finally, Leo Monckton had connections with Al Capone, although no one has been able to prove that Capone ever visited Monckton in Quincy.

When Prohibition ended but the Depression was still in full swing, Leo Monckton was left in the lurch as to how he was going to replace the income that he had made through the illegal production and distribution of liquor. He decided that he would go into gambling, both legal and illegal, and into prostitution. Since he had operated or supplied a number of speakeasies, he could make these into legitimate taverns. These taverns would then provide him with an easy transition to supply his latest products.

Congruent with the close of Prohibition in the 1930s, the first coin-operated pinball machines were being manufactured. Taverns and drugstores were the first places they were showing up. Another coin-operated machine that was showing up in taverns or "juke joints" was the jukebox (*juke* being a word that comes from Gullah, meaning rough, tough, and unsavory). Leo decided to become involved with these coin-operated machines that were cheap entertainment for those living during the Depression. These would become a front for another kind of coin-operated machine that was illegal — the "one-armed bandit," the slot machine.

A Port in the Storm

Enter the Settle family. My grandfather, Port Settle, had his own shop as a boilermaker, machinist, and all-round tool and die maker. He was hired by Leo to make the steel support platforms that held the heavy slot machines. Grandpa Settle probably knew Leo earlier because of the criminal activities of his brother "Doc" Settle (See Ch. 8). Of course, during the Depression with a wife and seven children to clothe and feed, my grandfather was grateful and loyal to anyone who paid him cash. Leo, on the other hand, knew that Port was a man he could trust and a man, who on occasion, could help out in a pinch.

The pinches had to do with removing troublemakers at some of the Monckton "juke" joints on Quincy's Southside (the tough region of Quincy). My grandfather was not a person to be messed with. As one person who knew my grandfather as a child stated to me, "Your grandfather was a man at twelve." He had spent his whole life with axes and hammers, which meant he could use equally well either hand. As in the song "16 Tons," he had "one fist of iron and the other of steel; if the right one don't get you, the left one will." There are stories of his removing bullies or rowdies from Leo's taverns — one time as many as three in one place. He could be a bouncer at a moment's notice.

Grandpa Port was not a bodyguard for Leo Monckton, however. This task was reserved for a number of thugs, one of who was the locally infamous Milton "Bucky" Batchelder — infamous because he was known for stomping a man (Skip Irvine) to death. A dance was named jokingly after him called "the Batchelder stomp." As you might expect from his connections, Batchelder did not go to jail for this. Nor was Grandpa an enforcer for those who owed Leo money. In general, except for the bouncing, Port steered clear of the Monckton gang's darker deeds.

And there were darker deeds. Occasionally there would be territorial disputes. Monckton, while a local mob leader, had affiliations with the Capone organization that came out of Chicago. If anyone tried to muscle in on his territory like the Shelton brothers from Peoria, the Chicago people sent down some thugs to take care of "business." For one man, "business" resulted in his being found in the local cemetery with his arms across his chest ready for burial.

Over the years, Leo and Port developed a friendship, and this friendship resulted in many odd jobs and dealings with Leo Monckton for the Settle family. My grandfather did caretaking jobs at the Monckton estate. He also became a collector for the money made from the slots — a 60/40 split with Leo getting the bulk because he made the payoffs that provided the protection, and he fixed the machines. My Uncle Merle was a "shaker." If one of the slot machines went on the fritz, it was often because coins got stuck in the mechanism. Merle was strong enough to turn a slot machine upside down and shake it, releasing jammed coins. He did this enough to get his job title.

The halcyon days

My father, Jack Settle, when he returned from WWII, joined in quickly with the "Baby Boom" phenomenon. I was born in 1946, and he quickly had to change his military uniform for a white shirt and tie to support a new wife and child. Since he was familiar with the bar trade through Uncle Doc and Leo Monckton, and, since he was an entertainer at many clubs previous to the war, opening a night spot was a good fit for him. Leo had a tavern that my father could lease, and Leo could provide him with all the gambling paraphernalia to make his new enterprise more profitable.

In the first years at the Coronado (his new place of business), my dad made a very lucrative living as a bar owner with supplemental income from gambling. He had slot machines, punchboards, dice games, and the spinning clock. The latter, a device that I have never seen since, looked like a mantle clock with one hand. The one-handed clock would spin every so often and randomly land on a number from 1 through 12. Customers would bet on a number in a similar fashion to roulette.

These were the halcyon days of gambling in Quincy. The town was wide open to gambling after WWII. Nothing was hidden. All was out in the open because the sheriff, police, and mayor got their cut of the profits. There was even a room in the Monckton mansion called the "Mayor's Room" because the mayor would sometimes spend the night there with one of Leo's prostitutes (the mayor and Leo weren't in bed with one another, but it was close). But there were dark clouds on the horizon with many anti-gambling forces putting pressure on Illinois governor Adlai Stevenson, the state's Attorney General Ivan Elliott, and state's attorney for Adams County John T. Reardon to end this illegal activity that existed and persisted most wantonly in Quincy.

As odd as it sounds, the number of slot machines and the number of places that had slot machines was easy information to obtain. Why? Because all the slot machine owners paid federal taxes. The federal government required all these gambling operations to buy a federal gambling stamp and pay taxes on their machines. Since no one wanted the Feds to come in, proprietors paid their U.S. taxes while ignoring with impunity all state taxes and regulations. The state of Illinois had all the records they needed to shut down gambling all over the state. But the state didn't act for the longest time, and I'm sure you can guess why — politicians were getting a windfall of additional campaign income.

As the pressure built, the state began at first to tepidly enforce the gambling laws. They realized the local officials weren't going to do it, so they sent out state law enforcement officers. The trouble with this system was that the gambling people knew when the state people were coming. Obviously, they had connections in the state capital, Springfield, Illinois, where these decisions were made. When the state people appeared in Quincy, lo and behold, they found either no gambling devices or the gambling rooms had been shut down. Of course, when the state officials left, the gambling activities started up again like children returning to school after Xmas break.

My father made accommodations for these visits by redesigning his bar towels with one side having the numbers for those betting on the clock and the other side blank.

When the state people came, he just turned over the towels and put his washed glasses on them. "No gambling going on here, Sir."

National attention was fomented by *Colliers Magazine*, because

Collier's, April 15, 1950

ILLINOIS SHAKEDOWN:
The Little Guys Lose

By GORDON SCHENDEL

In nickels, dimes and quarters, slot machines rob the people of the state of $100,000,000 a year

of articles about Quincy like the one above. This forced a decisive response from the state of Illinois to end the pockets of gambling that existed within its boundaries. Even the manufacturers of coin-operated machines, The Coin Machine Institute, kicked out the makers of slot machines (all of which were located in Chicago). They even went as far as providing assistance to the state in getting rid of these black sheep of coin-operated industries. Soon, the reign of the gambler barons was over. I remember going into the basement of the Monckton house on Locust Street and seeing hundreds of slot machines that had been retired from his businesses. It was like a Disneyland ride for me as I played the slots. Only a few places continued to have slots, and these were private clubs like the Elks and the VFW.

My father's gambling profits skidded to a halt, and he brought the clock and punchboards home to store in our basement. Over the years, these became toys for me and my brothers, toys I wish we hadn't destroyed because they would have been great conversational pieces for family history. In the end, my father opened up a new tavern sans gambling called "The Settle Inn."

Money, marbles, or chalk

One gambling tradition that was carried on in Quincy past the demise of slots was the dice box. Almost every bar continued to have a dice box where you could shake double or nothing for your drinks. You could walk into either a corner tavern or an elegant restaurant in the 60s and 70s in Quincy and find people shaking dice for their drinks. The game that was played was called "horses," and it required five dice and a leather cup. The game had its complications and strategies. To win you had to take two out of three sets or "horses."

My father loved this game for a number of reasons. First of all, he knew the odds on every shake, and he trained his bartenders what to do under all permutations of the dice. While it might appear to the customer we were being casual about our choices of dice to keep and shakes to take, we had no freedom at all in the Jack Settle system. Secondly, we always shook double or nothing the price of the drink. Nothing made my father happier than to realize he was shaking his cost for the drink against the customer's cost of double retail. Thus, a drink that cost my father $.50, which he sold for $2.00, suddenly had the possibility of becoming a $4.00 drink. A tidy little profit for Jack Settle, who won the majority of the time.

Even with just dice box gambling, we still had connections to the state capital through a network of liquor distributors. Word would always get to us when the state people were going to be in town and that we should put our boxes away. Then we would get an all-clear from our source, and we would be rattling the bones again. Certainly, the dice games for drinks were not a great evil. The money involved was slight in comparison with the old craps tables. Cheating was possible if you had a "whip box" and knew how to use it. My great Uncle Doc used one; however, I never came across anyone who did this.

Customers could cheat, too. I remember my father coaching me about odds. "When somebody's beating the odds too often, it ain't luck — *they're cheating*. Beware and watch closely." Indeed, I did have a customer that seemed to be winning at dice too facilely. There was something a little strange about the way the guy shook and released the dice from the cup. But I couldn't detect anything wrong in what he was doing.

Then I had my father observe unobtrusively while he was shaking. He smiled and walked away and said nothing. Eventually, he pulled me aside and showed me what was going on. The man was palming a die with a one on it (ones were wild in Horses) and skillfully placing it down when he released the dice. When we restricted him from laying down his palming hand when he released the dice, it was amazing how quickly his "luck" changed. It was, also, notable how quickly he abandoned our bar for another.

Finally, I realized that I could subtly cheat by assisting customers into making bad decisions by setting aside dice for them that would give them the lowest odds. They believed I was doing them a favor; of course, they didn't understand odds. I must admit I did this a few times just to see if it worked. It did, but I quickly returned to the freedom of good old honesty.

Despite the fact that the golden days of gambling were gone, Jack

Settle made a nice supplemental income from "money, marbles, or chalk" — a phrase that meant whatever game you wanted to play or whatever you wanted to bet on. During the day at the Settle Inn when my father was taking in inventory and making out payroll, there was always a card game going on in a round, corner booth. Mostly the game was pinochle, but it could be poker or gin rummy as well. These card games were never without money. Dad would never play unless there was money involved. He was a consummate card player, remembering every card played, and never giving away anything in his deadpan expression. On average, he came away with more money than he started with.

Betting, especially in sports, was rampant at the bar. You were almost a kind of bookie as a bartender. People were always willing to try to get you into some kind of bet. Here is where my father really shined, because he was a true gambler. Most people that bet are not true gamblers because they bet with their loyalties. My father never let his emotions get in the way of his wallet. He might goad a customer into a bet by playing on *his* emotions, but he saw clearly the point spread of the game (who was favored and by how much) and proceeded accordingly. Perhaps, to best explain a true gambler, let me pause here to give you an example, an example that I'm not particularly proud of but one that captures where objectivity leads:

A Story of a True Gambler

As I was growing up in Quincy, baseball was the prevailing sport in the nation. In our region, two major league teams were geographically close: the St. Louis Cardinals and the Chicago Cubs. So, the majority of fans were either for the Cardinals or the Cubs, and an intense rivalry developed between the two with a lot of betting going on.

As an unassuming child, I never questioned the fact that my father (and, therefore, my brothers and I) was a Brooklyn Dodgers' fan. Only when I came to be about twelve years old, did I begin to wonder about this. Why the Dodgers? We had no relatives in Brooklyn, no history, no friends, and no connections that I could determine with Brooklyn. So, I asked my dad, and he said, "Jackie Robinson." Jackie Robinson? I found that hard to believe because my father was a prejudiced man, who used the N-word and felt Black people were intellectually inferior. I knew he wasn't *on any band wagon to allow African Americans to play in the Major Leagues.*

But then he explained further. When he realized that the Dodgers had one of the better teams in baseball and that Jackie Robinson was a great addition, he decided to become a Dodger fan. With his bar being full of prejudiced people (like himself) and being either Cardinal or Cub fans, he saw a gold mine of potential for bets. Our customers wanted to see Jackie fail; they wanted their teams to beat the hell out of the Dodgers. Of course, my father took advantage of their desires by telling them to put their money where their biased mouths were. The only mouths that profited were the mouths in the family that my dad had to feed — the Dodgers prevailed for a decade and the money rolled in.

A true gambler never lets his or her prejudices and loyalties get in the way of an objective assessment of the odds. That was my dad — take him or leave him.

Never-can-tell with Oscar Figgins

Oscar Figgins was one of my father's childhood friends. He was a rough Irishman, who ran a tavern — actually more of a dive than tavern. Occasionally he would come to our place of business, unshaven in wrinkled, old clothes. At first, I misjudged my dad's old friend, thinking he was just a bum. But Oscar Figgins was more like a Jack London, a rough man but a very self-educated one.

When I went to college and thought I was quite the scholar, Oscar asked, "What are you majoring in, boy?" (He always called me "boy.") I told him proudly that I was an English major. Then, he proceeded to go through a list of the classics that he had read, along with commentary and observations. He had out-read me ten to one, and his insights were precise and cogent. I was embarrassed that I really couldn't carry on an intelligent conversation with him on subjects that were supposedly going to be my future profession. Thus, I got my first literary comeuppance from a man that smelled like a brewery. "Well, it seems to me, boy, that you're a little behind on your reading and thinking." It was a good lesson of "Never-can-tell," and it kept me humbler thereafter.

Besides being a voluminous reader, Oscar Figgins was a skillful card player and promoter of card games. The upper story of his tavern had a room for the *big* games. Every now and then you would hear that Oscar was hosting a day and night of high stakes poker. Card sharks from in and out of town came in to compete. This was serious business because the money was serious — into the tens of thousands.

Not only did Oscar provide the room, but he also provided the new decks of cards, food and drink, and the enforcement. He carried a pistol for these events just in case any disagreements might arise, or if anyone decided to renege on a bet. In these situations, he did not play but presided. Of course, he learned a great deal watching these high stakes games.

I loved to listen to Oscar and my father talk about *tells*, certain behaviors, gestures, or ticks that card players have that subconsciously reveals what kind of hand they are holding. For instance, if a card player shifts his position in his seat every time he is bluffing, an astute opponent will read the tell and proceed accordingly. If you are playing at the highest levels of poker, you cannot afford to give your hand away by tells. Therefore, professional poker players look for tells in the competition and try to make sure that they have none themselves.

Oscar had watched some very expert poker players, who believed they had no tells, but still if you were like Oscar and got to observe a player's moves hand after hand all night long, you would find the smallest of tells. But even more interesting, Figgins knew card players who faked tells like prostitutes faked orgasms. They would draw in their opposition to a point in the games where there was a lot of money on the table and then put out their tell like the lure of an angler. Those that took the bait found out that what they thought was a tell was a double agent. To me this was psychology at its highest level, and, while I admired the subtlety of these pros, I realized I could never join their ranks. I was an open book.

You would think that with all the gambling that I had been around that I myself would be a good gambler. Even though I sat at the foot of the masters, I was a lousy gambler. First of all, I played with emotion and would always be giving myself away to opponents. I could be read as easily as a dog's tail. Secondly, my brain could not remember every card played nor remember all the odds of so many games. I would be bluffing on cards already played, which meant a good gambler could take me to the cleaners.

Further, there was the money part that discouraged me. I was of the philosophy a dollar in hand was worth more than double or nothing on the table. Risk avoidance is not a quality that makes one go in for gambling. Finally, and most important of all, I didn't like table games in general. Whether it be Monopoly, Cootie, Scrabble, Chess, card games without money, etc. For me, these were not board games — they were bored games. I had friends who could spend an entire evening drinking beer and playing euchre, contented as grazing cattle. There was no way I could stay around and wait for the last trick. I'm not bluffing; I had to be on the move.

Backward Forward

The *Collier's* article "Illinois Shakedown[1]: The Little Guys Lose" by Gordon Schendel, which signaled the end of gambling in Quincy, was more sensational than factual. A follow-up article in *The Quincy Herald Whig*, "We Asked for It,"[2] pointed out that Quincy was quite prosperous with 75% of the population owning their own homes. The article goes on to say that "... a relatively small percentage gambles regularly...," and far from being plagued by violence associated with the gambling industry, Quincy was "...a place of security in which there is little major crime."

The first few paragraphs of *Colliers* tells a heart-tugging story of a mother holding her baby while addictively putting money into the slots. We find out she's spending the family's grocery money, and that her husband will have to eat leftovers as a result. The author claims that this dire story is common and that the state of Illinois must put a stop to this for the sake of morality more than anything else. The moral high ground argument was, certainly, his under-

[1]Gordon Schendel. "Illinois Shakedown: The Little Guys Lose." Collier's: April 15, 1950, p.13

[2]"Wound Is Fatal To "Doc" Settle Shot October 26." Editorial The Quincy Herald Whig: Nov. 2, 1931, p. 3A.

pinning argument and, I believe, the one that defeated all meager reasoned opposition of the gambling interests.

When I queried my father about the "poor family with a gambling addict story," he said he hadn't encountered such a thing. He did have a few customers who sat on stools with a roll of quarters, but these were people who were well off and just enjoyed the entertainment of pulling handles and waiting for a score. Most of his customers played the slots like they played the juke box, or to have something to do that was entertaining with their spare change. Finally, my father pointed out, the money spent on gambling in Quincy stayed in Quincy, which helped the city's economics.

What amazes me today is how congenial we are when the state is more ruinous to poor families with its gambling practices than illegal gambling ever was. Where is the moral outrage for state lotteries? Where are the preachers and priests shouting from the pulpits about these evils of betting? How many times have we seen people, who have all the outward appearances of being poor, with a fistful of lottery tickets? Isn't this the same scene drawn in 1950 magazine article? Victor Matheson, an economics professor at the College of Holy Cross and an expert on lotteries, says $325 a year is wagered on lottery tickets for every adult in the United States. However, Matheson goes on to say that it's the low-income people who spend a far greater percentage of their income than the rich.

I can't blame those who are poor for buying dozens of lottery tickets at a time because for most of them even the bad odds of striking it rich are better than no odds at all. The odds are very good, however, that invertebrate politicians have decided it is easier to take money from the poor than to battle those who are wealthy to pay their fair share of taxes. Of course, this shameless practice is justified by calling it in the name of *morality*, the "Educational" lottery, which is like calling a nuclear weapon a "Peacekeeper."

As a way of collecting taxes, the lottery is one of the most inefficient ways known to humankind. Of the 80 billion or so dollars that are collected per year, only about 20 billion goes to education. If most of it went to education, then we wouldn't have teachers around the nation picketing for better pay and more materials. Instead billions go into categories like "state general funds," which to me is a nice way of saying, "We don't know where in the hell it's going or whose pockets it's lining." If we think of all the bureaucratic costs and marketing costs of the lottery, we realize this is another place where billions are being spent. How many "cush" jobs does this money generate? Of the great lottery pie, only the thinnest sliver of 20 million dollars goes toward state programs for problem gamblers.

If my time in Quincy with the gambling forces has taught me anything, it is that big money is like nuclear waste that cannot be contained but seeps and creeps into all kinds of corruption. Favors and reciprocal favors begin to form a hidden network that is self-serving, and the members of this exclusive club hold tightly to their undeserved benefits. How much more money would be available for education and how many fewer good-ole-boy networks would exist if we decided to do away with lotteries and raise money the good, old-fashioned way with taxes. We already have a bureaucracy in place to collect taxes; we don't need marketing for taxes; we don't need to make or distribute tickets or to pay 6 billion dollars in commissions to retailers; and we can retake the moral high ground by instead of fleecing the poor, taxing those who can afford to pay and that justly should pay. All we need to make this happen is to see the true costs of lotteries, and to vote for politicians who are vertebrates.

SPRECHEN SIE DEUTSCH?

Quincy was settled by people of Germanic origins. As is the case with all U.S. immigrants, despite the fact that they would like to keep alive the language of their ancestors, these languages gradually become subsumed by American English. Their children, as quickly as possible, want to set aside their outsider status and become part of the main stream culture by mastering its language. By the time a second generation arrives, the use of the mother tongue has been diluted significantly.

In the Quincy of my childhood, one could always find the tattered remains of German words being used. For instance, after lunch at the house of one my childhood buddies, he told me to put "the dishes in the zink." *Zink*? After this happened to me on number of occasions and in different households, it was explained this was a German holdover — Germans often pronounced *S* like the English *Z*. Below are a number of holdover German words and phrases that I heard growing up.

Auch du Lieber: oh my or oh dear. Ex. *Ach du Lieber,* I left my wallet in the car.

Bier haben: I'll have a beer. (My father always used this phrase to order beer.)

Danka: thank you.

Dummkopf: stupid person. Ex. You *dummkopf* — you're in the wrong restroom!

Dunder vetter: thunderstorm weather. Ex. We're having *dunder vetter*.

Farshimmelt: mixed up, confused, or crazy. (When I married a Jewish woman, I found that we both used the word *farshimmelt*, which has both German and Yiddish origins.) Ex. After a wild party, everything in the house was *farshimmelt*.

Gesundheit: good health and is said after a person sneezes.

Gott in Himmel: God in heaven or oh my God. Ex. *Gott in Himmel*, how did you get done so fast!

Guten Morgen: good morning.

Kaput: broken or no longer working. Ex. The car went *kaput* and had to be towed.

Mach schnell: hurry or be quick. Ex. *Mach schnell*, the train is about to leave.

Raus: hurry and get out. Ex. *Raus, raus*, out of bed. It's time for school.

Scheissdreck or scheisse: shit, crap or load of shit. Ex. That's a bunch of *scheisse*.

Schweinhund: literally "pig dog"; a piggy, lazy person. Ex. *Schweinhund*, you've done nothing but drink beer all day.

Spiel: a pitch or persuasive speech. Ex. The used car salesperson gave us his *spiel* about how the car was only driven to church on Sunday.

Verboten: forbidden. Ex. Sleeping at the bar is *verboten*.

Wurst: sausage. Ex. The best of the *wurst* were brat*wurst*, knock*wurst*, bock*wurst*, and liver*wurst*.

Zink: sink. Ex. Wash the dishes in the *zink*.

I've saved the last German phrase to say good-bye:

Auf Wiedersehen

CHAPTER 10
CAUGHT IN AMBER

"If any man tells you he loves America, yet hates labor, he is a liar. If any man tells you he trusts America, yet fears labor, he is a fool."

—Abraham Lincoln

Quincy was primarily a German town. The majority of its citizens were German Catholic, and it would be no stereotype to say, "Germans loved their beer." The phenomenon of the family tavern was well established in Quincy when I was a child. These places that occupied corners on many of the streets of Quincy far outnumbered the churches. In many ways, they were more vital than the churches, performing sacramental services of communion and transformation through leavened barley. Whole families would attend certain neighborhood taverns as a way to relax after a day of labor, cool off in hot weather (the taverns had air conditioning before most homes), and listen to the juke box. The parents played cards and drank beer. The children played cards and drank soda.

Along with buying beer by the glass or bottle, many of these places had jug beer. There were no six packs to buy to take home; only gallon glass jugs to get filled. Purchasing a gallon jug didn't require an adult or an ID. Parents could send their ten-year-old to the family bar with an empty jug, and the bartender would fill it without question. Our clockwork German neighbor up the street, Herb Grieving, could be timed from when he came home from work. He would first send one of his children up the street with an empty jug and then take off his shirt. Next, he opened his lawn chair as his messenger returned with a golden lager. With jug and glass, he would sit contently until it was time for supper.

There were even a few places in Quincy that still performed an even earlier version of jug beer. Before jugs, you would buy beer to take home in buckets. They called it "shoot-the-can." My grandfather would rub butter on the bottom of his bucket so that when they filled it up, he'd get more beer and less foam. Foam was always the enemy of German beer drinkers, and bartenders were aware that customers were watching them like chemists for the correct proportions of foam to liquid.

Before the present era of craft beer, Quincy had a history of its own crafted beers, stretching from the latter half of the 19th century to the middle of the 20th. The German immigrants wanted to continue their old country's craft of making beer. Quincy had as many as nine breweries during this period of time, which was quite a lot for such a small town. The last and most successful of these breweries was Dick Brothers Quincy Brewing Company, which closed in 1951. At one time, Dick's had been larger than Anheuser Busch, but it never recovered fully from Prohibition and steadily declined until its closing.

You can still see the Dick Brothers buildings on 9th and York. Not only can you see, but you can go inside this historic building complex, which has a Ratskeller, tours, arts, and entertainment. Beneath these old red brick buildings is the remains of a maze of tunnels and caverns that were used to keep the beer cold before shipping. The train tracks remain underground where the trains pulled right up to the beer to be shipped. The artesian well that provided pure water for the beer still bubbles. It's rumored there is a tunnel that goes under 12th street to the home of the brew master so that he could walk to work underground in bad weather. Lastly, I've been told there was an old cock fighting ring down there that has been bricked up.

To walk into these old family taverns is like being trapped in amber, amber beer, that is. I get the spooky feeling that some of the people at these bars today have been there for a hundred years, unchanged like in an old fairy tale. I played on the bare wooden floors of such taverns when I was in diapers, as some of the furnishing of my father's taverns had that same ambience: twilight worlds that were neither night nor day. Time stopped at their patterned tin ceilings, the dim lighting, old, crusted ceiling fans, and the dark mahogany bars. The glow of liquid, glass, and ice created a crystalline spell for the viewer where nothing existed outside the walls. Only when you stepped out the door into harsh sunlight or a bitter, win-

Jack Settle (Father) at the Settle Inn

tery night was the spell broken with reality slapping you in the face.

Limbo Tavern

Somewhere
between heaven and hell
are timeless places
echoing twilights
filled with ice-cube laughter
and neon juke boxes.
Home not of the damned
but of the people
who might have been.
An amber eternity of forgetfulness

where songs of love lost
slowly bubble by,
and faces stare forever
into reflections
of liquid, glass, and ice.

Food Testaments

Behind the bar in these places were usually an array of various snacks — peanuts, cashews, gum, and candy. Commonly, there was also a jar of pickled pigs' feet that looked like something you'd find in formaldehyde in a biology class. Watching people suck out the jellies of the pig hooves confirmed to me than humans are, indeed, carnivores.

In addition, many of these corner taverns had grills to make burgers. These grills had been "broken in" for decades, which meant they could never be totally cleaned. When you ate a burger from these places, you ate eras of delicious build-up. The flavors embedded in the grills could not be reproduced anywhere else. Hot dogs at these places also reached a height of excellence. To get a sack of dogs from Gross's Inn was to bring home eating at its finest. Occasionally, taverns had deep fryers for fries and tenderloin sandwiches. Deep fried tenderloins came out of these fryers as big as elephant ears with buns to match. When I return to Quincy, I always reprise this eating by getting a tenderloin sandwich at Sprout's Inn. I'm still puzzled to this day why this sandwich has never reached national popularity.

A number of taverns had their specialties. Pig Ear Charlie's was named after its specialty — pig-ear sandwiches. Pig-ear sandwiches are not for the squeamish. If you think the pig-ear meat was disguised in some way to make it more palatable (fried in a crust or sliced and diced), think again. The whole pig ear was boiled in a flavored concoction, speared out, and placed on a bun. Mmm-mmm. And if that didn't get your salivary glands churning, then maybe identifying the species of pig by its mottled markings would.

The first time I confronted a pig ear sandwich was in high school. I turned a light shade of blue on this first encounter, but I was determined to carry on with my more experienced friends to the bitter end. My pig had black and white patterns on its ear, and I could still see some fine hairs on it. I watched the others put mustard and a slice of onion on theirs, and I did the same. Then, I took a deep breath and bit in largely. It wasn't the taste that brought me to the edge of vomiting; it was the texture. I thought I'd be ripping into a grizzled, stringy meat, but the ear was soft and contained gelatinous gunk that spirted out upon chewing. All I could think of was great quantities of ear wax exploding.

This sensation defeated me on my first try. But I came back later more prepared to face the obstacles of this specialty. This time I did not blanch upon the appearance of an amputated ear, and the jellied textures mixed well with the mustard, onion, and bun. I can't say I became a fan, but at least I'd overcome my disgust enough to make the ear palatable. All parts of the pig can, indeed, be eaten, if not savored.

Turkey nuts were another specialty that many taverns provided — and, yes, turkeys have testicles, but they're not visible, being inside the bird's abdominal cavity. The testicles are deep-fried to a crisp, reminiscent of fried mushroom nuggets. They go very well with beer. Some towns today have what are called Testicle Festivals, the oldest being in Byron, Illinois.

Even if named a bit crudely, at least turkey nuts were named accurately. Not so with an occasional specialty at my dad's tavern, "rocky mountain oysters," sometimes called "cowboy caviar." I can understand, though, the need to name this dish with a euphemism, since naming them "bull balls" or "testicles" does not sound savory. Somehow the psychological leap from eating turkey testicles to bull testicles is one of geometric proportions. Bull testicles are bigger and not so hidden as turkey testes. Most of us can envision quite easily a bull's hanging scrotum with testes the size of avocados, which is not exactly an appetizing thought. The bull's testicles do not come on the half shell but are deep-fried like turkey nuts and are served with cocktail sauce. Their taste and texture are like fried chicken gizzards, which are grizzled and crunchy.

My dad tells the story of some college co-eds coming to his bar and ordering rocky mountain oysters. Thinking he didn't need to provide any explanations, he served up an order. And then another order. And then another. They appeared to really love them. One of the young women commented to my dad, "These are delicious. I had no idea that the Rocky Mountains had oysters."

My dad grimaced but replied, "Well, actually these aren't really *oysters.* You mean to tell me you really don't know what these are?"

"No. What are they?"

"They're bull testicles, pounded and fried."

One of the women lost her "oysters" on her plate — obviously overwhelmed by the thought of her eating these huge testicles with such gusto.

Side note

If you don't believe these testicle stories are true, I must continue the theme of testicles and resort to a little biblical history and apocryphal linguistics. *Testify, testament,* and *testicle* have a long relationship. In the Bible, we have people swearing by holding the testicles of another (Ewww!); Abraham and his servant, for instance. And according to Dr. Dario Maestripieri in *Psychology Today* (blog 21/11/2011), "...men [Romans] held their own testicles as a sign of truthfulness while bearing witness in a public forum."

Therefore, I grab my crotch and testify that I have told you the truth, the whole truth, and nothing but the truth. So help my oysters.

Chili today and hot tamale

Finally, I end with the mystery of Simon's Tavern. Before I die, I would like someone in Quincy to enlighten me about the following: how Simon's Tavern had the best hot tamales I've ever tasted. The anomaly is that this tavern in the 1950s and 1960s was located in a Midwestern city of primarily German descent. We had no Hispanic population; in fact, I had never met anyone Hispanic in the entire city during this time period. Further, we knew nothing of Mexican cuisine. If you said to someone "taco" or "burrito," he or she would have stared back blankly.

At this time of my life, I accepted the reality of hot tamales in Quincy the way I accepted sauerkraut — in fact, I put both of them into the single category of German food. My father would occasionally send us to Simon's to bring home a bag of tamales. We always protested because Mrs. Simon, who ran the tavern, was a difficult old German. She'd be playing cards with her patrons, and when we approached her about buying some tamales, she'd slam down her cards as if we asked her to change the toilet paper in the men's room. For her the customer was not always right; the customer was an annoyance she had to attend to like a buzzing fly. Begrudgingly, she made our order and shooed us out.

Where did she learn to make these heavenly tamales wrapped in corn shucks, coated in corn dough, and filled with a seasoned meat? We had people who came down from Chicago to bring back her hot tamales. How in the hell did Mrs. Simon, who had not a smidgin of Hispanic background, know how to make a good tamale — no not a *good* tamale, the *best*? *Ich werde nie verstehen.*

All Work Does Not Make Jack's Boys Dull

Growing up I spent a lot of time in, around, and behind bars. This had its advantages. I got soda at the bar, which I didn't get at home. In the hot summer, my mother packed us up to spend the day at our tavern that was air conditioned (our home was not). My brothers and I could always play for free whatever game machines the Settle Inn had at the time — pinball machines, bowling machines, pool tables, etc. There were disadvantages, however, with the major disadvantage by far, at least for my brothers and me, being assigned some of the "shittiest" jobs known to humankind.

Cleaning in all its forms — washing, waxing, polishing, scraping, stacking, sweeping, mopping, replacing, stripping — were never ending tasks in the bar and restaurant business. One of the first jobs that I ever remember doing for our business was scraping gum off the bottom of the bar, bar chairs, surrounding tables and booths with a putty knife. Since I was maybe eight, I was short enough to get under these surfaces without a lot of effort. The view of gum fields beneath the bar was like the discovery of an asteroid belt.

Many people in these days chewed gum in lieu of smoking. Apparently, they thought it was inappropriate to put their worn-out gum among the cigarette butts and ashes in the ash trays, and so they furtively stuck it under the bar and tabletops.

Who knows the ages of some of the gums in this underworld? It was a large horseshoe bar that had a lot of age on it, and I doubt anyone had ever thought to remove these Wrigley fields underneath, except, of course, my detailed father. Some of the gum had calcified and had to be chiseled off with a hammer. Some gum of recent origin had some stick left on it, which required a constant re-cleaning of my scraping blade. Some gum was in wads the size of golf balls. They probably came from the minor league baseball players who frequented our place. Thankfully, I was not appalled by handling the shards of the archeology of chewers.

Another despicable job that my brothers and I got to be a part of at an early age was cleaning the large blind that hung over the picture window at the front entrance to our place. This was not a mere feather dusting, which was done on regular basis. No, this was a deep cleaning that had to do with removing a year's worth of smoke, ash, and grease that had been baked solid by the sun onto the slats. For this job, the venetian blind that covered the ten-foot-wide picture window had to be taken down and laid on the floor. The blind slats were narrow, around 1" wide, and there were 70 of them with intervening draw strings. We removed the gunk off each individual strip with a rag and bucket of cleaning solution. Tedious but easy enough. The *caveat lautus* (Let the cleaner beware) of this project was that metal strips cut the fingers and hands like razors. As slow as you might go and as careful as you might be, you always ended up with small cuts hatching your hands.

Being Paid Weakly

During the summer that I was going into eighth grade and my brother Larry was going into sixth, we became janitors. My father had lost his janitor and decided we were old enough to do the tasks required. Each morning Larry and I would arise early and ride our bikes to 8th and State, a few miles away. Our ritual was to unlock the door and then burst through it like mad men running around the bar and tables. The reason for this mad dash was that people drinking often dropped money and were too tipsy to pick it up or even to be aware they'd dropped anything — there were always coins to be found on the floor — sometimes the motherload of a dollar bill.

The finder did not have to split. Money was always scarce in the lives of the Settle boys, so dimes, nickels, and quarters had magnified value. Moreover, if you think we were receiving an allowance or payment for our janitorial services, you never knew the frugality upon which our family was built. A saying my father always used was "Poor people got poor ways." Also, he enjoyed telling us, "You'll be paid weekly," which sounded good, until he spelled out weekly as "w-e-A-k-l-y." For our janitorial services, it was less than weakly; it was nothing.

When I wrote "shittiest jobs" earlier, I wasn't being metaphorical. Our janitorial jobs introduced us to the bathroom behaviors of drinkers. First of all, we learned the sociology of men pissing in taverns. Tipsy men have bad aim and minimal control over where they pee — whether in or out of the urinal; in or around the toilet and toilet lid. Cleaning the men's room was always a smelly affair better done with a fire hose than a mop, bucket, cleanser, and brush.

Adding to the general squalor of the men's room were the butts — not the fleshy kind but the cigarette butts in the urinal. For some reason we never understood, men liked to pee and smoke at the same time and then cast their Lucky Strikes or Camel butts in the urinal drain. Fishing them out, even with rubber gloves, was no picnic.

The men, also, were graffiti prone. Phone numbers, pictographs of the crudest kind, and poems constantly appeared and reappeared on the walls and dividers. That classic poem that had to be washed off time and time again was:

> *He who writes upon these walls,*
> *rolls their shit into little balls.*
> *He who reads these words of wit,*
> *eats these little balls of shit.*

Even at 12, I knew these people had no future as poets, or comedians for that matter. Besides this poem, an image that constantly re-occurred was the "KILROY WAS HERE" drawing. This was a meme created during WWII and surfaced everywhere that American soldiers were stationed during the war. It continued to be used in the 1950s. The only witty — or at least I thought so at the time — piece of graffiti that I came across was one on the wall in front of the urinal. As you were urinating, the perpetrator would encourage you to follow the arrows, which climbed by degrees up the wall. As you reached the ceiling, there was a message, which stated, "You are now pissing on your shoes."

Kilroy Meme from WWII

A profound cultural change occurred when Larry and I entered the mysteries of the women's bathroom. It was neater and smelled much better with lingering perfumes to replace the urine smells that came from the outgassing of the men's urinals. There were no cigarette butts to fish out and a lot less graffiti.

However, this is not to say that cleaning the women's room was not without its gender challenges. More disgusting to Larry and me than cigarette butts in the urinal were the bloody Kotexes that spilled out of a full waste can or sometimes clogged a toilet. To us, women's periods were not so much a curse for women as it was a curse for us to have to clean them up. I preferred not being reminded of what I had recently learned about menstruation, and often offered a prayer of thanks to God that I was born male.

Although women didn't scratch phone numbers, petroglyphs, or poems on the wall, when they did decide to express themselves, it was usually in red lipstick on the mirror. It usually had something to say about a man in large, glaring letters — BILLY FLANNERY CAN GO FUCK HIMSELF. The impossibility of this request was almost as difficult as it was for us to remove it from the mirror. In our minds, Billy Flannery got away just in time.

Of course, we did all the things janitors usually do. We swept and mopped the floor. Emptied and washed the ash trays. Wiped down the bar, and, according to state law, we broke all the empty liquor bottles with a ball-peen hammer so that they could not be refilled with a cheaper liquor. We stocked all the coolers with the various beers of the day — Pabst Blue Ribbon, Schlitz, Budweiser, and Falstaff, which were the most popular beers at the time. Then, we'd take all the beer empties and soda empties down to the basement to be sorted into their proper cases.

A Case of Budweiser and The Cask of Amontillado

Descending into the basement of the Settle Inn was a journey into the mind of Edgar Allan Poe. Opening this cellar door that separated the world of the living from that of the undead, you encountered a merciless blackness. The switch for the light was shaped like a porcelain bone and sparked blue when it turned on a dangling, low watt bulb. The stairway was a worn, rickety creation with shaky, wooden steps and banister. Every speck of paint or varnish had been worn off to a skeletal smoothness. Almost every safety regulation you could think of was violated here. How someone was not maimed, electrocuted, or burned to death during our time at the Settle Inn was a matter of blind luck.

Larry and I made our way to the small circle of light that contained other cases for bottles. Our job was to sort through all the bottles and put them in their proper cases so that the delivery trucks could take them away at a savings to us. The basement was large, and beyond our working area yawned large areas of pitch black. Who knew what existed in these areas — rats, skeletons, torture devices, or a walled-up body? Whatever was there, we preferred not to explore, and we got our work done with alacrity.

My brother Larry was particularly jumpy in this environment, since he knew he had a sadistic brother who would like nothing better than to trap him in this dark pit of horrors. He was like a gazelle with a lion at a watering hole. Any quick motion by me toward the stairs, and Larry responded with a leap up two or three steps ahead of me. Larry kept positioned in his work so that I was always in front of him. It was the dance of predator and prey. I never caught him off-guard.

Da Agony of Da Feet

If you want a long and successful career bartending, you have to take care of your feet. Standing for long periods of time over the years makes one vulnerable to a number of ailments: sore feet, swollen ankles, achy back, calluses, bunions, corns, fallen arches, and varicose veins. In addition to these dangers, working behind the bar could be a slippery affair with spilled liquids and ice on the floor, which could cause falls and strained tendons. To obviate these kinds of problems at the Settle Inn, we made board walks that went over the linoleum floors.

Before my father assigned me the task of constructing board walks, I had a familiarity with hammering and sawing from making all kinds of constructions with neighborhood friends: camps, rubber guns, and crude, soap box racers. But I had never built anything that would be seriously used as part of our business. Therefore, building board walks was going to be a lesson for me in purchasing materials and accuracy down to the half inch.

It's a wonderful way to learn geometry, mathematics, and finances through real projects rather than the word problems given to us in school. I always identified with the story of the girl in school who was asked by her teacher whether she would like a third of a pie or a fourth of a pie. The girl's response was, "What kind of pie is it?" Now that's a person who is practical! These walks were made by lining up 1x2s of the desired length side by side with a half-inch between them. Then I'd connect their width with 1x2s at intervals of a yard. The boards were springy and kept a bounce in your step. They were like shock absorbers for your feet, knees, and ankles.

The satisfactions of a builder are considerable. I remember my father and I snuggly fitting my wooden walk between two others. It fit like the skin on a snake. I had learned numbers and that careful attention equaled lasting results. Every time I came behind the bar at the Settle Inn, I looked at my work with frissons of pride.

Another job involving feet that came my way occasionally was stripping and waxing the dance floor. Even though I was Catholic and had learned to be on my knees for long periods of time, this was a job that could defeat the most prayerful monk. The dance floor was not small. It had a juke box and could hold up to ten couples comfortably.

First there was stripping off of the old wax to get down to the bare wooden floor. This was done on hands and knees with a bucket of rinse water and a gallon of mineral spirits. You could only do two-foot squares at a time, and you had to apply some elbow grease to remove the previous layers of wax. I must say I got high before the 60s by breathing in the mineral spirits fumes. I tried to keep a fan running at all times, but this was only slightly effective.

The second stage of this process was applying a heavy-duty polish that was not liquid; again this had to be done on hands and knees. Once the polish was down (thank the gods), we had an electric buffer to bring out a sheen on the wax. I loved to let my friends or brothers give it a go with the buffer. If you haven't used a buffer before, it is not as easy as it looks — something like putting a stick-shift car into gear for the first time. When a neophyte first engages the buffer, it takes off like a dog on a leash that sees a cat. This trial thankfully was on a dance floor, and the dance between the buffer and the neophyte had lots of space to roam.

Once this base layer of wax was laid down, it was easy to keep up the dance floor for a year or so. All ye need do after that was to dry mop or put down a layer of liquid wax and buff. Of course, this job for the feet was just the opposite of the board walks, where the idea was not to slip. Dance floors were for slipping, sliding, and gliding.

The Dishes Ran Away With the Spoons

I think there should be a limit to how many dishes a human being is obliged to clean during a lifetime. This limit would be determined in miles. A stack of 12 platters/plates is conveniently equal to about one foot. This would mean that 5,280 ft. of platters would equal 63,360 platters. Considering this measurement, no one should have to clean more than two miles of platters or plates during his or her life. I reached this limit by the age of 16.

The first job for which I actually received pay was working as a dishwasher for my Aunt Dolly at the Patio restaurant. I was a freshman in high school and worked on weekends and in the summer. Even though the Patio was an upscale steakhouse, it had the most antiquated dishwashing equipment. They had no sprayer, garbage disposal, or automatic dishwasher. The dishes were all washed by hand and stacked in metal racks. The racks had hooks so that they could be hand dipped into a vat of water that was heated to 180 degrees, and then set out on a table to dry. The dishes then had to be put away.

This little back corner of the kitchen for doing dishes had a climate that was equatorial. And when you stuck your face above the heated rinse water, it was like sticking your face into a geyser basin at Yellowstone. The sweating was profuse and the replacing of body fluids constant. I always had nearby a glass of ice water or Coke. At the end of the evening, despite the fact that I was skinny, I had lost a couple of pounds, and I had enough food stains on my apron to frame it as a Jackson Pollock.

After the first week, I was going to beg my dad to let me quit this work in fire and brimstone; then my first paycheck arrived. Oh, ho, Hoo! You mean I suffer, but then I have my own money. It's amazing how pay becomes a palliative for suffering. Rather than quit, I asked for another night. The first thing that I bought was a wallet, of which I had no need before.

This was not my last stint at dishwashing. When our new restaurant, The Plaza, opened up, I was sent down to the kitchen located in the bowels of the basement to do more dishwashing. At least this time, I would be working with modern equipment — sprayer, garbage disposal, and racks for the dishes that slid in easily to an automatic dishwasher with a wash and rinse cycle. My corner of the kitchen was not so hellish as it was at the Patio's and not so isolated.

I could enjoy the company of my fellow kitchen troglodytes. The downside was there were many more dishes.

The Plaza was a larger restaurant that seated more people, and it was a busier restaurant with overflowing crowds on the weekends. We had a little elevator that sent up the food from the kitchen and took down the bus trays with dirty dishes from above. That elevator went up and down like a yo-yo on Friday and Saturday nights without pause. I had trays of dishes stacked around me like mine fields that I had to avoid stepping on. Even after we closed, I could still be doing dishes, and there were times I would come in the next morning to finish up the previous night's dishes. I couldn't even get away from dishwashing while I slept because the single-mindedness of the task entered my dreams, so that I continued to dishwash in bed. By age sixteen, I exceeded the two miles of dishes that I proposed earlier as a limit to the number of dishes one should have to do in a lifetime. Then, I was released.

As a junior in high school, I would enter the heaven of the upper regions of the restaurant business. I was to become a busboy. This was like in Catholicism going from purgatory to the Pearly Gates. I was dressed in nice slacks, a white shirt, and black tie. I worked in air-conditioning. I worked with people dressed up, laughing and celebrating. When I cleared a table of dishes, I sent them down the elevator to the fire and brimstone of the underworld from which I had been reprieved. My heart soared in this new realm of sunlit, cumulus clouds.

I got to listen to customers as I wheeled around my bus cart. I got to observe people's interactions whether they be courting, celebrating anniversaries, doing business, being refined or being tipsy. There were jokes and humor to be heard. And it was sexy work with beautiful women coming in dressed up and girls my own age that I could glance at as they ate demurely with their families. I sang "Happy Birthday" with my father multiple times per night as we graced celebrating tables with a small wine bottle with a candle lit on top and two-part harmony. All these stimulating things seemed like a privilege, and not only that but I was paid more, receiving tips from the waitresses. New work and better pay did not make Jack's boy dull.

Backward Forward

I hope my early years in the amber glow of bars don't sound like drudgery. I had plenty of time for play and did not become a dull boy. But I will say these projects in and around bars did develop in me a work ethic and a sense of pride for my contributions to the family. My parents were back-patters and expressive of their appreciation of work well done. Praise was always more important to me than the money, and because this was work for the family enterprise, I felt deeply my contribution to something greater than myself.

I think it's good to be toughened up by physical labor and responsibility at an age earlier than our society allows. I remember a story a social worker told me about a ten-year-old child that was so out of control that they could not find a foster home that would keep him. In such emergencies, they resorted to an Amish community in a rural area nearby. The social worker left the child there with some trepidation about how he would adjust to the Amish way of life, but when she came back two weeks later, she couldn't believe the transformation in him. He was working in the fields bringing buckets of water to the laborers. When they called him in to talk with her, she said he was dressed in bibs and a straw hat like the other Amish children and that he was as calm as a stand of wheat. What the Amish had done for the boy was to have him work alongside them and have purpose. Apparently, that was all he needed.

It was the same for my daughter when she began working at 16 for Starbucks. I could not give to her my experiences with the restaurant business nor could she join in with the work that her mom and I did as college professors. To get her to take out the garbage was an ordeal. I held my breath as she started her first job, which required her to get up at 4:30 in the morning. But she took her new responsibilities without complaint or neglect. I remember walking into Starbucks one day, and there she was on her hands and knees with a small brush, cleaning the grout between the tiles. My heart did a pitter-patter because I knew that she was learning about toil and what was required to live in this world. It made her career path that much easier, knowing that she was a competent barista and, therefore, could be competent in any area she chose with a little hard work.

The initiation into hard work early in life is a passage into adulthood that many do not go through today. Early competency, no matter what the skill, from making coffee to stripping a dance floor, gives a person a sense of control and self-worth better than psychologists can provide. Somehow it should be included in every life's journey, no matter how rich or poor, no matter the race, no matter the gender or religion. Work is not something to avoid, but something to learn to relish. When I retired, I knew sitting beneath a cabana with an umbrella drink and watching the waves come in was not going to be the life for me. What is going to sustain me to the end will not be relaxation but work where I can be of service — service, which is the next step after love.

The Plaza Restaurant Menu in 1963.
See next page for some laughable prices.

DINNERS

CHARCOAL BROILED STEAKS

(ALL U. S. CHOICE GRADES)
Ask Waitress for Special Cut Steaks

Top Sirloin Steak (for two) (38 oz.)	8.75
New York Strip	4.50 — 5.50
Top Sirloin Steak (20 oz.)	5.00
Choice Sirloin Steak (18-oz.)	4.75
T Bone Steak (24 oz.) 1 Person—5.00 Two Persons	5.75
T Bone Steak (18 oz.)	4.75
Filet Mignon 1-Pc. (10-oz.)	5.75
Filet Mignon 2-Pc. (8-oz.)	4.75
Special Club Steak (12 oz.)	3.75
Steak and Mushroom Shish-Ka-Bob	3.00

Slaw or Salad — Potatoes — Hot Rolls with Above Orders
75c extra charge when one dinner is divided for two
Steaks broiled past "Medium" not guaranteed

From the Barbecue Pit

Barbecued Ribs	3.50
Barbecued Chicken Breast	1.75
Barbecued Ham Steak (BBQ ½ Ham Steak 1.90)	2.60

Slaw or Salad — Potatoes — Hot Rolls and Butter with Above Orders

Palate Sea Foods

Shrimp — Stuffed with Crab	2.95
French Fried Shrimp, with Tartar or Hot Sauce	2.50
French Fried Scallops, with Tartar or Hot Sauce	2.00
Fresh Fried Oysters—Fresh Selects—(in season)	2.50
Mississippi Channel Catfish	Ask Waitress
African Lobster Tails with Drawn Butter	Ask Waitress
"Special" Lobster Tails	Ask Waitress
Deep Sea Fish (Haddock)	1.50
Ocean White Fish	1.50
Filet of Sole or Shrimp Steak Dinner	1.60

Slaw or Salad — Potatoes — Hot Rolls with Above Orders

Chops and Specialties

Sugar Cured Ham Steak (½ Ham Steak 1.25)	2.00
Breaded Veal Steak Cutlets	1.75
Charcoal-Broiled Chops with Apple Sauce	2.50
Charcoal-Broiled Chops (1 Center Cut) with Apple Sauce	1.75
Ground Sirloin Steak Topped with French Fried Onion Rings	2.00
Pan Fried Steak	1.75
Breaded (Center Cuts) Tenderloins	1.75
Ham and Eggs with Buttered Toast	1.50

Potatoes—Hot Rolls and Butter with Above Orders

We Cater to Banquets, Private Parties, Sales Me

DIETER'S SPECIAL
Small Broiled Filet
Wedge of Lettuce or Jello Salad
Cottage Cheese With Peach
Coffee, Tea or Milk
$2.50

The Pl

RESTAURANT AND COCKTAIL LOUNGE

. . . . *Ask Waitress*

Our Specialty

½ Golden Brown Southern Fried Chicken	1.60
¼ Golden Brown Southern Fried Chicken	1.10
Pan Fried Chicken Livers or Gizzards	1.75
Potatoes—Hot Rolls and Butter with Above Orders	

❧ A LA CARTE ❧

Soups and Appetizers

Cream of Tomato	.25	Barbecued Rib Tidbits	1.50
Split Pea	.25	Fresh Shrimp Cocktail	1.35
Vegetable and Beef	.25	French Fried Onions (Platter	.60
Chicken Noodle	.25	Fried Chicken Livers or Gizzards	1.35
Homemade Soup	.40	Sauteed Mushrooms	1.25
Chilled Tomato Juice	.25	Charcoal Broiled Mushrooms	1.25
Chilled Orange Juice	.25	Mushroom Pops	1.25
Garlic Bread	.15	Cream Style Herring	.75
Oyster Cocktail	1.35	Toasted Ravioli	1.35
Basket Crackers (8 pkgs.) & Butter	.25		

Refreshing Crisp Salads

Jello Fruit Salad	.30
Fresh Cottage Cheese with Peach	.40
Combination Vegetable Salad Bowl	.55
Caesar - Salad	.55
Sliced Red Ripe Tomatoes with Lettuce Leaf	.55
Creamed Cole Slaw	.30
Pickled Beets	.30
Large Salad Topped with Ham — 1.25 with Shrimp	1.30
Plaza Special Dressing or Roquefort	.20 extra
Chipped Dry Roquefort Cheese Topping	.25 extra
Extra Bar-B-Q Sauce with Sandwich—.05 with Dinners—.20	

Your Choice of Potatoes

French Fried Potatoes	.35	Lattice Potatoes	.35
Hash Browned Potatoes	.35	Baked Potato	.35

Delicious Sandwiches

Strip Pork Tenderloin	.60	Mushroom-Steak	.55
Super Strip Pork Tenderloin	.80	Pepper Steak	.55
Hamburger	.45	Baked or Fried Ham	.40
Hamburger Deluxe	.50	Ham and Egg or Cheese	.55
Cheeseburger	.50	Grilled Cheese	.25
Cheeseburger Deluxe	.55	Plaza Special	.60
Bar-B-Q Beef (On Bun)	.50	Ocean White Fish	.40
Bar-B-Q Ham (On Bun)	.50	Fish (Haddock)	.40
Special-Steak-On-Toasted-Bun	.90	Filet of Sole or Shrimp Steak	.50
Filet Mignon Steak	1.75	Corn-Dog	.25

Soft Beverages

Coca-Cola	.25	Seven-Up	.25
Root-Beer	.25	Pot-Coffee	1.00
Tea — Coffee — Sanka	.10	Milk	.20

itings . . . *Managers Personal Attention Call* 222-0690

```
SPECIALS
PALMINA'S ITALIAN SPAGHETTI . . 1.75
TOASTED-MEAT-RAVIOLIS . . . . . 1.60
Dinners include — Cole Slaw and Garlic Bread
```

vza

12TH AT LIND · QUINCY, ILLINOIS

Party Time

Have your business meetings, bowling parties, and other group functions in our private party room, seating up to 110 people.

We are proud to be your host, and appreciate the privilege of serving you . . . we pledge the same high standards of quality you have learned to expect from us.

Carry-Out Orders . . .

Available from any selection on the menu

CHAPTER 11
A VIEW FROM BEHIND BARS

"I have never let schooling interfere with my education."
—Mark Twain

My rite of passage into manhood came Settle-style in 1965. I would be able to belly up to the bars of my uncles and aunt as an equal warrior of the bartending trade. Further, I could swap stories of drunks with them, I could discuss the latest drink trends, I could exchange the latest jokes, and I could talk about crazy customers. It was a privilege that came early in life for me, for I was able to serve liquor before I was old enough to drink it legally. How? Because state law did not apply to me as a member of a family business. Thus, as a minor, I was carding people older than myself and denying them legal status to purchase liquor.

To be a part of the Settle clan as a bartender was to be a part of Quincy history. The name Settle was synonymous with bar life in town. There was a time in the 1950s that you could almost a drink a six-pack by having one beer at each of the bars run by Settles.

You could start with your first drink on the outskirts of Quincy at my Uncle Porter's place called the Rainbow Inn. Then you'd drive into town on 12th Street and catch another beer on the north end of town at my Uncle Ralph's Plaza restaurant on Lind Street. For beer three, you would continue on 12th and turn left on Oak until it reaches 17th St., where you could say hello to my Uncle Dick at the Congress Tavern. Next, you'd return to 12th Street and continue on to State Street on the south end of town and make a right. Around

8ᵗʰ and State, you could stop at the Settle Inn and get a cold one from Jack Settle (my father) and then drink it next door at Jax Grill where my Uncle Merle had a connecting grill. That would get you up to beer four. From there, you would head to the river until you could go no farther on Front Street and have your last drink with Aunt Dolly at the River House. If you brought a stranger in town along with you, he might think he was in a Twilight Zone episode where one family was bred to serve alcohol.

Indeed, my father and his siblings were ideal for work behind the bar. They were all extroverts, lively, and entertaining. All of them could tell a good joke, and my dad and Uncle Dick could sing and dance. Secondly, they could handle any shenanigans from drunks to brawlers because they were a tough lot with the size and attitude to throw you out on your ear. Their bars were always safe havens without troublemakers. Finally, they had a sense of independence that made them unsuitable to work any job with bosses or that didn't have a sense of play. They felt like 9-5 jobs were for the dull, and they could make a living on their personalities. And, indeed, they all had formidable, if not educated, personalities.

From left to right and in birth order:
Granpa Settle, Ralph, Merle, Giles, Dolly, Porter, Jack (my father) and Dick

Arriving at the position of bartender was for me reaching the summit of a steep climb in the restaurant business. Having started in the basement as a dishwasher, I had made my way to the cooler climbs of the air-conditioned main floor as a busboy, and from there I continued the climb past the tree line to the craggy world of cashier. The summit was arriving behind the bar, and I was dazzled by the expansive view. For years to come, I would see the gamut of humanity in their nocturnal habitats. It was to be an enlightening experience that continues to *in-form* me.

I Profess

Bartending was more complicated than any of my previous jobs. There was more to learn — to the point you might even call it a profession. First of all, the array of drinks to prepare was quite extensive. When people in this historical period went out for dinner, they drank more cocktails than they did beer and even less wine. Commonly we made whiskey sours, Tom and John Collins, Bacardi cocktails, Manhattans, martinis, Singapore slings, old fashions, side cars, Long Island teas, and many more. We made the whole spectrum of ice creams drinks — grasshoppers, golden Cadillacs, pink squirrels, brandy alexanders — all topped with umbrellas stuck through with a maraschino cherry. The bar was always a kaleidoscope of rich colors in a variety of differently shaped glasses filled with colorful liquids — pink, red, green, blue, beige, and dark browns. If we didn't know a drink, we referred to our bible *Old Mr. Boston: Official Bartenders Guide.*

Besides encyclopedic, mixology skills, there was panache to be learned behind the bar. The Plaza restaurant was not a corner tavern or a grill. We were more upscale, and we played the part with more elegance in our dress of white shirts and black ties and our choreographed manner of making drinks. We shook drinks, not in front of us or to the side, but dramatically above our heads. The sound made for a Latin beat of maracas. Then, as a flourish, we cracked tin and glass apart against the bar edge. Together with blenders, liquid being strained over cubes of ice, the tinkling of mixing spoons, the intermittent chorus of waitresses calling in drinks, you felt like you were participating in a musical.

Our bar stations were arranged like the panel of a Boeing 747. In emergencies, we never had to even look for gin, bourbon, vodka; or glasses, lemon peels, limes; or muddler, strainer, bar spoon. We could talk to customers as our hands found what we needed as surely as we could find "qwerty" on a typewriter. We used powdered sugar rather than simple syrup, which as far as I'm concerned put us a step higher in class and taste. We actually muddled our old fashions, which most places did not do. When you really knew what you were doing behind the bar, you could be in sync with the bartender next to you. It was like a ball room dance when you could anticipate the other bartender's moves and hand him a glass just as he was ready to pour off a martini. My father and I were particularly in sync, and when we were percolating together on a busy night, we would often glance at one another like a basketball player who scores and points to the other in recognition of the assist.

Drink, Drank, Drunk

Drinks of Seduction

Along with mixology, over time one learned the behaviors associated with the drinks. For instance, the drink of seduction was Southern Comfort and Coke. Hustlers, who wanted to score with the women they were with, would "considerately" order them this sweet drink. Southern Comfort is an odd liqueur — sweet and whisky-flavored but deceptively 100 proof.

If you're not familiar with alcohol, two-proof is equal to one percent alcohol by volume. Thus, 100 proof means 50 percent of what you're drinking is alcohol. That's quite a bit. For comparison, beer is around ten proof and wine around 20. Putting a Coke on top of a sweet liqueur makes for a drink that will sneak up on you, if that liqueur is 100 proof. This was exactly what hustlers wanted to happen.

Men were not the only ones who used drinks seductively. There were women who liked to order a Sloe Screw with full knowledge of how it would be received. It's hard for me to imagine anyone wanting to put sloe gin and orange juice together for a tasty drink, but the name gave the drink cache. As a bartender, I never flinched when an attractive woman asked me, "May I have a Sloe Screw?" The banter was too easy from that point, and I always acted like they'd ordered a Budweiser.

The last drink of seduction is the martini. Most people do not realize that dry vermouth is a wine, and when you mix wine with gin, it's a chemical experiment that results quickly in the loss of your sobriety and, perhaps, your virginity. It pushes people over the edge faster than any cocktail, except maybe a Long Island Tea. I must agree with this poem falsely attributed to Dorothy Parker:

> *Martinis, my dear, are deceiving.*
> *Drink one at the very most.*
> *Drink two you're under the table.*
> *Drink three and you're under the host.*

Truer words were never spoken.

Martini Timber

Besides seduction, martinis have other attributes that I would like to expand upon. First of all, I call it the "Timber" drink. I have seen drinkers at the bar having a great time imbibing multiple martinis. They might seem a bit tipsy to me but nowhere near drunk. Usually, they are people who have never had martinis before and seem to think they have found a wonder drug. Then, still laughing and smiling, they get up from their bar stool and drop like they've been felled by a lumberjack. Splat! It is usually these people, once recovered, who cannot stand the smell of gin for the rest of their lives.

There is a joke about a guy talking to a bartender about backpacking in the wilderness, and he's trying to make sure that he has everything he needs.

The bartender says, "Have you packed the fixings for a martini?"

"Why would I pack the ingredients for a martini? I'm going into the wilderness by foot for god's sake," the guy responds.

"In case you're lost," the bartender replies.

"So rather than panic, I can sit under a tree with a martini and calm down?"

"No so you'll be found. As you're making the martini, someone will always come out of the woods and say, 'That's not how you make a martini.'"

That is the way of martini drinkers. When a person orders a *dry* martini, "dry" is a code word for no vermouth. What martini drinkers like is chilled straight gin or vodka accompanied by olives for nutrition. But they are too embarrassed to order shots because that would sound a bit alcoholic. So, in order to sound sophisticated, they order an elegant drink, a dry martini. The sophistication doesn't stop there; martini drinkers like to pretend they're connoisseurs. They'll have the waitress take the martini back to the bar, saying it's not dry enough. Of course, I know they're drinking pure gin, and it doesn't get any drier than that. What I'll do is put their drink below the bar for a moment, and then hand the same drink back to the waitress, who will bring it back to the table. Usually, I'll get a thumb's up signal from the drinker that says, "Now THAT'S how you make a martini." I'll smile back and wink in return, thinking to myself, "Now THAT'S a dumb ass."

The Whine Connoisseurs

As you might expect from my previous expose' of dry martini drinkers, I don't believe in connoisseurs. Many people like the idea of being discriminating in their choice of wines, liqueurs, and brand names. They want to be seen by others as people who gravitate toward quality; in fact, they want to see *themselves* as finer people, who measure quality with a micrometer rather than an ordinary ruler like others.

The first rule for a faux connoisseur or "con," as I like to call them, is **the brand makes the man**. They would never stoop to ordering just a bar bourbon for a cocktail. Thus, we have the con order a brand name that exudes quality. Crown Royal whisky, for instance. I could accept this as a bit discerning, if one were going to drink shots or mix it with water. But, the con mixes it with Coke. If you're going to mix Crown Royal with Coke, you may as well drink the most rotgut whisky you can find and save yourself some money, because you'll never taste the difference.

Rule two for connoisseurship is **the class is the glass**. Never drink a beer from the bottle, a glass of wine from a tumbler, or a liqueur from a shot glass. As evidence of this rule, I remember serving a customer, who incidentally was a friend, a new liqueur called King Festo. I told him it was expensive, but he could have one on the house, since we were trying to promote it. My friend held up the King Festo to the light to observe its pale amber color, took a sample smell, and then raised it to his lips for his first, tentative taste. He paused, and then said, "This is good, *real* good!"

When he finished his King Festo, he told me, "Give me another of those. I'll buy this one. They're delicious — light with a winey twang."

"Glad you liked it," I said, as I pulled out a bottle of beer that had gone flat from beneath the bar and refilled his pony glass.

"What's this?"

"Flat beer," I said, "or as I like to call flat Budweiser, the king of beers, 'King Festo.'"

We laughed together at the fact that he accepted flat beer as an expensive and exotic liqueur because it was in a cordial glass. The human psychology is easily swayed.

Rule three of connoisseurs is **the higher the price, the higher the quality**. Wine drinkers are particularly susceptible to this rule. This is borne out by both my observations and scientific research. Observationally, I once worked with a French waiter, whose accent and suavity indicated that he was an expert in wines. Our manager would tell Pascal (who was both Italian and French) that he wanted to get rid of a case of wine that wouldn't sell and that he would give him five dollars for every bottle he sold. By the end of the night, Pascal had sold the entire case by convincing customers that this wine was one of our finest: "Thees wine ees like a breeze on the Seine — light with a bouquet of spreeng." I would cringe with an embarrassment as he pitched the wine, but the customers bought it; moreover, they LOVED this loser wine. They were sorry to hear later that we didn't carry it anymore.

Scientifically, anyone who wants to spend the time looking into the research about wine tasting will find a revealing, comprehensive literature. As just one example in 2001, Frederic Brochet of the University of Bordeaux brought in fifty-seven wine experts and asked them to write down their descriptions of two separate glasses of wine, one "red" and the other white. The catch in the experiment was that both wines were the same white wine, except one had been turned red with food coloring. The "experts" described the red wine in red wine terms, showing that just a change of color threw the judges off. Brochet didn't stop there; he continued with a second experiment where he took the same wine and put it into two separate bottles, one with a table wine label and the other with an exclusive wine label. The professional connoisseurs described the "expensive" wine in glowing terms and the table wine as "flat and faulty."

All this science of tasting indicates there is a lot of subjectivity in the area of wine. I have seen people who pretend to be wine connoisseurs spend exorbitant amounts of money on the "best" wines, while they could have saved a lot of money (but maybe not face) by purchasing something a lot cheaper. I have always used a variation of James Thurber's quote about wine when I'm trying to sell people a cheaper but quality wine: "A naïve wine without any breeding, but I think you'll be amused by its presumption."

Bar Maxims

Wine and whiskey –
mighty risky.
Wine and beer –
never fear.

Martinis, my dear, are deceiving.
Drink one at the very most.
Drink two you're under the table.
Drink three and you're under the host.
(Often spuriously attributed to Dorothy Parker)

In vino veritas;
in cervesio felicitas.
(Latin for "In wine truth; in beer joy.")

Malt does more than Milton can
to justify God's ways to man. – A. E. Housman

Alcohol is an aphrodisiac that often heightens the dress rehearsal
but spoils the performance.

Drink to make other people interesting.

Always carry a flagon of whiskey in case of snakebite and further-
more always carry a small snake. – W. C Fields

Taxonomy of Bar Species

You can get Linnaean with your observations about customers in bartending. There are distinct groups, or species if you will, that seem to populate every bar. Here are a few that I've identified:

Ambrosia theologicus

This species of drinker sits most of the night silently at the bar and then blurts out, "There's got to be a God. I mean, look at the stars."

I always nod approvingly, "Yeah, there's so many of them."

"Somebody had to make 'em. Who did that, will you tell me? God, thass who."

"Gee, you never know when insights like this will visit you. That's pretty profound." I think to myself about the mysteries of liquor-induced meditations at the bar and hope *theologicus* goes outside and stares at the stars on his way home. I want to tell him this, but I pour Thomas Aquinas another glass, who knows but that while he's taking a piss, he may come up with a new episstemology.

Hustler erectus

Erectus is usually a middle-aged man recently divorced who thinks he still has what is takes it takes to hustle young women. Usually, he has begun balding and carrying a little paunch. In my time, he wore a shirt with the top two or three buttons open to expose a hairy chest overlaid with a gold, chain necklace. *Very sexy* — to maybe women his own age. But he's not going for women his own age. However, he wants his virility to appeal to younger women, whom he missed out on because of a youthful marriage.

Hustler erectus will spend all evening in pursuit of his prey. He buys drinks for younger women, hoping to strike up a conversation and impress them with his "wealth" (he usually has a sports car parked outside). Most women, however, take *him* for a ride, getting their drinks for free and them leaving him like a de-clawed cat. His last hope as the evening goes by devoid of success is for a woman to get drunk enough so that she's indiscriminate in her choice of companionship.

One night I remember a member of this species sitting at the bar near closing time. I glanced over at him and received a momentary vision of who he was. His face had dropped from the exertions of being young — every wrinkle exposed and the circles beneath his eyes pronounced. This was who he really was behind the mask — an aging man who was trying his best to defy time. He should really be sleeping contentedly in his bed. When he saw me looking at him, he quickly recomposed his face. In compassion, I refilled his glass — on the house.

Aggressasaurus wrecks

This species can be very deceiving, appearing at first to be governed by the cerebral cortex, but after a few drinks, you can see his R-complex start to kick in, the reptilian part of the brain. I learned from previous dangerous situations to become aware of "the look," as part of his transformation. "The look" is a puffed up, cobralike stare that says, "I can whip anybody in here. Please somebody give me a chance to kick your ass."

Aggressasaurus wrecks comes from the Creeptaceous period. Alcohol releases his violent nature. When I saw "the look," I became very wary about serving *wrecks* another drink. Also, I prepared myself for trouble. As I said previously, my Aunt Dolly was a genius at turning tigers into pussycats. So, I forewarned Dolly that we had *Aggressasaurus* in the house and be on the alert.

Other bars that I worked at that didn't have Aunt Dollies had other devices. One place had a blackjack beneath the bar. If you don't know what a blackjack is, it's a short leather strap with a metal ball enclosed on one end. One quick swat with this on someone's head, and he drops like a bowling ball off a chair. The problem is, though, is that you could kill someone that way. I never used a blackjack on anyone. More often at most places, you would join up with another bartender (sometimes other employees) and take the bullying customer down and throw him out the door.

My choice of a swat team member was a Quincyan named Louie Cookson. Louie was a soft-spoken person with nothing to recommend him as a tough guy — average build about six feet tall with an obvious toupee. That's why when he tapped *Aggressasaurus* on the shoulder and told him he had to cool it or leave, *Aggressasaurus* thought Louie was easy prey. Big mistake.

Louie Cookson was a street fighter par excellence. He would ask politely for Mr. Tough Guy to step outside, and Mr. Tough Guy would usually do so, smelling a chest-thumping victory. Usually the fight was over in about a minute. Louie's fists were a blur and his movements calculated and choreographed. After being hit about twenty times in a matter of seconds, Louie would ask our trouble-maker if he wanted more. Suddenly, *Aggressasaurus* was jolted into using his cerebral cortex again; he slunk off into the darkness in such humiliation that he never darkened our door again.

Barstooli domestica

How *domestica* can sit at a bar an entire evening from 5 p.m. to 1 a.m. has always been a mystery to me. If I weren't bartending, I could take being a customer at a drinking establishment for about two hours at most. By then I would be bored out of my squash. But these marathoners of sitting and drinking, also known as Barflies, can endure to closing time.

They are never any trouble, nor are they drunks. They sip steadily and drink in all total maybe three cocktails or four beers a night. I found some of them quite remarkable in their ability to not urinate during their duration at the bar. With such healthy kidneys, they would have made great kidney donors. The barflies are pleasant and occasionally make comments or tell a joke. But basically, they are silent, contented to sip and stare ahead.

What motivates them, I don't know. They never revealed their stories to me. As far as I knew, they contemplated tragic chapters in their lives while staring off: war, lost love, lost careers, bad decisions, etc. Or maybe rather than achievement, they chose contentment in life. All I knew is that they were great customers, we had their drink ready for them before they sat down, and we greeted them by name. Then we left them alone.

Extraordinaire cheapus

This species makes sure that they get every drop coming to them. You can identify this species by their distinctive calls: "fill'er up, fill'er up, fill'er up"; "full shot, full shot, full shot"; and "less ice, less ice, less ice." The theme of their lives is "get mine, get mine, get mine."

Extraordinaire cheapus has hawkish eyes that will watch you make a drink to make sure they get a full shot and that you fill their glass to the brim; in fact, they would like you to go beyond the brim, using the meniscus, or surface tension in a liquid. They often asked for less ice, so that you could fill their glass with more liquor. They request not one olive for a martini but three; on the side, of course, lest the olives raise the volume of the liquid. (Archimedes had nothing over them.)

In order to do battle with *cheapus*, we had our strategies. First of all, we made sure that all our drinks had glasses that corresponded to the volume of the drink. This may sound simple, but I've seen bars that had fancy glasses that did not hold a drink properly. Customers always felt they were being shorted. We did this even with wine and didn't use the barely half full, bulblike glass. All our drinks went to the brim.

Secondly, we used shot glasses with false bottoms that appeared to hold a full shot. Actually, they held three-quarters of a shot. This was not to cheat; this was to appease *Extraordinaire cheapus* by letting the last quarter of the shot spill over into the glass. This illusion deceived close observers into thinking they were getting more than a shot, which avoided a lot of complaints about our being chintzy.

The final ploy of *cheapus* was to ask us to "top" her drink before exiting — for free, of course. After a *cheapus* left, his glass was entirely devoid of even a drop of liquid or an uneaten garnish, and his place setting, as you would expect, devoid of any tip.

From the Liquor Cabinet of Curiosities

Besides those customers who were true to type, we did have our curiosities that belonged in a display case as one of a kind. They chose to make the Plaza their place of habitation for a variety of reasons — some were lonely, some alcoholics, some bored, and some "not quite right." Whatever the reason, I enjoyed collecting them into my cabinet of curiosities.

The Chemist and the Psychologist

Dr. Lang was a chemistry professor at Quincy College. When I first came across Dr. Lang as a student, I told him that we needed toilet paper in the men's room. I thought he was the janitor the way he was dressed in plain, gray T-shirt and work pants. But he cared nothing about what he wore or about anything else in the world except chemistry. He was always in his mind with the periodic table swirling around in various configurations.

He would come in our place of business late on a weekday night and sit at the remotest table he could find. For light reading, he would bring along the latest copy of *Scientific American*. Our waitresses were afraid of him because he never spoke to them beyond ordering, and his black, staring eyes said to them, "serial killer." He'd order a sandwich and iced tea. When he got his tea, he would stir it, clangety, clangety, clang, for about an hour. All of us began wincing after about ten minutes, but Dr. Lang kept on like his tea was in a Pyrex beaker and his long spoon was a glass stirring rod.

The only time I ever heard him speak was when he came to the bar to watch our TV for a moment as the news was reporting on the recent Nobel Prize winner in Chemistry. "That was my teacher," he said with a great deal of pride. "You must be excited," I responded. That was it.

Just as odd in his own way was another professor that came to our bar on a regular basis, Dr. Dooley or as we called him "Dooley." Dooley was an odd combination of many elements. He had been a Marine who had gone to college on the G.I. bill. He was an experimental psychologist, or as I liked to call him a "rat psychologist." Besides these things, he was well read in literature and had a broad knowledge of all sorts of fields. Finally, for a guy who was short and thin, he could really put away some beer on a night out. He always sat at the bar and chatted.

One night as Dr. Lang was stirring his beaker of iced tea, Dooley observed Lang's rather aberrant behavior. As a psychologist, it intrigued him. We talked about Dr. Lang and his isolated behaviors. Dooley had crossed paths with Lang at school and had never got a response to his greetings or nods. This provoked Dr. Dooley into his experimental mode. Dr. Lang became a specimen like a rat for Dooley, and he wanted to know what it would take to break Lang out of his single, electron shell.

Not long after our talk, Dooley came in, ordered a beer, and then said, "Marty, he defeated me."

"Who's he?" I said, forgetting about our previous conversation.

"Dr. Lang. I'm at an impasse with him. I can't ethically go any farther."

"What happened? The rat escape the maze?"

"You could say that."

What Dooley had done was plan to be going down a set of stairs at the college while Dr. Lang was going up. There was a railing separating the two sets of stairs. Before Dr. Lang could go past him, Dooley leapt over the railing, blocking Lang's way. "Good morning, mother fucker," Dooley spouted into his face.

Dr. Lang didn't even look up but took two steps sideways in a military fashion and continued unabashedly on his way. Dooley, deflated, sat vanquished on a step, not believing that he couldn't shake this electron loose from its belt. Final score: Chemist 1, Experimental psychologist 0.

Where Were You at Guadalcanal?

Like Dooley, Mr. Hicks was a former Marine, but he was quite a few years older and had made a career out of the military. He was always dressed in a tan sport coat and wore darkened glasses. The first time I saw him I looked for a white cane because I thought he was blind. His appearance was reminiscent of Peter Sellers's portrayal of Dr. Strangelove without the wheelchair.

He had a low, formal, booming voice like he was still giving commands to his troops. "Barkeep!" he'd bark like a drill instructor. "I'd like a beer." His deliberate way of talking always made me believe he had some kind of head injury from a war mission. He'd sit at the end of the bar ramrod straight like a big game hunter. His topics of conversation were limited mostly to the military and war. Occasionally, he'd blurt out, "Where were you at Guadacanal?" My brother Larry would always say, "In the left bunker," which seemed to satisfy him.

His assessment of the enemy in the Vietnam War was that they had "native cunning." In his mind, it was like the U.S. Calvary trying to corral the American Indians. Mr. Hicks would have been more than glad to brandish a sword and charge into enemy lines, if they had lines. But as it was, these cowardly natives slunk around in the jungle, afraid to come out and fight man to man.

The ritual of Mr. Hicks, which we all enjoyed watching, was when he vacated his seat to go to the restroom. He'd stare at the painted cat on door of the men's room, and then draw two fingers like a gunslinger and poke the cat in the eyes to open the door. I suppose he perceived the cat as an enemy with native cunning, and he would take him down. After all, he was a battle-proven marine from Guadalcanal who would never let down his guard. *Semper fi*, Mr. Hicks.

Come to the Cabaret, Old Girl

"What good is sitting alone in your room? Come hear the music play." We had many people who came to our bar because they were lonely. And why not? You could be in the middle of hubbub, observe people of all kinds, listen in on a variety of conversations, and get attention from our bartenders. You could break out of your isolation and forget your worries for a short period of time. This was especially true for older women. An older man, who sat at a bar for a couple of hours, would receive no particular kind of scrutiny. But there was still a stigma in the 1960s of women being out by themselves and sitting at a bar.

If ever there was a place that tried to bring down that stigma and to make visible the invisible, it was the Plaza. Women could dress up, have fun, and relax at our bar without a second thought about its appropriateness. We ran a safe haven, and we kept all riff-raff out. Of course, with this kind of reputation, we had senior women as regular customers. The most memorable of these were the dynamic duo of Helen Wernicke and Maude Broeker, and the queen, Ruby Browner.

Maude and Helen would usually come in as a pair. Helen was a widow and the gregarious one of the duo. She was like a terrier ready for a walk. She gloried in the sights, sounds, and smells of the bar. She loved humor and was capable of telling some very salacious jokes. Larry and I adored her, and even in her late seventies, she had some sexiness about her. We would have done anything to fix her up with a comparable man.

Maude was her curmudgeon, know-it-all friend. I don't believe she was ever married. She bossed Helen around, and Helen took it because she could never imagine being out by herself and needed Maude as a drinking companion. Both of them were capable of putting down two martinis without obvious effects. But number three was the one Larry and I liked because it set Maude off to wax poetic on her *vast* educational career, and Helen to snipe at her about its exaggerated value. Helen with a few drinks in her could zing Maude, and Maude often was not bright enough to know she was being zinged.

Maude's educational career consisted of one year at the Illinois Institute of Technology, a secretarial school. Without doubt, it was a profound experience for her and enabled her to reminisce without limit. She got more out of this one year of education than most PhD's at Harvard. And she held it as the reason for her superiority over Helen, who had no college experience. When Maude began pronouncing her alma mater as "the Ill-noy instiTOOT of tech-NOWL-ology," we knew it was time to call a cab. We didn't want a graduate of such a prestigious school as the "Ill-noy instiTOOT of tech-NOWL-ology" to drive into a telephone pole.

Another woman in this category of only-the-lonely was Ruby Browner. She had lost her husband, Bill Browner, and came in every Saturday night. She worked hard as a hairdresser, and Saturday night was her treat night to dress up and let her hair down. I liked her well enough, and we treated her as Plaza family, but she did have some annoying characteristics.

First of all, she carried herself very imperiously, as if she deserved more than our warmth but our royal obeisance. Second, I wanted to feel sorrier for her, but she was of the species that I described above as *Extraordinaire cheapus.* You had better let the last drop come out of the strainer of the martini tin when filling her glass, else she'd take it out of your hand and shake it herself. Once a new bartender, not realizing he was in the presence of royalty, did not fill her drink to the brim. She said to him, "Obviously, you don't know who I am."

One night I made a critical error with Ruby. I had an extra martini, and as I knew how Ruby liked all things free, I placed it in front of her.

"What this?" she asked.

Flippantly, I said, "This is from a secret admirer." I really thought she would realize that I was joking, but she took it as gospel truth.

"Who, who, Marty? You've got to tell me."

"Ruby, I promised not tell, and I'm keeping my promise."

Ruby began searching the crowd to see if she could pick out her secret admirer. I was busy, so I hadn't had time to repair the damage I had caused. Before I knew it, she had left for the night.

I was hoping in a week's time that this would be the end of it. But Ruby came in for the next six months and mercilessly interrogated me about the identity of her secret admirer. I was feeling guiltier by the day, but I didn't know how to extricate myself from the situation. Finally, I decided to tell her the truth.

When I nervously told Ruby how I had lied to her from the beginning and how this lie had become more burdensome as time went on, she looked me harshly and said, "I don't believe you. You made this up so that you wouldn't have deal with my questioning. I'm not falling for that ploy."

"Okay, okay, you've got me. I give. The man's name is Michael Haversham, and he's a traveling salesman for Beamis Bags. He used to come in once a month on Saturday and see you sitting at the bar. He's married, but he still wanted to know your name because he enjoyed your stylish dress and the bravery you displayed in coming to the bar by yourself and having such a good time. I haven't seen Mike since he bought you that drink. His territory must have changed." It was rehearsed lying that I had hoped to use only as a last resort. It seemed to placate Ruby, though, and after that she left me alone.

I made a resolution then and there never to do such a thing again.

I had mistakenly tapped into the well of Ruby's deepest fantasies. Who knew that behind the eyes of the old there was a person much younger and still filled with so much desire? Now that I'm old, I realize that I view myself as around 34 years old and as still an attractive figure. In my cabinet of curiosities, I keep the heart of Ruby Browner preserved in wrinkled foil. When I hold it, it still beats.

Backward Forward

I often told my father years later when I taught at the University of North Carolina at Charlotte, "Thanks for the bar degree." I learned as much at our bar as I learned in any of my formal schooling endeavors, which included two master's degrees. In the bar profession, I got a privileged view of society. This view allowed me to be a psychologist, a social worker, a philosopher, a storyteller, a comforter, and a confessor. The wealth of human insight in bartending was cornucopian. The combining of relaxation with liquor enabled people to reveal themselves from the bar stool as they would on a psychiatrist's couch. The gamut of psychological states would surface — joy, tragedy, bawdiness, flirtation, salaciousness, sadness, song, truth telling, aggressiveness, loneliness, sentimentality, and blessedly to embrace them all, humor.

In addition to my own insights about human behavior, I had the added benefit of my father beside me, coaching me about appearance and reality as eloquently as Shakespeare. "See the large diamond ring on that rich woman's finger — zircon; see that large diamond ring on the woman who works at Motorola — real." "The older guy at the bar who's telling two younger men about his battle experiences in WWII never made it out of the States." "See that waitress steering what she thinks will be a poor tipper to another waitress's table; that guy's a farmer who has more money than god and is a great tipper." "That man in an expensive suit with an ascot and Rolex watch, that's John Benyea, an amazing architect; the two beauties with him are prostitutes. Never take a check from him." "There are only two categories of bartenders — those that don't drink and alcoholics; never drink behind the bar." The catalog goes on, and I learned more than I can say at the foot of the master.

A recommendation that I would make to all college students aspiring to be writers, psychologists, ministers, social workers, etc. is to be a bartender for a short stint. It will lay a foundation for your future career that does not deal in abstractions. View life from behind bars for a while.

10 Experiences of a Real Bartender

1. You make a martini with no vermouth in it and it's sent back to you because it isn't dry enough.

2. You can be making drinks, talking to a customer, and listening for drink orders – all at the same time.

3. You learn to like lemon juice in small cuts on your hands.

4. You can work a ten-hour shift with two hours of sleep.

5. You appear to be champagne when you feel like flat beer.

6. You can lie over the phone – "He's not here."

7. You can spot an asshole faster than a proctologist.

8. You can steal car keys from a drunk better than a pickpocket.

9. You know the best all-night diners in town.

10. You know when peanut butter is really bullshit.

CHAPTER 12

A MAN WALKS INTO A BAR...

"The universe is made of stories, not of atoms."
—Muriel Rukeyser

"A man walks into a bar..." is the way many jokes begin, and I might add it could just as well be a woman. To be immersed in the bar culture, as I was, there was no need to use made up stories; we had real people who provided us with an unending supply of true-life narratives. Being from a family of bartenders was to be on the New York Stock Exchange of such tales. Each night I always found something worthy of telling, but not always worth preserving. The stories I will tell here are the classics worthy of a continuing life. Some reach the level of instruction, some legend, some mythology. Most are humorous, but often not without a wince while laughing.

It's All Relatives

Dolly Settle

Excuse You

My Aunt Dolly may have been the most forceful woman I ever knew. When I think about her being raised with six domineering brothers, I figure she had two ways that she could respond: become a shrinking violet because she would never be heard in the morass of dominating males or become a steeled woman who could contend with all the behaviors of men. She chose the latter path.

When I worked with my aunt as a bartender, occasionally I would have an aggressive guy who was either getting too loud or looking for a fight. If he was getting out of hand, I learned quickly that if I tried to handle it, it only escalated the situation. So, who you gonna call? "Aunt Dolly! Could you come here for a minute." She would take this frothing tiger and turn him into a kitten. They really didn't know what to do with her. She'd treat them like a child, sit them down, and ball them out. Sometimes she'd call a cab, and they went to their new destiny heads down like lambs.

Perhaps, the story that characterizes my Aunt Dolly the most is the one where she was having a battle with flatulence one evening. These farts were not the loud, thrumming kind, but the silent and deadly ones. As a hostess, she was doing her best to seek moments of refuge between escorting customers to tables and making her rounds of schmoozing with those sitting at the bar, where she could release a toxic mixture in the remote recesses of the restaurant.

But when she came to the bar, she lost control for a moment and one of her deadly concoctions slipped out. She was talking to a well-dressed gentleman, who jerked spasmodically when her fart rose to his nostrils. My aunt, undaunted, said, "George, did you fart? My god, that's a nasty smell."

The man blanched, "No, Dolly, I swear that wasn't me."

"Well, it wasn't me. And there's no one else around. It had to be you, George. Sometimes they just slip out. You can admit it, George. No reason to be shy about it."

"I guess I...I...I must have eaten something that disagreed with me. I'm sorry, Dolly, I didn't even realize I farted."

Of course, he hadn't. Later that night after George left, we all had to laugh with admiration for a woman who could convince a man that he farted and then apologize for it. Now that's a forceful woman.

Dick Settle

The Ubiquitous Barkeep

I did say that the Settles ran quite a few establishments in Quincy, but this story takes it even further. My Uncle Dick ran a tavern called The Congress. The Congress was on a corner and had a front and side entrance. One afternoon, he looked up from the bar as a guy staggered through the door. He weaved around some tables, knocking over a chair. My uncle came around the bar and said, "I think you've had enough for today, old buddy. You need to go home." He grabbed him by the back of the pants and guided him to the walk outside. A couple minutes later the same drunk came through the side door, thinking he was in another tavern. Again, Uncle Dick grabbed him by the pants and started escorting him out the door again, when the man looked up and said, "Shay, Mister, you work everywhere."

Porter Settle

Careful Where You Urinate

Between Quincy and Lima, Illinois, in the countryside, Uncle Porter ran a steakhouse called The Rainbow Inn. This spot was subject to break-ins because there were no streetlights around, and it was remote and not policed very well.

Porter decided he'd been burgled enough, and to discourage break-ins, he bought a dog to watch over his property at night. Brandy was a huge dog, even by a St. Bernard's standards. When we dined at The Rainbow Inn during the day, Brandy would be chained up by his doghouse. We knew Brandy, and we always parked our car near enough to him so that he could stick his head, which was the size of a basketball, through our car windows to get love. At night, Uncle Porter would unchain Brandy and let him roam around the property. Brandy was not so nice at night and quickly took to his work as protector of the realm.

As Uncle Porter was closing up one night and after he'd fed and freed Brandy, he decided to have an outdoor smoke before he locked up. Suddenly, car headlights rolled off the highway and slowly approached his parking lot. Porter watched intently, as this might be one of the thieves he was intent on catching. The man got out of his car, furtively looking around. *Where is Brandy?* my uncle thought.

Brandy was there but hidden behind his doghouse, where he liked to take five. The man was actually not a thief but a traveling salesman who had to pee. As soon as he unzipped and began to relieve himself, Brandy came out from behind his doghouse with the fury of a wolverine. The salesman jumped on the hood of his car and then on the roof, trying to save himself. All the while he continued peeing — on himself, on his windshield, and on his roof. But there was no escaping Brandy whose head reached high over the roof, and he got him by the shoe.

Before Porter could get to the scene, Brandy had shredded one shoe and was circling the car for a taste of another. Finally, while Uncle Porter calmed down Brandy and chained him, the man had jumped off the roof of his car and dove into the driver's seat. He took off, tires smoking, as he did not want to know what the rest of this story forebode. In the parking lot, there lingered the smell of urine and one tattered shoe. "Good boy, Brandy," said my uncle as he patted the dog on the head.

Jack Settle at Settle Inn

One Size Fits All

During the 1950s, many men bought their prophylactics (we called them "rubbers") not at the drug stores but at taverns. The stigma of having sexual intentions in the 50s was much easier to live with from your local barkeep than the woman in white who worked at the drugstore. At the time, my father didn't have a machine in the men's room, but he kept packets of rubbers in a drawer behind the bar at the Settle Inn.

Early in the evening, a young man appeared. He angled shyly up to the bar. My father thought he was going to try to buy a drink as a minor, but instead he whispered, "I'd like to buy a rubber."

"What," my father said in loud voice, "I can't hear what you're saying. Speak up, boy."

"I need to buy a rubber," the young man croaked out in a louder voice, which got the attention of a handful of men sitting at the bar.

"So, you need a rubber, do you," my father continued in a booming voice. "What size do you need — large, medium, or small."

Obviously, the poor kid hadn't ever used a rubber before and hadn't anticipated size as part of the decision (which, of course, it wasn't, but my father was having his fun). He thought for a moment and then came out with "I'll take a small." His answer was greeted with a wave a laughter from the men at the bar as the teen turned beet red.

Then my father threw him a couple of rubbers. "These are on the house," he said. "And from now on rubbers don't come in sizes. One size fits all."

Side note to prophylactics in taverns

Later in the 50s my father eventually sold rubbers in the men's room using machines. These long narrow machines with silver knobs were very mysterious to my brothers and me. We thought they were a kind of gum machine with gums that men gave to women to "satisfy her."

Later when we were older my father told us about an unsavory character who ran a popular bar in Quincy, who put these machines into the women's room. At first you might think this guy was a forward-looking feminist. *Au contraire*; his gamut was that he never filled the machines with rubbers. When women put money into these machines, they got nothing. He made spending money every month from these machines. Why didn't the women complain? Because in these times, "nice" women didn't buy prophylactics and would be too embarrassed to say, "Your rubber machine is empty, and I want my money back." As much as my father was into making money, he never stooped so low as this.

Tales from the Full Moon

Now I'm not one to go in for astrology. When I'm with people who put their faith in it and they want to know my sign, I either give them the wrong sign, whereby they always say, "I knew it"; or I tell them "I'm a Herpes," which sends them quickly off to other groups of their ilk. That said, I may have a little leaning toward the full moon as a celestial body that may affect people's behavior.

My dad was a great believer in the full moon's ability to pull out the strangest people from the cracks and crevices of society to our bar. I tried to pooh-pooh his theory, but I must say that he was more often right than wrong. So much so that when he said, "There's a full moon tonight, Mart," I would brace myself for bizarre company.

Full Moon and the Mongoose

On a full moon night when business was rather slow, a man dressed in dark clothes came out of the darkness and ordered a beer. He seemed to want to talk and, before I knew it, he had me and two other regular customers engaged in a conversation about animals — their strength, speed, and danger.

Then he said, "You know the quickest animal on earth is a mongoose."

We all agreed that a creature that could kill a striking cobra had to be fast.

"Would you like to see one?"

"What are you talking about," I said. "You got one under your coat."

"No, but I do have one in the car. I could go get it."

"Hey, man, I don't want any mongoose in here! What if it bites somebody?"

"Oh, don't worry. He's caged up safely. He wouldn't be able to hurt a soul."

Ralph, one of the other customers, who was a bit tipsy, said, "Let him bring it in, Mar (he could never pronounce the "t" after he had a few). There ain't nobody here. Wha', wha' could be the harm. I never seen no mon, mongoose."

J.D., the other guy at the bar, began begging like a child, "Aw, come on, come on. It'll be fun. Won't cha, won't cha, huh?"

I relented finally under this pitiful whining. "Okay, bring in your mongoose, but for god's sake make sure it doesn't get loose."

"Not to worry. Not to worry," he repeated as he went out the door to fetch the critter.

A few moments later, he hoisted a wire cage about the size of a bale of hay onto the bar. We all gathered around it, looking in intently. The mongoose seemed to be curled up in some straw at one end. All we could see was its tail, and we were all a little disappointed. Our mystery man shook the cage and tried to awaken our guest, but to no avail. The mongoose seemed to be either shy or in a stupor.

"I was afraid he'd be like this in the late evening. That's why I brought in the stick so I could poke him. I'll just release the door a crack and rouse him."

"Whoa, whoa," I said, "there'll be no opening that door. You said he was fast and that's enough for me."

"Well he's fast but he can't get through a crack. It'll be all right."

I had gone this far so I sighed a reluctant, "Ooo-kay."

He very cautiously opened the door a crack and prepared to slide in the stick. We were all glued around the cage with anticipation. Faster than the blink of an eye, the cage door slammed open and a tail streaked out. Mongoose on the loose! The guys on the bar stools dispersed almost as fast as the mongoose, spilling their drinks and knocking over dining room chairs. I wish there was an Olympic event for jumping sideways, because I managed a leap of about six feet sideways in the opposite direction of the mongoose — I'm sure it would've been a world record.

Suddenly silence, rather than the screams of someone having a mongoose go up his pantleg, we all took a moment to comprehend that the tail was just lying on top of the cage. There *was* no mongoose, only a fury tail attached to a spring-loaded cage door.

Then, came the cackle of the full-moon man, who apparently went around with this little contraption to scare the bejesus out of his victims. There was a moment when we all thought of beating him senseless and stuffing his head into the cage. But as the adrenaline subsided, we realized that we'd been had and that we may as well succumb to a very masterful performance. The man took his apparatus into the night, and I never saw him again. But I can imagine him as some sort of Johnny Appleseed going around the nation and planting the idea of the fastest creature on earth, the mongoose, into people's heads. They would learn about fast, all right.

Bull Whip

"155-160," he said.

It was another full moon night. I didn't have time to look up and watch for the crazies because the place was packed, and I was making drinks at ultra-sonic speeds, trying to keep the waitresses satisfied and my bar customers with fresh cocktails in their hands.

Again, but a bit louder over the din this time, I heard, "155-160." Sitting directly in front of me was a man with a weathered, leathery face in a cowboy hat (unusual in Quincy). But it wasn't the abnormality of his hat that gave him away as one of the lunar crazies, but his eyes that burned with the steadiness of black olives. I didn't know how to respond to "155-160," so I said, "Hike."

"That's your weight, Chief. You weigh somewhere between 150 and 160."

First of all, I hate being called "Chief." Secondly, I was really busy, and didn't have time to be bantering with Wyatt Earp. But I did manage to say, "I didn't know the circus was in town."

He tried to digest the sarcasm of this remark when he came back with, "You think you're pretty fast, don't you?"

I was moving at high speeds making drinks, so I thought he was referring to this. So, I returned, "Yeah, I can put a drink order together pretty quickly."

"Not fast enough for a bull whip, boy."

Being called "boy" was even more insulting to me than being called "Chief." But I held my tongue. I could tell that Mr. Looney Tunes was coming to the attention of Larry Waterkotte, the bartender working beside me. I saw him raise his eyebrows and begin to move farther away from me. There would be no support coming from him in this encounter.

"If I wanted to, I could take that whiskey bottle out of your hand faster than a frog's tongue with a bull whip."

How to respond? "Gee, that's great," I said, hoping some positive acknowledgement would end this conversation.

But no. "I could take the straw out of that woman's drink before she got it to her lips with my bull whip."

"Okay, well then, that's pretty..." Larry was drying a glass some distance from me, amused and refusing to intercede.

"You don't believe me, do ya? It so happens I got my bull whip in the car, and I'll give you a little demonstration, boy."

"I believe you, I believe you. No demonstration necessary, heh-heh." But Hopalong Assidy was off his stool, weaving through the crowd to fetch his bull whip.

"Aunt Dolly!" As I've stated previously, my Aunt Dolly was my go-to person in these situations. I explained to her what we were up against. Of course, she was undaunted by these situations. When the man returned to his bar stool with his bull whip in hand, my aunt flew into him like a fighting cock. She had him out the door in minutes with plenty of warnings about what returning might mean.

I looked over at Larry. "Where were you in my time of need, oh faux friend of mine?"

"Marty, you're 160 lbs. and you're fast. You don't need any help against a bull whip."

"Larry...fuck you."

Good Witches

When my brother Larry reached bartending age, he was my favorite person to bartend with. We always kept track of full moons, having adopted our father's belief in its power to call the undead into our bar.

In the glow of Diana, I arrived to work a few hours after Larry, who had opened the restaurant. I could tell from his body language that he was in the presence of the abnormal. Usually, he's all vivacious with his interactions with customers, but I could see him putting distance between himself and two quite good-looking women at the bar. This put up even more red flags for me, since Larry never kept his distance from attractive women.

Immediately, I said to myself, "Shields up, Scotty."

"Larry!" the one woman exclaimed. "This must be your brother. You look alike. So *very* handsome. Introduce us, introduce us," the older woman of the two women said, clapping her hands in child-ish delight.

Reluctantly Larry came over. "Ah, this is Connie. She claims to be a good witch. And this is Bonnie her daughter, also, a good witch."

"Okay then, witches. Good ones at that. We haven't had any of those for a while." I glanced at Larry, who stared back with brows aloft. "Well, I must say you're very beautiful witches. I'm already under your spells." A tinkling laughter bleated forth from them.

The red-headed mother, it seemed, was the spokesperson for them. She wanted to know all about me. When I told her that I was an English major in college and enjoyed writing, she squealed, "Bonnie writes! And draws, too! Bonnie, show him your journal."

Bonnie, a beautiful brunette, had up to this point never said a word. From a large purse, she removed a scrapbook-looking man-uscript, stapled together. The poems and sketches in it were on the level, I would say, being generous, of a ten-year-old. At first, I thought it was a fond childhood production that she always kept with her. But no, this was current material, hot off the press.

It's times like these that even loquacious people like Larry and I were struck speechless. We nodded as we paged through her deep-est thoughts and renderings searching...searching for some encour-aging words to give Bonnie.

"I've never seen anything quite like it," Larry finally blurted out.

"Me either," I said continuing this line of thought. "It's unique, Bonnie." Both of them beamed as if we had told them Bonnie's art reminded us of the childlike qualities of Paul Klee and e.e cum-mings. Thankfully, an order from a waitress broke the spell, and we no longer had to dig any deeper for honest but deceptive phrases.

As we got busy, Connie and Bonnie did not require our company. Two attractive women sitting at the bar brings in men like chum brings in sharks. Soon they were circled by a group who continued to buy them martinis. Their sweet little voices rose among the fray, and occasionally I could hear snatches of what they were saying. I was shocked.

Could it be mother and daughter witches, Bonnie and Connie, hustled together as a team? It appeared the younger Bonnie was the bait and Mom was the flirtatious speaker. I could hear heavy sexual innuendo and salacious speech coming from their quarter. These good witches looked like they were out to ride somebody's broom and maybe even together. I couldn't quite tell what they were looking for with these men — sugar daddies, a night out (all expenses paid), or making a living. But it was unnerving to see this odd combination of childishness, carnal knowledge, and incest.

By midnight, the dynamic duo hadn't accompanied any of the men out the door, and they were thoroughly smashed from all the free martinis they'd downed. Larry and I didn't have time to pay but cursory attention to them for most of the night but, when we saw Bonnie by herself at the bar crying, we were forced to break the boundaries we had given ourselves.

"What's wrong, Bonnie? Why are you crying?"

"Momma hasn't come back. I don't know what to do?"

"Now, now calm down, Bonnie. We'll find your mom. Here's a napkin. You need to clean up your mascara."

I stayed with the panicky Bonnie, while Larry went outside in search of Connie. He circled the Plaza parking lot until he saw her across the street by a Coke machine. She was staggering and cursing. When Larry came up to her, she asked for his help in dialing up a cab. Apparently, she thought the bright machine was a phone booth ("Hello, give me Dr. Pepper, please").

We reunited the broken coven and poured them into a cab. What dark continent of sexuality we witnessed that night was beyond anything we had ever experienced. A mother-daughter, hustling team! Does Freud or Jung have a term for this? An Oedipal-Electra-Tinkerbell complex. Hopefully, the witches of Eastwick wouldn't return soon.

After we closed up the restaurant, we breathed deeply of the night fresh air, trying purge ourselves of cigarette smoke and twisted personalities. As we walked toward home, Larry pointed to the sky.

"Yep," I said in its glow.

Mary Lee Inzerello, Miss Illinois 1966

A Chary Tale

"The moon shines bright. In such a night as this. When the sweet wind did gently kiss the trees and they did make no noise, in such a night." It was an evening as Shakespeare just described as I walked, whistling to work. The moon bulged with its false, secondhand light, and I took no precautions about this being anything but promising. And, indeed, it seemed to be just that as I joined my companion bartender Neil Smelzer.

Sitting at the bar when I came in, glowing with the radiance of an angel, was Mary Lee Inzerello. I recognized Mary Lee for two reasons: 1. I had seen her in my classes at Quincy College — we were both English majors; 2. she had recently become Miss Illinois 1966 and would be participating in the Miss America pageant. Sitting next to her was her roommate, who was another very attractive woman. I had never approached Mary Lee in all my activities at school because you have to be able to say words with your mouth when you communicate with someone. She moved me to muteness.

But good ole' Neil was a hustling fool, and he had both of them laughing as he provided them with drinks. Neil pulled me over to the girls.

"This is my partner in crime, Marty Settle. I'm teaching him some guitar." (Neil had some notoriety on campus with a folk group similar to Peter, Paul, and Mary.)

I nodded and said something that sounded like, "gulltomeeoo."

"Don't I know you?" Mary Lee said in dulcet tones. "You look familiar."

Somehow my first attempt at speech broke a barrier, and I had found voice, although a raspy one. "Yeah, we take a lot of classes together in the English Department."

"That's it! You always sit in a corner and doodle."

"That's me."

"I got Paul Edward next semester. What do you think?"

The name Father Paul Edward, a professor priest in the English Department, struck terror into every English major at Quincy College. I had never got higher than a C in his classes. You couldn't be one second late to his class without being ejected. He would ask questions in class and then go down the rows of class until he either found someone who had the answer or he had run out of students (usually it was the latter). And he gave long essay questions for tests that were answered in vile blue booklets.

"Well at least you'll have him in the fall. You know he always keeps the windows open, no matter the season. In the winter, I remember him giving a lecture as the snow blew in and gathered around his podium. He continued lecturing on *Canterbury Tales*, unphased as enough snow piled up to build a Chaucer snowman."

Mary and her companion Deborah responded with tinkling laughter. *They laughed at what I said!* I thought. I began to get confident and surreptitiously poured some vodka in a water glass to further bolster my confidence. The conversation went swimmingly between the four of us, and Mary Lee and Deborah stayed until closing time. Then they said, "Why don't you come over to our apartment? We want to share with you a recent album that we picked up. Both of you are poetic. We think you'll enjoy it."

As I was stuttering a response at such an opportunity, Neil stepped in, asking for directions and telling them that we would bring the wine. On the way over to the apartment, Neil was singing "Tonight" from *West Side Story*. He looked over at me, "Settle, it's our night tonight. Don't fuck it up." When we arrived, Deborah was going around lighting candles, and Mary Lee was drawing the drapes. We uncorked the wine and chatted for a moment before the pièce de résistance.

The lights were turned off with only flickering candlelight to see by. This promised to be a romantic evening. Neil I'm sure would make his move on Mary Lee, and I hoped I could make mine on Deborah. I could see Mary Lee sliding the record out of its cover and holding it like an archeological relic. With fingertip delicacy, she placed it on the turntable and gently put the stylus in place. "Everyone silent, now," was her final demand.

The beginning of this piece was the sound of the ocean's surf. Waves beat rhythmically on the shore — soothing, susurrus waves. Soon seagull cries were heard in the distance. I waited with a relaxed anticipation in the velvet darkness, refilling my glass of wine. Unhurriedly, a clarinet in soft tones blended in with the sea's meditation. After a full minute, a wistful male voice began:

Do you know my friend the sea? [waves continue]
He watches everything we do
You, rolling over in your beach-bank sleep [piano begins rain-drop notes]
Me, chasing seagulls down the dunes
You, your skirts held high
Wading in the water
The lovers; those who go alone
He sees them all
If we've ourselves to know
We should get to know the sea

At this point, I burst into laughter. I couldn't help myself. This guy, who turns out to be Rod McKuen, is cornier than Illinois in August. Really bad stuff. Suddenly, the lights flicked on. Obviously, I had disturbed the mood of the evening.

"I'm so-so sorry," I said stifling my laughter. "Please continue. I...I...must have had too much to drink. But you got to admit this guy ain't e.e. cummings." The hole got deeper.

"I think we've had enough for the night. We need to get up early tomorrow," Miss Illinois said, gathering glasses. Deborah gave us a stiff "good night" as she corralled Neil and me out the door.

Neil took me home. A seething silence filled the car. When he pulled up to my house, he said gruffly, "Get out." Then he spun off into the darkness. And there I stood alone on the curb, reflecting under a smirking moon. Indeed, the moon had a dark side and a dark sense of humor. Like vodka and wine, romance and literary criticism don't mix well.

Backward Forward

"If you've heard this story before, stop me." That's a sentence that you would never hear in the Settle family. We always said, "Tell it again," like small children never tiring of revisiting the same old stories of family legend. I was shocked to find out as I grew up that many families did not have many stories to tell, and the stories they did have, they felt didn't deserve repeating. My wife's family is like that. I can be with them and not one of them will start with the phrase, "Remember the time when..."

A good question to ask yourself in the present is "What do you think will sustain you as you journey toward your eventual demise?" I have asked this question at many dinner parties. And as we would go around the table, there are a variety of answers — children, grandchildren, religious faith, making art, reading, watching sports, etc. For me, it would be family stories. Cut me off from those, and I would shrivel into a meaningless existence.

The Settle tribal drum beats in my heart. We need campfires to sit around and tell stories while sparks fly into the stars. These tales are our connectors to the universe. Most of them worship a laughing god, who has made it possible for our family to belong to the priesthood of bartenders. We are votaries of the humorous tale, and we pass it on to our patrons, who are able to endure this cold universe with a few moments of warmth around our bar hearth.

CHAPTER 13

MY PARENTS:
THE TELEOLOGY OF DUNES

"Time binding in semantic form permits each generation to advance from the point at which the preceding one left off ..."
—Edith Cobb

If you think I'm going to narrate perfection here, I am not. If you think this will be an idyllic Norman Rockwell chapter, it is not. Much of the grief borne by my mother and father permeated the family, but it was covered over in the typical fashion of a non-psychological generation. They did not like to share their mental suffering. Perhaps this was the result of having lived through the Great Depression, where nobody wanted to hear about your "sniveling" personal problems in the midst of trying to make ends meet.

Would I describe my family as dysfunctional? No. There were second helpings of love available all of the time and no abuse of any kind — physical, verbal, or otherwise. Most of the sting of the pervasive grief in our household was soothed by a poultice of warmth, freedom, and humor. However, our tendency to cover up more deep-seated problems within the family unit caused a lot of unnecessary suffering. But such is the complexity of the love-hate relationships of family and the yearnings and conceptions of each member of the family. My entire life I have looked for that undamaged family. They must exist somewhere. However, as soon as I think I've found the smooth, porcelain family, cracks begin to appear upon closer examination, and it's back to the quest again.

Father: Bearing Acquaintance

If I were to describe my father with one salient feature, it would be talent. As a child of ten, he had his own radio show for WTAD called "The Jackie Settle Show," where he sang the old standards (probably to little old ladies around the city) two or three times a week. He learned popular songs from both his mother, who played the piano, and his father, who occasionally sang old folk ditties like "We Shall Be Free," a song that both Lead Belly and Woody Guthrie sang together. Even before ten, he would sing at the local "snake oil" medicine show behind St. Rose Church. Old man Stock had a small stage where he hawked his miracle medicine — Stock's New Tone Tonic Medicine — while at the same time providing entertainment.

As he grew older, he continued to sing in school musicals, where he did some acting and dancing as well. He was comfortable on the stage, and he nurtured his desire by learning as many skills as he could to improve his chances of becoming an entertainer. From Jake Merritt, an usher at the Orpheum Theater, he learned some tap dancing steps — the single and double timesteps. Dad was a close observer and, when he went to the movies and minstrel shows, he would, using a phrase of his dad's, "steal with his eyes." He was quite adept at imitating what he saw. Gradually, without any formal training, he became a competent tap dancer.

From his sister Dolly, he learned how to walk on his hands. They had competitions to see who could walk the farthest. But walking on one's hands is easier than standing still on one's hands. Furthering his knowledge of handstands, he went to a Bernarr Macfadden book, a predecessor of Charles Atlas and Jack LaLanne. The book recommended he do handstands against a wall and continue to tap away from the wall until you didn't need the wall anymore. Once he had conquered walking and stationary handstands, he built a set of wooden steps, which he placed in the backyard. On these, he practiced going up and down on his hands.

However, the pièce de résistance of his quest to become an entertainer resulted in one of the most creative and unique acts that I've ever heard of. What Jack Settle did was to combine his tap-dancing skill set with his handstand skill set. He would wear white gloves while tap dancing and then suddenly go up on his hands and continue tapping — the gloves had taps sewn on them. Of course, the tap steps were different and less complicated on his hands, but he could keep a rhythm going.

After high school, he became a featured tap dancer in local minstrel shows. And, yes, he was in blackface (not a part of family history that I'm proud of). Dad was a man of great energy and physical strength. It makes me tired to think of how he was able to pursue his dream as a song and dance man while working at his father's boiler maker shop, and then sculling after work for the Southside Boat Club and then going to a nightclub to perform. In more ways than one he was a man of steel — steel job, steel body, and steel will. As he began to get a little traction and reputation in Quincy as an entertainer, he made plans to leave town for brighter horizons in bigger cities.

ENTER: WWII

Jack Settle was a reluctant soldier. No volunteering for him. Uncle Sam had to come and get him. While the war had changed many of his ideas about God, country, and patriotism, it did not change his desire to be on stage. When he came back from Germany with a purple heart and five oak leaf clusters (meaning he had been wounded six times), he was not the worse for wear. He tried out for the Muni Opera in St. Louis and out of the 500 applicants, he and another woman were selected to be part of the chorus.

This should have been the break that would lead him to greater things. But circumstances worked against him. First of all, when he came back from the war like many soldiers hungry for the love of a woman, he immediately married and had a child (that would be me). I was an early Baby Boomer. My father was no longer the free and easy young man in entertainment with no family. How was he going to go to St. Louis and leave his new bride and family behind? His salary was not going to be enough for the move.

The local gangster Leo Monckton (See Chapter 8, "Built on Bluffs"), a very good friend of my father's father, said he would put up the money. It wouldn't even be a loan but pure patronage. My father thought that my mother and I could live with Grandpa, which she had done before the war ended. Then came the betrayal that would change Jack Settle's life forever. Porter Settle, his dad, told Leo not to give his son the money. In his mind, Jack had no business going to St. Louis with all the beautiful show biz women and the temptations of the city. He belonged in Quincy beside his wife and child.

And that was that. It would be his last opportunity to climb this ladder of success, and he talked about it with bitterness to the end of his life at 96. It took something out of my father to be betrayed by his own father, and I could always feel somehow his disappointment with life. I think it's one of the reasons he never challenged anything that I wanted to do with my life.

Another aspect of my father that I found rather remarkable was that he was tender. Yes, a man who came from a family who prided themselves in having tough, rugged men, and a man who killed people as a soldier in WWII was unabashedly tender. He was physical in his expression of his love, always touching and hugging us. I remember one time surprising him at the bar after I had been gone for a few weeks. He came around the bar and gave me one of his bear hugs and kissed me on the lips. One of our customers, a psychologist, was almost breathless in his comments of this masculine display of affection. It had opened up a new territory for him in viewing how manliness and tenderness could co-exist.

I'm not sure what the psychologist at the bar would make of the physicality of the following poem. I'm sure a Freudian would have a field day in interpreting this poem, but I stand by the poem's innocence and naturalness of a son learning some deep lessons from the father's body.

Showering with my Father

I loved being naked with your naked body,
rivulets running in joy spray,
god and god's son sculpted in fountain myth.
renaissance proportions.
your body landscape instructions –

here's how to stand, pillar on plinth,
here's how to wash your testicle bag,
not shyly,
both hands cupped in froth suds,
buttocks flexed forward in cornucopia.

male mysteries revealed in muscle mass.
start with the curvature of vertebrae channel
and build the surrounding terrain.
a god arranges his own geology.
the expanse of back, for example,

crescendos at the shoulders
with trapezii and triceps stacked like boulders.
compact heft, a man's language.
your pectorals rock shelves for lookout.
forearms and fists posture justice.

my body streamed smooth,
innocent of narrative.
but yours,
yours had hair, had history.
forested regions full of stories,

scars clearcut from war shrapnel,
razor domestications,
meadows my mother had lain her head.
the delta bramble of penis harbor
and hull that had been to sea.

faucets twisted abrupt.
our final asperges
jumping up and down to shake off like dogs,
hands covering flapping privates
like Adam leaving paradise.

sitting with draped thighs
you'd towel me dry,
rubbing into my breast a birthright
of carnivore tenderness,
anodyne to ready me for the wounds of a man.

As a businessman, my father was entrepreneurial, shrewd, and hard working. When he returned to society after WWII and when he realized that his dreams of being an entertainer had been crushed by his father, he assessed his talents and decided that they could be best used in the bar business. He was a risk taker, and a greater believer in his ability "to bear acquaintance." This latter phrase was something that he learned from his father Port Settle, who meant by it that you had to be outstanding at something so that people wanted to meet you.

I would say Jack Settle not only had faith in his ability to attract people to his places of business, but he was a bit cocky about it. Once he told me that if he had a board and a couple of chairs, he could make a living. And I have to say that this wasn't hyperbole. He chose well his new profession because with his singing, dancing, joke telling, and doggerel recitation abilities, people flocked to see him and be around him. Often, he would hire a piano man for the weekend, so that he could sing and dance for his customers. If you wanted to be in on the action in Quincy, Illinois, you went to the Settle Inn where you would get the most bang for your buck.

But having a good personality and being entertaining is not good enough if you're going to be in the bar business. One of the great dangers in this business is that in a sense you're always partying with customers who are out for a good time. They want you to have a good time with them, and that means drink with them. Many a solid bar business has failed because the owner became an alcoholic. Dad hardly ever drank at home and NEVER drank while he worked at his bars.

Further, he was always there. Another sure way to lose money in the bar business is to, once you have established your business, have others take your place while you take more days off. When the boss is away, the mice will play. The result is poorer service, sultry attitudes from employees, drinking on the job, and stealing. I have bartended at many places besides our family bar, and I have watched this kind of erosion set in with the owner's absence.

A solid work ethic and disciplined business practices were a package that made my dad a success in the bar trade. However, they were conflicting qualities for a wife and a family. Because he had a night business with hours that went from 5 p.m. to 2 a.m., he was absent from many evening family events. He was absent from many of the weekend events that other families had because he had to work on the weekends, which were our most profitable workdays. Even at that, he never replaced weekends by taking two alternate days off during the week. He allowed himself one day off a week, and often this was spoiled by some work-related incident or an employee calling in sick. And as far as vacations were concerned, there were none. We never went anywhere.

His absence was a burden for everyone in the family. I know it was a burden to me because I bonded with my father in the deepest sort of way, and I could never get enough of him. This is not to say that when he was with us, he was psychologically absent. He was an engaged and enthusiastic father *when* he was present. He played sports with us and wrestled with us and the neighborhood kids on the lawn, taught us magic tricks and card games, told us jokes and sang us songs, and he was an expert in telling bedtime stories the one night a week that he put us to bed. He was able to fill my head with so many dreams and fantasies about living in the wild like the old pioneers and Native Americans and going to Alaska and starting a new frontier. Because he was such an entertaining father when he was around, it made his absence that much more painful. It might have been better if he were like many of the fathers I knew who, although they had more time around the house, they had little inclination to spend it with their children.

I modeled myself upon my father, and as I was growing up, I wanted to learn everything that he knew. Thankfully, he was a willing and patient teacher. I learned tap dancing from him. Unlike other students of tap, I didn't have the luxury of wooden floors or store-bought tap shoes. I got my lessons on our smooth, concrete, basement floor, which required a certain amount of balance just to stand up with metal taps on. And my tap shoes were not Capezios, but an old pair of shoes refurbished by the shoemaker. "Stomp-hop-one/two-one/two-one," he would say to me as he was teaching me the timestep, unlike a formal dance teacher, who would say, "stomp-hop-a flap-a flap-step." Yet despite all the "crudities" of my instruction, I could out-dance people who had taken years of tap by the time I was in the sixth grade. It was a skill that helped me "bear acquaintance" for my entire life.

Handstands and hand-walking are two skills that I learned to emulate my dad. I remember spending an entire winter at his behest throwing myself up against a wall in my bedroom into the handstand position. With the wall for a support, my first goal was to just be able to hold myself there. Once I could do that, I was to tap myself away from the wall and see how long I could keep myself from either falling back into the wall or returning to the starting position.

After a week with little success, I complained that I couldn't do it. "Patience, Marty, patience. If it were easy to do, then *anyone* could do it. You want to be *anyone* or do you want to be *someone*. You choose." And I did. Gradually, I could hold a handstand for five seconds, then ten seconds, then 20 seconds. Finally, I didn't need the wall at all. I was exhilarated — exhilarated by the accomplishment and just as exhilarated to know what extra effort in *any* area might bring.

But I save the worst about my father until last. He did have some fatal flaws. One, he liked women too much; two, he could be duplicitous with a poker face and not lose a moment's sleep over it. In college, I had been told by my youngest brother Kirby that Dad had been seeing a woman for years. Of course, I didn't believe him. Not the man who I modelled my life on; not the man who I was too strongly attached to for my own good. "If you want to see her," my brother said, "just wait until Dad closes the restaurant. She'll pull up outside and wait for him to come out. Then they'll go out dancing and who knows what else."

I remember shivering in the cold on a February night, waiting for a car to pull up in our empty parking lot. And sure enough, she came. And I knew her! Without thinking, I jumped into the car and confronted her. She was afraid as I told her what I'd do to her if I found her with Jack Settle again. Then, I slammed her car door, walked home, and waited in the kitchen for my father's return. He came soon, and we went for a walk, where he professed to love Mom and that he would no longer participate in this dalliance. It molli-fied me, and although the pedestal I had him on was shaken, he was not toppled off.

Although I was the oldest brother, I was so smitten by my father that I had not seen the obvious. I could always feel his woundedness and frustration at not being who he wanted to be. This more than anything else made my blindness easier. Both of my younger broth-ers had known for years about Dad's unfaithfulness. They could always better assess who he was and his furtive ways. Even with such an Oedipal moment as the incident above, you would think that I would have had glowing insight into my father like Biff in *The Death of a Salesman*. But it would take me decades before I could honestly see my father's dark side. He was a dream weaver, and I had been caught in his net. He was the greatest love of my life; he was my greatest disappointment.

Mother: Mangia, Mangia, Mangia

My father was myth; my mother was milk. Not only milk in the literal sense of breastfeeding; she was the nourishment that was as ubiquitous as air. She was always present as a background to me and my brothers growing up. She was the magical food that ap-peared at our table, the folded clothes in our drawers, the pillowed breasts of our comfort, the soother, the procurer, the defender, the supporter, the supplier, and, and, and, and.

My mother met my father in the dramatic theater of WWII. It was the familiar movie scenario of soldier meets the local girl at the U.S.O dance. My father was stationed at Fort Indiantown Gap, which was only 15 miles north of Hershey, Pennsylvania, where my mother lived. Because this was the last stop for soldiers before they embarked to the European front, the fort tried to provide some last entertainment for the "boys." They sponsored free buses for the women who lived in the area to come to the fort and dance with the soldiers. My mother and some of her friends fatefully took one of those buses.

Yes, they did swirl and have a good time, but as far as each of them were concerned, this would be the last time they would meet.

But as destiny would have it, they met the next morning at the local Catholic Church on Mother's Day. After church, my mother invited Staff Sergeant Jack Settle over for dinner. It was on this day he became enamored with the Other.

My mother's name was Palmina Modesto (I have never met another Palmina), and she was Italian through and through. She lived in an Italian neighborhood in Hershey, where hardly anyone spoke English, and where she didn't learn English herself until she went to school. My grandparents, Antonio Modesto and Maria de Angela, had emigrated from Italy to the U.S. during the 1920s with Antonio finding work in the quarries in Pennsylvania. They had five children, with my mother being the youngest.

That Sunday, when "Pal," which is the name my mother went by, introduced my father around the neighborhood, Jack Settle was in a culture more foreign than any he had ever experienced. The older Italian women loved him because he could eat, and he loved them because he was a champion eater. My father thought that "mangia, mangia, mangia" was a long Italian word that meant to eat, rather than the word *eat* repeated three times.

And eat he did. Every house he went into had a pot of some kind of pasta boiling, and for the first time in his life, he had spaghetti, ravioli, and gnocchi. He took to this new food like a barnacle takes to the hull of a ship. He had never been so stuffed in his life. During his stay at Indiantown Gap, he gained ten pounds and saw my mother quite often. When he left, they were unofficially engaged to be married.

Much that is to be understood about Palmina Modesto must be predicated on her Italian background. After the war, my father married my mother and brought her to Quincy, Illinois. The people who she encountered in Quincy were very different from the gregarious community that she had lived in all her life. They were mostly German in origin and much more reserved and disciplined than her Italian counterparts. Even my father's family did not mesh well with the kinds of people she knew in Hershey. Of course, in the beginning, she was homesick, but her homesickness did not subside over the years. She always felt out of place in Quincy, and she always longed for her old home.

I would always tell people that I was the product of this unholy alliance between the Italian culture and the German culture, which meant I loved spaghetti, but I had to cut it up into organized, bite-size pieces. I think my mother would have had a much better life if my father would have moved to Hershey to make a living. Quincy isolated my mom with few resources to link her to her previous existence. There were no Italian communities in Quincy, and no one to speak Italian with. We didn't take vacations, so my mother only returned to Hershey once upon her father's death. Occasionally, we did get a visit from Italian friends and relatives, but this was rare and awfully spread out. Thank heavens for the telephone where she could keep some semblance of her past by talking with her favorite sister, Aunt Pat.

If we add all this culture shock to the fact that my father was in a business that not only took up sixty plus hours a week but took up evening and weekend hours, we can see she was alone a lot. While other families were having family dinners, my father was at work. When other families were having weekend outings and holiday celebrations, my father was napping so that he would be awake for his long night shift. The only society my mother got was from her children, and, unfortunately for her, she had all this masculinity around her with three boys. Not having a daughter I think was another unlucky break for her.

It's no surprise then as I look back that she suffered from depression. The depression was not clinical, but it was pervasive. In the present age, she would have sought out psychological treatment and medication. But the people in her generation were not very psychological, and their very best psychological advice was "suck it up and get a good night's sleep."

I was probably the hardest on her because of my adamantine attachment to my father. My mother and I fought a lot when I was growing up because I saw my mother stifling my father's good nature, his sense of fun, and his time spent with me. I always defended my father no matter what he did. I didn't realize how far his neglect went. In later years (as I mentioned above) when I discovered how much time he had spent with a mistress and how isolated my mother must have felt, I was struck by how complicitous I had been in Palmina's suffering. My blindness and coldness during these times gnaws at me to this day. In this difficult environment, she drowned her sorrows by eating and becoming overweight.

Yet she loved my brothers and me fiercely. She was a mama lioness and born to be a mother and housewife. In the present age where fewer women aspire to such things, it is easy to denigrate a pure aspiration of this sort. Yet for my mother it was more than a job to raise kids and take care of her husband, it was a vocation as sacramental as priesthood, and she performed her role with confidence and without doubt. As smart as she was (and she was smart), it never occurred to her that she could make her life more complete by having an outside job. She implicitly trusted my father would do his job in bringing in money and that she would do hers in child-rearing and keeping house.

Halcyon Days of Eating

As a cook, Katie bar the door! People always assumed that most of our meals came from our restaurant. "Au contraire," we would say. "Why eat *good* food, when you have your own personal chef to make *great* food." There was nothing that my mother fixed in the way of ordinary dishes that she didn't improve on.

Other people made potato salad, for instance, that was too creamy, or dripping with mayonnaise, or drowned in relish; Mom's potato salad had a firm consistency that you could almost spread, was lightly salted, had a tincture of mustard, a patina of mayonnaise (I hope you notice that my prose is getting poetic here) and geometry. Geometry? Yes, whatever Palmina Modesto made was always cut with care; thus, her potatoes in potato salad were almost the same size, which made for platonic beauty.

The same could be said of her fried chicken, her egg sandwiches, and her vinegar and oil salads (my brothers and I despair to reproduce something so simple as Mother's vinegar oil salad, which she always slapped together with no measurements with results good enough to drink). Then, too, she could make gravy out of any meat. And these weren't ordinary gravies, but gravies that complemented the worst cuts of meat, and she made mashed potatoes, boiled pota-toes, and breads come alive. Sometimes I'd pour her gravy over my whole dish, including the vegetables.

Pie, pie, me-o-my! I would put up her two-inch thick pies and crust against any entry in the state fair. They were never cloyingly syrupy; you could taste the quality of the fruit, along with the flak-iness of the crust. Her lemon méringue pies stood up six inches in the refrigerator. To come home from school and find one of these pies on the counter, still warm, was an assault to the salivary glands. Then, to eat a hunk of this pie (my mother did not believe in slivers) with a cold glass of milk was to enter a black hole of pleasure. (At the moment I salivate on my computer in remembrance.)

As you would expect being Italian, my mother had her special sauces and pasta dishes. Almost every Sunday, we had some form of pasta after church. You might think this got tiring. No one ever complained; only anticipated. We liked to say that some of these spaghetti dishes "set on you" like concrete. It took an hour or two after the Sunday feast to be able to go out and play. Often my broth-er Larry and I made our way to the couch to watch football with our father, who, to relieve the discomfort of being stuffed, had released his belt buckle, pants button, and zipper.

If you were invited to our house for dinner, you might think my mother was cooking for ten people instead of five. *Heaped* would be the key word. Every service bowl or plate was *heaped* with food — chicken piled high, mashed potatoes peaking like Mt. Fuji, stews in pots usually reserved for the military cafeterias, and pasta in dishes that took up two place settings. It was always a shock when we ate at our neighbors' houses to see the small portions on their table. *Maybe they can't afford more food*, we thought.

Were Mama Mia Modesto's little bambinos up to the task of eat-ing her offerings of love? Oh god, yes. First of all, we were not like many children I see today, who would rather be with their iPhones than savor a good dinner. We were not finicky, and we ate like field hands. It was not a matter of survival of the fittest at our table (there was plenty for all); it was a matter of staying out of each other's way, lest you get a fork in the hand reaching for a favorite piece of chicken. One would think that the way we ate we looked like little sausages tied tight at both ends, but we were all skinny as saplings — in fact, it looked like we came from a nation suffering from famine. Metabolism can work for you or against you. We had the metabolisms of birds, burning off every ounce of fat we ate, while we had friends who ate half as much and were overweight. Unfair? Indeed.

I always tell people my halcyon days of eating are over. I will never eat food like that again. I have been spoiled with the best early in life, and I must resign myself to food that is "okay" for the rest of my life. I'm so sorry that I did not have a sister who could have taken up the torch of family recipes. Although my brothers and I were very much involved in eating, none of us took an interest in cooking. Today, we can only remember and say, "I would pay $500 today for one of mom's pies."

Tomorrow and Tomorrow Creeps in This Penny Pace

We had parents who had lived through The Great Depression. They knew poverty and they didn't waste. Recycling and repurposing are concepts that I was introduced to by my mother before they became societal words. Our mother was a master of home economy.

During the Eisenhour presidencies, there were no supermarkets in our small city but only corner grocery stores. Within a block of our house, I can remember three — Kalmers, Bowls, and Krienburgs. My mother would often send me to one of those stores to pick up some item that she needed, and she would always give me the exact change. She kept track of her pennies, and she knew the cost of every item to the penny. Occasionally, she'd be off a penny because of a raise in price, and I had to go back and forth again with the extra penny. (Notice the grocery store did not forgive being a penny short.)

If you were the butcher, you would quake as Mama Modesto came bearing down on you. She had no problem telling you your prices were too high, the cuts looked too gristly, or your scale was off. She got the most beef for her buck. If there were sales, she'd stock up. She'd outwait high prices for fruits and vegetables until they were in season and cheaper.

The gastronomical magic that she could perform with first meals, I covered above. What I didn't cover was the ways that she could take leftovers and put them into new forms that would amaze an organic chemist. These recycled meals were just as compelling to eat. Have extra spaghetti sauce? Then make pasta fagioli (we never pronounced the "i" on the end). It was a simple Italian peasant soup made with spaghetti sauce, ditalini, red beans, seasonings, and water. What wasn't simple was its taste, which you could soak into your side of crusty bread. Have extra chicken? Well, there was chicken salad, chicken soups and stocks for other soups, and the giblets were great for gravy. Leftover ham and hock made for soups that were hardy and filling — lentil soup, navy bean soup (with corn bread, of course), and pea soup. I often preferred the soups and stews to the main courses made on the first go-around. If we had lived during the Great Depression, those searching in our garbage would find sparse leavings for something to eat.

In the family album, there is a series of pictures that I think are very revealing. My first pictures were of a child with brand new clothes, and my first two years took up about half the album. Next came brother Larry. He was dressed in all my hand-me-downs, which still looked nice but were a bit frayed. His pictures were still fairly formal and took up about a third of the album. The last sixth of the book started off with my brother Kirby playing in the mud with the same clothes that had now become relegated to play clothes. You could easily see in this documentation of our early lives that my mother was getting busier and busier and that there was less and less time to be devoted to photography and less money to buy new clothes. You could also see that we didn't throw anything away. My clothes lived three lives and they still had one left even after they were no longer worn because they went into the rag bag, which provided cloth for picking up bad spills, cleaning windows, and wiping excess paint from brushes.

Mother was queen of the yard sale, the thrift store, and the consignment shop. Our clothes were often secondhand. We seldom got anything new. Yet we were always dressed nicely because of her shrewdness in finding the bargain. It was a treat to accompany her, which we often did, to these venues that sold secondhand goods. It was like watching a dog trained to point out prey for the hunter.

She could assess in seconds if a garage sale was worth her time. And she could negotiate price with the best of them. She knew all the tricks of haggling, walking away, returning later in the day when the sellers were tired of frying out in the sun and having sold little, or of bundling two or three items at a lower price.

When we went into secondhand stores, she was immediately recognized by the salespeople. In fact, she had a network of thrift shop workers who worked for her so to speak. I can still hear them say confidentially into her ear, "Pal, we set back some nice school clothes in the pricing room. Why don't you look at them before we put them out?" Or she'd receive a call from a place like Caldwell's, telling her to get down there fast because they had just got in some dresses in her size.

Besides clothes, she had every kitchen utensil and gadget known to humankind — cherry pitters, garlic presses, noodle machines, basters, blender bowls, thermometers, grapefruit sectioners, melon ballers, whisks, graters, timers, tongs, colanders, and much more. All purchased with pocket change.

If there was a way to cut corners or to stretch a budget, Mama Settle knew it. I remember us sitting down and having a pasting party to make bulging books of green stamps so that we could claim some item we needed from the Green Stamp Catalog. Many stores at the time had lagnappes or giveaways that rewarded you for your purchases. We obtained a whole new set of dishes this way, and perhaps, most valuable of all, an unabridged dictionary. Each week they handed out a new letter for your dictionary if you shopped at their store, until you had the letter Z. Throughout high school and college, I referred to that dictionary like a preacher refers to the Bible.

We could never really waste money on air conditioning, since we had no air conditioner. However, we could waste money on heat. My mother had a rule for this situation, which she enforced unswervingly — never turn on the heat before Nov.1st. Sometimes that worked out okay, but sometimes we were breaking through ice on our cereal because of Mom's arbitrary date had not yet come, even though the frost was on the pumpkin. These mornings we did everything with alacrity to get to school, which had the *quaint* luxury of having heat. This lack of heat was never a problem for Pal, because, as we would always say, "She's a hot-blooded Italian." On cold mornings after having fixed our breakfast for school, you could find her outside sitting on a lawn chair in a house dress, sipping her morning coffee, her breath curling around her. She liked nothing better, and it made us cold just looking at her.

Finally, Mom supplied us with a healthy collection of books by going to garage sales and thrift shops. For her, reading was a means to sustain herself through her loneliness, especially her romance novels with book covers that always displayed a woman with a plunging neckline which exposed her bosoms almost to the nipple; the woman was ready to be ravaged by a ruggedly handsome man standing behind her (a pirate, a soldier, a cowboy, a nobleman, etc.). For us, Mother purchased a spread of eclectic reading: classics, best sellers, *The Book of Knowledge*, medical books, comic books, history books (H.G. Wells's *The Outline of History* was one of my favorites). She never made any effort to get us to read, except by example, yet she was the source for all three of us loving to read.

Backward Forward

The question in life as children become adults and then parents themselves is what to pass on from parents and what to forgive and let die. This is a sacred choice we all have — to leave behind and not repeat what was bad about our parents and to advance what was good and nourishing about them. If all of us do this well (and it is very difficult to do because much of this is unconscious) we leaven the Great Unconscious of society. The goal of these choices is to, as the generations advance, have a lot of more goodness passed on than evil.

What I would choose to pass on from my father is, first of all, his tenderness as a male. Because of him, I was not caught up in the silent, tough guy stereotype of what a man should be and could express my feelings without looking upon myself as a "sissy." This sense of masculinity has served me well in my marriage. Also, from my father, I learned that you can up your game in any area with a little extra persistence. Why settle for being mediocre in anything. Go to the next level by holding out a little longer in your pursuits. This is different from being *the best* in your ambitions; it is about attainable things that do not make one obsessive. Thus, I learned handstands, tap dancing, and memorizing doggerel — all of which contributed to my eventual achievements as an English teacher. I wasn't *the best* teacher, but I was good enough "to bear acquaintance."

From my mother, I found the sustenance of unquestioning love. Through the really, really tough patches of life (and I've had some), it was not my father's persistence that saved me from suicide but the inner layers of nourishment that my mother had laid down long ago. My disturbed brain in crises was like a geode that looks ugly on the outside but if you crack it open you see a beautiful crystalline world. Those crystals of ubiquitous care, attention, and nourishment are what my mother left to me. I have tried to pass on this kind of all-accepting condition to my daughter. No matter what the situation, I'm there in her corner ready to serve like a bucket of water in a fire. Devotion.

From both Mom and Dad, I learned to love economy and the small pleasures in life —the smell of spaghetti sauce on the stove, sheets dried on the clothesline, harvesting apples from our backyard tree, burning the trash on crisp autumn nights, going to double-feature movies with a cartoon at the drive-in, sleeping in the same bed with a brother, etc. I did not envy anyone. There was little drudgery in our lower-middle-class existence.

Somehow the drama of our lives was as satisfying as traveling the world. I'm sure we would have loved to go to Disneyland, but when I became an adult and went to Disneyland, I saw more children spanked there than I ever had anywhere else in life (the disgruntled children just weren't reacting to this privilege as their parents wanted). All I know is that going to garage sales as a child was always an adventure and making our 25-cent purchases was as good as buying a new pair of Air Jordans today.

As last words, I would like to say that even though my mother and father did not have a marriage made in heaven, I had been introduced to the broad swath of history that brings improbable people together and shuffles genetics like the four decks of cards for a blackjack table in Vegas. If it weren't for Hitler, I wouldn't be here. The likelihood of Jack Settle from Quincy, Illinois, and Palmina Modesto of Hershey, Pennsylvania, meeting would have been impossible had it not been for WWII. America is a large deck of cultures, languages, and traditions that can be dealt out randomly like hands of poker to disparate people. Seldom do we stay within the cultural origin of our family like a poker flush. It all has to do with boy meets girl and being smitten by the "Other."

My grandfather Settle, a hard-shell Baptist, met a Catholic girl Olive Vandenboom in another city and was determined to marry her. So, he became Catholic. My father's traditions were miles apart from my mother's. In the same tradition, I, an Italian-German Catholic, have married a Jewish woman, and we have raised our daughter in the Jewish tradition. In similar fashion, it would be nice if my daughter marries the Other. I can see a future where our family genetics will be so mixed that we will be unable to hate any ethnicity. This, I believe, is the American dream and the global dream of unity. The following poem tries to capture on a personal level my sense of the movement of history and the confluence of peoples.

The Teleology of Dunes

dunes can walk seventy feet in one year
so much for permanency
we like to think of our seventy or so years
as purposeful leaps
rather than accident and accumulation
yet our skin is sand sloughed in the wind
wrinkled as the tide recedes
our swash food for ghost crabs

maybe a child will find a shell of us
place it in a garden to be rototilled into a tomato
reincarnation churning, churning, churning
maybe our hearts are cockle shells
maybe our yearnings are pulled by the moon
maybe our last breaths provide moisture for clouds

my mother is dead yet she still moves
she crossed the Atlantic to speak English
her skin olives from the Mediterranean
at the USO dance she made my father swirl
her kiss was the last shore he knew
before he crossed the ocean to kill Nazis
the Nazis stacked human hair into dunes.
the dunes were spun into rugs

I am Catholic, my spouse Jewish.
what confluences for such currents?
the forces that shape shells shape hearts
our daughter has made her home in our spiraling genes
our faces are moons pulling her tongue toward language
she has begun to walk on her own
with each step she slightly shifts
the boundaries of Jerusalem

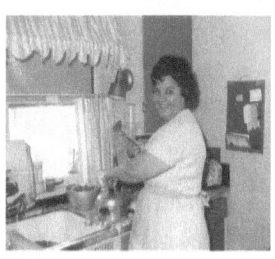

lmina Katherine Modesto/Settle

Edmond (Jack) Joseph Settle

Jack Settle   *Pal Settle*

CHAPTER 14

BROTHERS, CAN YOU PARADIGM?

My brothers and I are all in our seventies, and time and distance has not separated us. We gather at least once a year without spouses and spend a week together. A week! To some that might sound horrifying. Not all people have siblings as close as we are. Yet the bare truth is that we never run out of conversation or are bored by the retelling of the family lore for seven days straight. Laughter fills the air like pollen in the spring. No one, even our spouses and friends, know us like we know each other. We come together as separate entities and then become this composite symbiosis.

I've always seen this triumvirate of MLK (Marty, Larry, and Kirby) working like the trio on Star Trek — Captain Kirk, Mr. Spock, and Dr. McCoy. I label Larry, the middle brother, as Dr. McCoy because he was the most emotional of the three brothers. He took things the hardest while at the same time he was the happiest. Kirby, the youngest, was the rational Mr. Spock of our family *Starship Enterprise.* He could put aside emotions and approach a problem through study and research. As for me, I was Captain Kirk, the oldest brother, who in some ways was a blend between the propensities of the other two. While we were growing up by dint of my greater size and experience, I had a leadership role, but once my reign was over, I still was the brother who bridged a gap between the poles of my bros.

One reason, I believe, for the intensity of our relationship had to do with our isolation. We were in some ways like the Bronte sisters. Although we weren't nearly as isolated as Charlotte, Emily, and

Anne, we did have a form of isolation that brought us together. As I said previously, our father was absent a lot, and our mother was caught in the housework of a time that did not have the labor-saving devices of washer and dryer, microwave, pre-processed dinners, and more. This left us with a dependency on one another to amuse or entertain. When youngest brother Kirby created his own Catholic altar in our basement and his own priestly vestments, he did not have to go looking for congregants. Larry and I were there as dutiful worshippers, receiving communion and receiving his blessings.

Another very forceful reason for our closeness over the years was our Italian mother's deep desire that we always support one another. She made this known on a regular basis how important it was to her that we never abandon one another. When Mom made a toast at our Sunday dinners, it was always the same, "Familia!" This was not the case with my father, who while he claimed great love for his siblings, never did anything socially with them, even though they lived in the same town. One of Dad's brothers lived less than a block away from another brother, but they never visited each other. In addition, these people never visited us, we never had picnics with them, never vacationed with them. Once a year, they gathered for Christmas and that was it. Of course, this made our family more nuclear and isolated; brought my brothers and I closer with resolutions never to be like my father's brothers and sister.

Nature, Nurture, and Birth Order
Marty Larry Kirby

Marty the Elder: the once but not future king

"Power tends to corrupt, and absolute power corrupts absolutely." Thankfully, only the first half of this quote by Lord Acton describes my position as the eldest sibling. My reign as eldest brother was, indeed, tainted by corruption. It was difficult being bigger, stronger, and more experienced for me not to take advantage of the power that came with my birth order. I could, for instance, easily take any item I wanted away from my brothers if my parents weren't around. Their screams and hollers at this injustice never touched my soul. I was the alpha that had a sadistic streak that could wrestle a brother to the floor and then tickle him until he could barely breathe. Or I could put my brother Larry into a closet and hold the door shut, knowing that he was claustrophobic. Truly, I had my moments as Ivan the Terrible.

My brothers were not entirely without their means of self-defense. Brother Kirby, the youngest, could cry at the drop of a hat. He proved to me on occasion that it did not require my doing anything for him to just up and loudly cry with Mom coming in and immediately blaming me for aggravating my "poor, helpless brother." She never believed me when I told her Kirby was the instigator (as well she shouldn't have, since I was responsible for 95% of the tumult and the shouting among the brothers). When Mom left after chastising me, Kirby would give me a malevolent smile, having delivered his warning like a rattle snake.

I bullied my brother Larry more than I did Kirby because we were closer in age and many of our interests overlapped. I was constantly punching him in the shoulder, which left a bruise mark like a permanent tattoo. Finally, one day when he had had enough of me, he vowed in tears that he would get me back. I sloughed off his warning like brushing away a fly. But later that day, I went out into the yard to take a nap on a lawn chair. I put on suntan lotion because I wanted to tan and look good for my fellow eighth-grade girls.

A serpent in the grass, Larry crawled to where I dozed, took the bottle of suntan lotion and jammed it up my nose. Then he squeezed with both hands the poison into my nose. Suddenly, I was a whirling dervish, hacking and coughing and spitting out suntan lotion that had made its way to my mouth. As I was in my death throes, I glanced up at the perpetrator smiling ever so satisfactorily. He had gotten his revenge. He had also sent me a warning that while he couldn't beat me up, I had to sleep *sometime,* and this was when I was vulnerable to some awful counterattack. I took note of this escalation of our warfare.

More than physically, I loved to mess with my brothers' credulity. We all slept in the same bedroom, and we all had a definite bedtime. We never went straight to sleep. And as long as we were in bed with the lights out, our mother didn't care if we chattered until midnight. Mostly, the conversation sent us gently in the arms of sleep, but occasionally in the darkness an evil djinni took possession of me.

For example, my brothers slept in a double bed that abutted a double set of windows. In the quiet, just before sleep, I commented:

"Are you going to sleep with the curtains open?"

"What do you mean?" Larry said. "We always sleep with the curtains open."

"I just meant that there's a full moon tonight. And I thought... Oh, never mind. Do as you choose."

The bait had been presented.

"Yeah...so... who cares if there's a full moon?"

"Well, it's shining on your bed and on your faces."

"Hahahaha. What's that supposed to mean?" My skeptical middle brother said.

"Well," I said, "it *could* make you go crazy."

"You're making this up to scare us," Kirby commented with a loud but less than confident courage.

They were now circling the hook.

"I'm not. You know the word *lunar,* don't you? It refers to the moon, just like *luna-tic* does. You sleep under that full moon and you could become a *luna-tic.*"

I can see their temptation to bite. "He's lying," bro Larry says. "Yeah," little bro adds, but weakly.

"Okay, suit yourself, but I'm glad I'm sleeping over here."

The bobber shakes at their nibble.

In the silence of about a minute, they lay with thoughts of the possibility of going mad. Suddenly, both of them bounce to their feet, staggering on their mattress, while they hurriedly shut the curtains.

The swallow — hook, line, and sinker.

Their gullibility could be also financially useful to me. Both of them had received metal banks one Christmas with combination locks. It didn't take me long to realize that you didn't need to be Alan Turing to break the code. When they put their small savings into these banks, they believed their money was secure from all intruders. Soon they realized an awful fact about savings — despite what our parents told them about the virtues of saving money, the money in their safes dwindled rather than accumulated.

The source of this anomaly, the thief in the night: Marty, the elder. Money was always hard to come by in our family. When it did come, it came in change — pennies, nickels, dimes, quarters, and the granddaddy of them all, the fifty-cent piece. Once in a great while, we got a dollar bill at Christmas from our Aunt Pat in Pennsylvania. When I became old enough to start running around with friends after supper, we would go to places that had pinball machines and sodas. My buds all had much more spending money than I had. It didn't take me long to run out of dough and be relegated to watching them play pinball and drink sodas while I abstained. This led to my raiding Larry and Kirby's savings to support my new nighttime lifestyle. I never cleaned them out (I was too smart for that), but I did take enough to buy a soda or play some pinball.

Yes, a true rat — not a lab rat, a wood rat, but a gutter rat. Later in life, I have told my brothers to think about the value of my thievery to their future economic wisdom. "I taught you guys early in life — trust no one. Hasn't that served you well?" From their response, apparently not.

I would not like to leave my reign as King Martin with the impression that I was Attila the Hun. I loved my brothers and they loved me. I remember getting into a fight after school when I was in seventh grade. As I was in the midst of the tussle, suddenly my opponent was being bashed by school bags and lunch buckets. As the victim wriggled his way out of three dervishes, he ran like a dog with his tail between his legs. We had a great laugh because we all realized you fight one of us, you fight all three.

We played a lot together during our childhoods — board games, cards, baseball, hopscotch, tag, hide-n-seek, etc. And while I got out of line at times, mostly it was harmonious. Finally, if you look at our family albums, I always had my arm around my brothers in a protective way. It wouldn't be long before my parents trusted me as a babysitter, and I did the job responsibly. So, even though I could transmogrify as a rat, I mostly was a friendly canine with my brothers.

Tween Larry: Court Jester

At this point, I would like to say that while birth order matters in some areas — for instance, the raw physical and mental domination of the first born over later siblings — I think it loses its steam when we enter into the mysteries of personality. While I happen to fit rather well into the profile of the older brother, my brother Larry did not fit into the middle brother profile.

First of all, he did not have the reputed "rebellious streak" of the middle born. He was gentle in his play, getting along with both Kirby and me. And he was obedient, receiving fewer reprimands than Kirby and I. Another middle-child profile feature that he did not fit into was having a large, social circle. Larry was shy and preferred the intimacy of a few select friends. It was not hard to imagine him living at home forever. I remember when he first learned that he would have to be a busboy at our restaurant. It was as if my father had told him, "Tonight you will be executed." He spent the entire day in morose contemplation of his life being torn asunder.

Middle bro exuded a certain contentment within the family confines. You could apprise his undisturbed internality when he ate. As the rest of us were eating with gusto at the supper table and talking with our mouths full, you could hear Larry humming as he did his work of packing away food. The way he ate was also an indication of his Zen involvement with the act of eating. He was a civil engineer of his plate, building roads, dams, and bridges. There were roadways constructed between the creamed corn and asparagus. The basin in the mashed potatoes was a retaining dam for the gravy. Occasionally, he would open the dam to let gravy spill on the population of meat below.

His food had to be just so. When he ate a bowl of ice cream, he ate it symmetrically. He held the bowl with his fingertips and then rotated it around as if it were a Lazy Susan. In this way, he could chisel bites off the mound to keep its platonic, spherical shape. In his preference for the sphere, our mother once tried to serve him Neapolitan ice cream cut into a rectangle with the visible stripes of strawberry, chocolate, and vanilla. This was a sin within his theology of eating. He wouldn't eat it unless it was scooped into a mound that he could carve.

He was, as you might deduce, the pickiest eater of us three, approaching new food with a wariness that bordered on a king's fear of being poisoned. I can still remember my brother Kirby and me watching him as he tasted cream puffs after years of rejecting them. We were hoping he wouldn't like them once again because there would be more for us. He took a bite and his face went into all sorts of contortions as he chewed. You would have thought he were eating earth worms. Then as we waited in anticipation of his verdict, which we supposed wouldn't be positive, he swallowed and said, "I like it." Kirby and I almost killed him.

Icarus Will Never Fly

As you can see Larry amused Kirby and me immensely. Larry's idiosyncrasies were unintentionally very entertaining. Mechanically, he was, perhaps, the most challenged person I have ever met and would certainly not be Scotty on the *Starship Enterprise*. He had a real knack of breaking his toys. Both Kirby and I were reluctant to let him borrow any of our toys that wound up or took a battery lest they end up in the dumpster. If he were frustrated with a toy, he would either push it to its maximum capacity or angrily gut its mechanism.

One of our great pleasures was to look out the window and watch Larry attempt to start the lawnmower. This melodrama began with Larry being out in the blistering heat with his shirt off, a momentary god. He made his first rope pulls and the engine made a few sputtering promises as he gave it more gas. But then it would fizzle out again. You could feel a titanic restraint set in as he let the engine breathe like a good bottle of wine. Then he'd go at it again.

Now the engine didn't make a sound because he had flooded it. This was the point of no return for our hero. He took the gloves off now — no more Mr. Nice Guy. He began pulling the rope repeatedly in fast succession like a mad man, all the while sweating profusely and cursing Briggs and Stratton. Once in a while, the mower would mumble at its suffering. Kirby and I had to applaud his animation during this part of the drama. The denouement occurred in one of two ways: Mom went out and started the mower on the first pull, or he pulled the rope out of its housing and we had to get the mower repaired.

Who Goes There — Friend Or Enema?

As vulgar as it sounds, our parents had great faith in the enema to relieve constipation and sometimes the accompanying fever that went with it. No "sissy" Ex-lax for us. No siree! We were sacrificial victims of the god of rubber tubing. When the judgment came down that we were to be one of the chosen for the ritual of Enema, we contemplated our destiny with the hope of *deus ex machina.*

Everything was laid out before the ceremony to heighten the experience — the lukewarm saltwater, the rubber bag with hose and nozzle, the towel laid neatly on the bed for the human sacrifice, and the Vaseline to make for smooth entry into the body cavity. At one time or another, we all received enemas from our parents, and I will not deny that they worked. But by far the person who received the most enemas was brother Larry, who for one reason or another got impacted the most. He was, also, the most terrified of the process.

Children are ghoulish, at least we were. So, whoever got the enema, the other brothers were in attendance, enjoying the ordeal. Larry was the most fun to watch because he resisted the most. I can still see brother Larry walking toward the gallows in the bedroom, naked except for a white undershirt. Mom and Dad followed up from behind as priest and priestess, while Kirby and I were last, dancing votaries like Hari Krishnas.

The ordeal had begun with Larry taking his place on the towel. Mom raised the bag high, so that the water flowed easily through the tube; Dad took the slender, four-inch nozzle and greased it down with Vaseline. Larry did not go gently into that good night. Try as my father might, he could not at first insert the nozzle into Larry's anus. Middle brother tightened up like a snare drum.

"Relax, Larry. You have to relax, if we're going to get this done quickly," our father would cajole.

"Relax! How can I relax when you're trying to put something up my butt!"

We all agreed he had a point there. When the deed was done, Larry would spend whatever time it took in the bathroom until he could show proof of the operation's success. There was no more horrifying thought to him that they might have to repeat the procedure.

Pitch-and-catch in Eternity

If I have ever experienced eternity, it was playing pitch and catch with Larry — thwack...toss... thwack...pop up...ground ball...throw to first...thwack...play at the plate...curveball...knuckle ball...fast ball...thwack.... We were as immersed as dolphins in their underwater world with ball gloves for flippers. Who knows how long we could remain at this activity if we were not called to supper or the sun hadn't gone down? Thwack...thwack...thwack...thwack. Timeless.

I played a lot of sports with Larry. He was a good athlete, and even though I was older, I had to keep a fine edge to beat him. If he were not so shy, he could have played on his school's teams. We played all the major sports together — baseball, basketball, football, and tennis. Tennis was where we had epic battles on the neighborhood park courts.

There was housing adjacent to these courts, and sometimes residents set up chairs to watch Achilles and Hector go at it. They didn't watch because we were so good; they watched because of our antics. Neither of us were good losers, and after all, there was so much at stake — little brother bringing down Goliath; older brother retaining his role as king. In hundred-degree weather, we would slash forehands and backhands, throw rackets, cuss blue streaks, and argue about boundaries. When these storms were over, the audience had packed up their chairs, and Olympus was at peace again, we made our way to our restaurant (which wasn't open during the day to the public) and reveled in the air conditioning and milkshake concoctions we'd make. All was forgiven...until the next time our rackets rattled like sabers.

A turning point came in Larry's life when he went to high school. When he arrived as a freshman, the teachers all asked him if he was as smart as his older brother (I had already gained a reputation of being a straight-A student). My brother replied, "Smarter," which was his ironic way of saying, "I'm not going to be anything like my brother." What he discovered about himself in high school was that he was funny... really funny. At first this comic element of his personality may have been a compensating device for his shyness. But it wasn't long before it was a full-blown growing spurt into his clown shoes. He had a reputation in high school not for being a scholar like me, but for being a comedian. In his comic way, he claimed that both his older brother and he had something in common — both of us had graduated from high school with only one B.

Kirby the Youngest: the Dark Knight

FBO

The third brother's birth was surrounded in a cloud of anxieties and ironies. First of all, my parents made it clear when we discussed our birth stories that Kirby was a mistake made on an evening of wine and song. Despite her resistance, my mother would say my father convinced her to make love on that evening — the result Kirby. As they would tell this story, I would look over at Kirby's face, which was frozen in horror. Knowing my parents, they had no notion that this story was disturbing to Kirby. After all, in the pre-birth control era, most babies were the result of mistakes, and no one need take shame in it.

Then, too, came the part of the story where Mom did not want to see Kirby after he was born. She was emotionally committed to the idea that this third child would be a girl, and when the nurses told her as she was coming to after giving birth (they drugged women in these days when they were delivering a child) that she had a bouncing baby boy, she refused to see him or hold him.

Ordinarily, birth stories like these would have little affect years later when they were recounted. "Okay, so you were a mistake, so your mother wanted you to be a girl. So what? All births are mysterious and dependent on a million accidents." I myself wouldn't have been born had it not been for Adolph Hitler. Further, Palmina Modesto was pregnant with me before she was married to Jack Settle, a returning soldier of WWII. The power of sex is seldom logical.

But for Kirby these stories could not be sloughed off. They ran deeper because of a phenomenon called Fraternal Birth Order or FBO. According to research, FBO states that there is a higher likelihood for a child to be born with a homosexual identity the more brothers he has. For Kirby, this turned out to be the case, and it had profound consequences for his early years, which in turn shaped much of his life.

You wouldn't think that such a quirk of birth would have such early influences, and yet we realize that children identify as male or female by the time they are two years of age. Kirby identified as male while at the same time identifying as "different." He knew very early in life that there was something different in his maleness from that of his brothers. Unlike Larry and me, Kirby had different interests. He didn't like sports, and he didn't use Dad as a model for maleness; he didn't use Mom either as a model for his sexual identity. However, he did take an interest in household work, decorations for the house, and chattering with Mom about neighborhood figures and families.

This sense of being different that he felt very early was confirmed later when he went to school and played with other males. He felt profoundly that he didn't fit in. What do you do when you feel disoriented in your relationships, when you feel you're walking with one foot on the curbing and the other in the street, when your interests don't match the cultural landscape? Kirby's response was a kind of pervasive anxiety that colored his days. In addition, he felt that he mustn't reveal his true self, else those around him wouldn't love him. His birth stories seem to reinforce this belief that he was not wanted in the first place. This is how Kirby became the dark knight, the boy who lived with a protective shield and helmet with a visor.

In Kirby's own words:

> *Growing up in the fifties and sixties in a small Midwestern town I began at a very early age stage managing my life and creating roles for myself that would ensure my safety and acceptance.*
>
> *For me the greatest tragedy in all of this was that I could never accept that I was truly loved by anyone. I believed that if they knew who I really was they would reject me out of hand. I got them to love the parts I played rather than the person I was.*

[Note: Before I proceed with Kirby's profile, I want to pause to make a few points clear. Number one I have no doubt that people are born heterosexual and homosexual. The explanations for this are becoming more refined, and I would guess it has to do with epigenetic factors in utero. Thus, let's put to rest the myth that sexual identity is a choice. Number two, the pathway that Kirby took as a response to his knowledge of his difference is specific to his family experience and his times. Being born gay today is thankfully more understood and nurtured than it was in the 1950s. As a society, we are still not entirely able to accept homosexual identities, but we've come a long way. Finally, I have already written about some of Kirby's dark nights of the soul from sixth grade to his sophomore year in high school in Chapter 7 "Minority Report."]

Comic Relief

I do not want to dwell too long on the tragic side of brother Kirby. Being four years older than he, I always took his behaviors not as odd or different so much as what could be expected in the realm of a spoiled, younger brother. He seemed to have privileges that I never got when it came to staying up late, being excused from school, and having his own room. When he became increasingly marginal in my life as I got older, we played together less and less. Larry became Kirby's main playmate, and together they managed to have a couple of their own adventures.

Economics 101

Eventually most kids have an entrepreneurial period where they seek means to make money. These are usually short-lived, mainly because they're boring with the cruel realization that they require real work. However, when I see kids today setting up a lemonade stand, I never pass it by. It pleases me greatly to see them swarm to my car and take my order. Usually, it takes at least three of them to pour me a glass lemonade and make change, which I never take.

Kirby and Larry had such a period, but it wasn't lemonade that they chose to sell, but something more cutting-edge, Spudnut donuts. Spudnuts at this time were the latest in donut technology, being made not with ordinary wheat flour, but with potato flour. A brand new Spudnut franchise moved into our neighborhood, and we frequented it in the beginning like connoisseurs of fine wine. Indeed, Spudnuts did have effects that made them different from your ordinary donut. After eating a couple of potato donuts, you were put out of commission for about an hour. They sat in your stomach like a glob of clay. Your body went into a kind of digestive shock, where all its energies were diverted to break up the mass in your stomach.

Kirby and Larry became friendly to the owner of the store, who encouraged them to buy a box of Spudnuts at a wholesale price and then go sell them door to door, keeping all profits. Ah, a business of their own! They bought a box and smartly went into neighborhoods that looked upscale. An hour later they had sold all their donuts and had money jingling in the pockets. *Could it be this easy?* they thought. They tried it again, and again they were successful.

Dollar signs bled out of their eyes. Why mess around with this pocket change when there was folding money to be made. They decided to quadruple their investment, purchasing four dozen donuts. Here is where they got into economic hot water. When they returned to their original customers, they found that repeat business was not to be counted on. Many of the adults were like me with lemonade stands and would purchase a donut in the beginning just because they thought it was cute that these little guys were trying to earn nickels and dimes. But the second time around, they lost interest in cute; they couldn't sell one Spudnut. For Larry and Kirby, it was a stock market crash. They tried to take the Spudnuts back to the shop owner for a refund, but that was a no-go. Now what? They couldn't bear to throw them away. So, they snuck them back home and stored them in an old Victrola case in the basement.

They decided that they must eat them all, and they worked on it with little pleasure, forcing themselves to eat four donuts apiece per day like a Tour de France. Mother became concerned because they were listless with their food, which was usually a sign they were sick. But no fever. On and on they continued, even though the Spudnuts became stale. Finally, victory came, and they broke through the end ribbon. This was economics lesson 101: Do not expand at initial success. It was a lesson, even for Spudnuts, the company, which only lasted a few years after their expansion into franchises.

No Frigate Like a Book

Kirby was quite capable of having adventures of his own. One summer he had managed to make a deal with the owner of an outdoor trampoline center. He would rise early on his own and bicycle to the center. Then he would take the protective tarps off the trampolines, fold them, and put them away. For this task, he was given as much free time on the trampolines as he wanted. This activity was strictly his own thing, as no one in the family knew about it. Only decades later did he reveal where he had gone so early in the morning.

Also, Kirby did not shy away from becoming an altar boy. As I mentioned in Chapter 3 about the ordeal of becoming an altar boy, he got up at the ungodly (or should I say "godly") hour of 4:30 a.m. to serve at "Duck Mass." Of course, this meant no food and trudging to St. Francis Church in the pitch blackness, sometimes in the most inclement weather. He, also, like me had to face the rites of passage of serving Mass for Father Cyrenus (Chapter 3). Thus, while Kirby shrunk from sports, it did not mean he was not tough or unable to expose himself to difficult activities.

More than Larry and I in grade school, Kirby had intellectual adventures. He read voluminously and knew the pleasures of the intellect and imagination far earlier than his brothers. The reading that our mother provided around the house — best sellers, a colorful collection of *Reader's Digest Condensed Classics*, H.G. Wells's *Outline of History*, and noteworthy novels by authors like Thomas Wolfe and Sinclair Lewis — Kirby had consumed before he finished grade school. To our amazement, he actually used the library and brought books home. Books provided a comfort and sense of accomplishment for him that many outside activities could not.

A Brief-case History

I believe Kirby would have continued on his unhappy way had it not been for an incident that occurred during his sophomore year of high school. Like Larry and I, Kirby enrolled in the all-boys Catholic high school called Christian Brothers. His intellectual bent in grade school continued into the rigors of Catholic education. He was a top student and respected for that, being elected as vice president of his class.

He did, however, have a teacher, Brother Phillip, who did not like him. Perhaps he could see a sexuality in Kirby that he denied in himself (at least Kirby maintained this years later). Whatever the reason, Kirby tried to avoid Brother Phillip's snide remarks and sarcasm. To do so, however, was nearly impossible in a school of such small size. A day of confrontation was brewing, and it came during his sophomore year.

Kirby had missed a pop quiz in Brother Phillip's class because he was at a meeting of the Student Council. Only later did he find out about the quiz. Being a student concerned about grades, he wanted to make sure that he could make up the quiz. This was a dilemma for him because he would have to make his entreaty face to face with the dreaded Brother. As Kirby practiced his pitch, he decided that he wasn't going to take any "shit" off the good Brother. He had dieted long enough on his sour offerings, and he wasn't going to swallow any more.

When the time came after class the next day, Kirby approached Brother Phillip, explaining the circumstances of his missing the quiz and asking for a make-up time.

Brother Phillip's response: "Sorry, Settle. There'll be no make-up test. Better luck next time."

My brother's response: "Sorry, Brother Phillip. But there ain't gonna be a next time."

Kirby picked up his briefcase and walked through the school and out the door. The authorities, Brother Pius (principal) and Brother Matthew (vice principal) screamed after him to get back in class. But Kirby kept walking and never turned back.

When Kirby got home, he thought he would be in grave trouble. After all, his oldest brother not only graduated from Christian Brothers, but went on to join the religious order, while the other brother was about to complete his senior year there. As it turned out, when Brother Matthew called and told our father about what had happened, Dad, instead of his usual — "if you get punished at school, you'll be punished a second time when you get home" — said, "It's about time one of my boys quit your school. He won't be coming back." Not just Kirby, but all of us were stunned by our father's response. When he decided to step to the plate, Dad could hit a home run.

The next day found Kirby in the morass of students at Quincy Senior High School — a school of almost 3,000 students. He suddenly realized that he could immerse himself in a new identity there. Nobody knew him or knew his past. It was an exhilarating thought. Then, he became aware that to become invisible he would have to ditch the briefcase he had brought to school. Nobody carried a briefcase there; that was strictly a Catholic school practice. So, instead of standing there like an insurance salesman, he promptly went to his newly assigned locker and stuffed his satchel in it, tearing it to pieces to make it fit.

When he slammed the locker door, he slammed shut his past life as the scholarly, good boy. His new identity was to be a free and loose cut-up in class. What about grades? He had saved up enough knowledge in his intellectual larder in Catholic schools to pass his classes without study. In addition, Kirby was handsome (it pains me to say this, but he was the handsomest of the brothers). One of the wildest girls and most beautiful in high school took a liking to him, and he hung with her and the fast crowd she was a part of. He never revealed that he was gay, and they never perceived that he was. He even had sex with the wild beauty, which ironically meant that he preceded his older, straight brothers in sexual intercourse with a woman, and a stunningly beautiful woman, at that. (Gee, I'm so glad I went to a rigorously academic, all-boys school — not.)

At home, we were unaware of Kirby's new-found identity. His propensity to be furtive about his life continued. This would be a pattern for him, because when he went to college, he took on another identity, which included changing his name to "John." With his college identity, he returned to being scholarly, but for the first time, he added *gay* to this identity. Southern Illinois University at Edwardsville had a gay student union, which he was able to participate in. And he could now go to gay bars in nearby St. Louis's Gas Light District.

In the Gas Light District, he could experience a kind of relaxed freedom that he never had before. He could hold hands publicly with a date, dance, and kiss. In this gay island of the city, people could take off their societal masks whether they be teachers, lawyers, doctors, policemen, actors, students, waiters, etc. Further, they needn't worry about being raided by the police or being harassed by gay bashers. Why? Because the mafia ran these bars, and they had a "Guido" as a bouncer at their doors. If you came to "roll some queers," your next stop might be waking up at the nearest emergency room.

Again, we knew little of "John's" new life at the university. In retrospect, which it could only be in thinking about Kirby's life, I was glad to learn that he had more than survived the ordeal of being gay in times that were unaccepting of homosexuality and reprehensible in their treatment of homosexuals. Even though we didn't know it at the time, he had some key experiences that brought him to people and places that would nourish him and allow him some happiness. But the pernicious effects of his early years would never and could never wear off. Kirby today prefers his own company. He is solitary and intellectual. When you're alone, you don't have to pretend to be anybody else.

Backward Forward

It is a dark and stormy night [with a nod to Edward Bulw-er-Lytton] and three men in their sixties are outside holding hands and dancing around a bird bath. They are nude and chanting lines from the witches in Macbeth — "When shall we three meet again/ In thunder, lightning, or in rain?" and "Trouble, trouble, boil and bubble." Occasionally, they raise their fists and shout defiance to the heavens — "Is that all the lightning you got?" or "You can do better than this in calling down your wrath!" They are not in the country but a suburban neighborhood that prefers quiet. It would seem they are mad.

The old men dancing like Druids are my brothers and me. We were visiting our father and his new wife in late fall, when one of us said, "I'd like to dance nude in the rain." Another responded, "Let's do it," while the third was stripping off his clothes and going out the door. Soon he would be followed by two other buck-naked brothers. My father and Joyce just sat there stunned as we left them with their mouths open at the kitchen table.

What does this say about Kirby, Larry, and Marty? Are we moving into early dementia? Is nothing sacred to us? Do we value shocking people? I would choose none of the above for an answer. What it means to me is that through all our separate pathways of tragedy and triumph, we have remained a trinity with bonds adamantine. We are a synergy that is the triumph of many kinds of love, especially our mother's love. I have no doubt that we would die for one another and, more disturbingly, kill for one another.

More of a mystery to me than our closeness is the mystery of how many people I meet who have little use for their siblings. Maybe it's a sign of the times where many struggle to leave home and break bonds as soon as possible. Sentimentality is looked upon as a weakness, and the stories of their childhood not worthy of repetition. Yet we never tire of the stories of our youth, despite the painful elements of some of them.

Relationships, if they are good ones, provide more freedoms than restraints. I think this is another misconception of the present.

In our era of intense individualism, most do not want to be "tied down" by wife, children, church, place, etc., ignoring the synergistic possibilities of long-term partnerships. The feelings of freedom that I have within the triumvirate of my brothers, releases behaviors that I would never be capable of on my own. We come across to others as wonderfully "certifiable" — a madness that others like to be around. The opening scene of "Backward Forward" indicates what heights (or depths, if you prefer) we are capable of when together. This could only have happened through years of remaining faithful to our past, of forgiving one another for trespasses, and of renewing ourselves by the retelling of the old stories. Without sounding blasphemous, I do understand something of the mystery of the Trinity.

Kirby   *Marty*   *Larry*

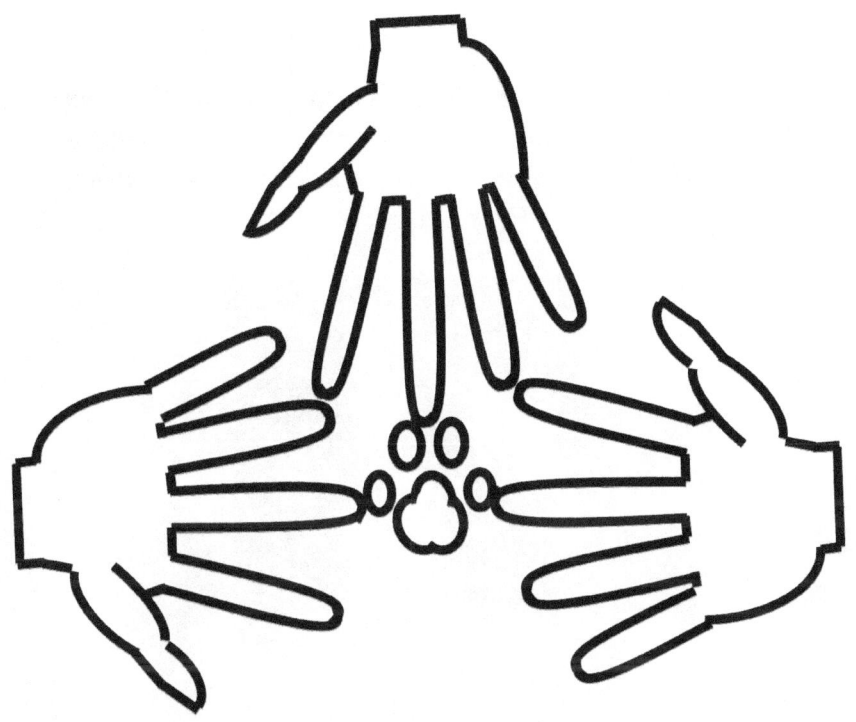

Three Brothers and Another

CHAPTER 15
THE HAIRY BROTHER

"Unhonour'd falls, unnotic'd all his worth, Deny'd in heaven the Soul he held on earth: While man, vain insect! hopes to be forgiven, And claims himself a sole exclusive heaven."
—from Lord Byron's "Epitaph to a Dog"

Schultz — The Royal We

I am not being sentimental, I am not being neurotically needy, and I am not being hyperbolic when I include Schultz, a reddish-brown dachshund, into the family circle. He is the hairy brother, like Esau, and I do believe he was cheated out of birthright by god. While Jonathan Swift makes his Houyhnhnm horses into a superior species, I would do the same for the canine species. Their purity of spirit is unequalled in the animal world (I include humans in this category). If you want to know joy, unquestioning love, and untiring acceptance, you will find them in the emotional fount that is dog.

If you count me and my family as fools in our love of these creatures, then I would enjoin you to think about those who have endorsed the human-canine bond in the highest terms: Lord Byron, Franz Kafka, Gertrude Stein, and John Updike, just to name a few. Franz Kafka claims, "All knowledge, the totality of all questions and all answers is contained in the dog." That is why I would have an ethical dilemma if my car lost its brakes, and I had to choose between running over a dog or a human. Begrudgingly, because I am loyal to my species, I would run over the dog, but it would not be a choice without some hesitation. If it were not a generic dog, but the family dog Schultz, I fear to speculate what I would do.

Without any mental fumbling around, I proclaim Schultz was a family member — not a warning system, a hunter, a herder, or a pet. He was little brother and a cohesive element in our family dynamics. Each of us had our own role and relationship with him. And he made all of us better for it. He was not a rescue dog; we were rescue humans.

I've seen a certain neglect set in from the time people purchase a puppy until they have a full-grown dog that remains tied up most of the time in the backyard. Not true for Schultz. From the time he was brought home from a litter of puppies to the time of his death, he received constant attention and stimulation from us. And he in turn gave us unending amusement and psychological nourishment. We continue to talk about him 50 years later.

Paw Prince

Marty, the walker

For me, Schultz was my companion in nature and meditation. He knew I was the source of his forays into the nearby park, and he was always up for a walk, sometimes when I was not. If he were ready for a walk, he would make himself quite noticeable to me. Wherever I turned, "somehow" he was in front of me stretching, as if to say, "In case you've forgotten, wouldn't this be a great time to stretch your muscles on a walk?" Or if I happened to be reading the newspaper spread out on the floor (I always read the newspaper from a kneeling squat position on the floor when I was a child), he would come by and "just happen" to want to lie on the paper. In these battles to be taken for a walk, he always won.

The magic words for a walk were: "Do you want to get a squirrel?" Squirrels were Schultz's nemesis, and he would have given anything to catch one. He would approach a park squirrel (he was never on a leash) crouched down and slow moving as a cat. The squirrels in Berrian Park had long ago realized that this short-legged creature could neither catch them nor follow them up a tree. Thus, they took the most vulnerable postures as they watched his stealthy approach. They'd let him get quite close. When Schultz burst into attack mode, he made a high-pitched yiii, yiii, yiii. The squirrels easily outmaneuvered him as they made their way to the nearest tree. However, this did not end the game. The squirrels liked to torture "shortstuff" by heading back down the tree, staying just out of reach of Schultz's leaps (a retelling of the Tantalus story). Squirrels are not nice people.

On these walks, I found much to ponder and observe. There is something about walking that can bring out the most profound meditations. I was a thinker and observer, so these walks were as good for me as they were for Schultz. Birds, plants, animals, mushrooms, and insects all came under my perusal. What could have been a duty for me became a form of mental liberation. Not all walks provided me with these ruminations. Schultz always kept the action lively.

Once in a while, the walk would come abruptly to an end when he found the "right" stick. Usually, it was a branch three times longer than he was and almost too big to get his mouth around. As a salmon finds it necessary to return to its breeding grounds, Schultz felt obliged to take this branch home. You could not make him put it down to continue the walk or rip it out of his mouth; he was determined to get it home as awkward as the trip would be. Once home, he dropped it and took no further interest in it. Why some dogs do this, I have often speculated. Perhaps, there is something in it of the ancient pride of bringing back the kill to the den.

Another behavior that requires speculation is why dogs like to cover themselves in the most disgusting odors. If I weren't keeping an eye on Schultz in the park, he would wonder toward the pond that always seemed to have a dead fish on the shoreline. The irresistible smell of guts and gore were like a perfume to him, and he would roll his body over the decayed fish like he was flattening pie dough. It was times like these I wanted to kill him — giving him a bath was one thing; giving a bath to a leper was another.

I also had to watch out for other dogs off leash, as most of the dogs in the park were. Without fear and without the least sense of how small he was, Schultz would approach the largest and most fearsome of dogs — rottweilers, German shepherds, Dobermans, and crossbreeds the size of donkeys. I always prepared myself to pry open their jaws so that they would spit out what to them would be a snack.

Along with this fear of being in the middle of a dog fight, there was the realization that Schultz was socially inept. Indeed, he did go through some of the rituals dogs have in getting acquainted with one another; his problem, though, was that he went beyond courtesy. Most dogs would take their sniff of the other's rectum and that would be that. Then, they could move on to other business. But imagine a person continuing to shake your hand beyond your introduction. This is what Schultz would do. He continued to poke his nose into the other dog's behind until it could stand it no longer. I came to the rescue many times before he got bitten in two.

Larry, the nemesis

While I was the walker, Larry was the nemesis. Early on in Schultz's life, he realized he could get handouts from Kirby, Mom, and me (I do not include our father because he was often gone for family meals). But Larry was another story. The concept of sharing food (one of the hallmarks of the human species) had somehow passed Larry by, especially sharing food with animals. And while Larry loved our wiener dog deeply, he never fed him under the table or dropped down crumbs or a spoonful of ice cream on the newspaper we had out for this purpose. Once we complained about his "selfishness," and he reluctantly gave the dog some ice cream from the tip of his spoon that was so small that Schultz couldn't see it.

We fed him, in addition, when we came home from a late shift at the restaurant, which was around one or two in the morning. Most often we brought some food to-go with us. Schultz, when he heard eating going on, would arise from his bed and make a sleepy and dramatic entrance. I say "dramatic" because in order to go from the bedrooms to the kitchen, he would bang against the two black interior doors. The doors burst open with such force that you expected the appearance of a Chinese emperor. But instead, there was this diminutive creature blinking in the lights. He would quickly assess if there were possibilities for food. If he saw Larry alone, it was "abandon all hope ye who enter here," and he would turn around and go back to bed.

What this meant was that Larry was not welcome around *his* food. If Schultz had a bone from the restaurant, all of us could bend down and pet Schultz without the least reaction. We could even take it out of his mouth. But not Larry. First of all, if the dog did get a new bone and Larry came into the room, he would first clack it around in his mouth to get Larry's attention. It was his way of saying, "The tables have turned and now I have food and you don't. If you think I will share with you, think again."

Larry developed a game with Schultz in these situations. He feigned interest in the bone and began getting closer to Schultz, cajoling him to give up the bone. The growls at first were rather weak and low-pitched. Then Larry would get ahold of Schultz's body from behind. As his hands went up Schultz's spine, he would narrate how he was shifting gears on a motorcycle. With each new position of his hands, Schultz would respond with a higher pitch of ferocity, until Larry reached his mouth, when the dog's engine was wide open. When he demonstrated this motorcycle to visitors, they were all concerned that middle brother would be bitten savagely. Of course, he never was. In fact, I think for Schultz it was a therapeutic game, allowing him to let out his repressed killer instincts. Could any of the rest of us of play this game? No, this was reserved strictly for the food Scrooge of the family.

Kirby, the confessor

When we first brought Schultz home, Kirby was quite young and to him Schultz was more of a doll than a pet. Thus, he would dress him up, put party hats on him, and wheel him in a wagon. Schultz never shirked from these indignities but willingly became the little brother of the little brother.

For a child that held a secret and that felt unloved as he grew older, Schultz became a confidante for Kirby. Schultz was Kirby's confessor that he could talk to and reveal his confusion and pain. If Kirby had doubt about being loved by the other family members, there was none about our dog's love. What Schultz could imbibe of Kirby's tears and frustrations seemed inexhaustible. He nudged him into better states of mind, curled up with his discontent, and let him ramble with affirming trust like a psychiatrist listening to a patient on a couch. Schultz was essential therapy for Kirby.

When Kirby returned home one summer from college, he felt armed with new knowledge about humans and animals. He had become a behaviorist, a Skinnerian, interested in the stimulus-response possibilities in describing the psychologies of all creatures. What Kirby did not yet know was that he had barely scratched the surface of this psychology and that the complexity of it was far greater than he imagined. The source of this new learning would not come from books or a professor, but a dog.

One of the duties Kirby occasionally received during his summer stint was to watch over Schultz when the rest of us were away from home. This task could be for an entire afternoon, and Kirby had a restless nature that in no way wanted to spend the afternoon imprisoned in the house. The behavioral problem for him was to sneak out of the house without triggering any of Schultz's response mechanisms, for when Schultz perceived that he was alone, he would set up a yowl that would disturb the whole neighborhood.

Okay, then, Kirby thought, *first put the dog on his chain outside*. In this way, he could make noises inside the house to confirm to Schultz someone was in the house. Next, when he supposed Schultz let down his guard, he thought he could ever so quietly go out the front door. His first attempt to leave was thwarted by a creaky front door. At the first smidgin of a creak, Schultz responded to the stimulus with a howling response.

Okay, then, thought Kirby, *turn the radio on at high volume*. Again, Schultz's heard the creak and howled. As his next plan of escape, Kirby thought, *How about going out the window on the far side of house, ever, ever so stealthily?* When he dropped to the ground, the howling began like an alarm on a car. Kirby began to feel like Wile E. Coyote. All his experiments had gone awry. He could not outwit, despite his college training, a dog. Besides Schultz's finely tuned senses, he had an ability to intuit his keepers' plans. From the beginning, Kirby attested, Schultz recognized that he was the subject of an experiment and was on high alert. This proved to be more complex than Skinner's black box, and Kirby, a wiser man, had to resign himself to afternoons in the house.

For Schultz, Mom was mom. He knew she was the fundamental

Mother, the cradle rocker

source of his love and care. For Mom, Schultz was her child and anodyne for her loneliness. She talked to him as if she were trying to
teach him language. Sometimes she cradled him like a baby. Whatever accommodations that needed to be made for Schultz, she made
them. She had a pillow on the windowsill in front of the kitchen table so that Schultz could watch what was going on outside. She had
a sweater for him to keep his chest warm in the snow. She would
make special dishes for him and made sure he ate a variety of foods
(except dog food).

Mom was Schultz's advocate. Whenever we came in the door
from school, college, or work, her first command was "Pet the dog."
Her second was "Pick up the dog," because Schultz like to be eye
level when we were standing and talking. After all, he did not like to
be reminded that he was not actually human and, thus, not able to
participate in the hullabaloo of our greetings.

The mafioso side of my Italian mother came out if any person
or dog tried to do harm to her hairy child. Ordinarily a fairly meek
person, our mother would become a tigress in Schultz's defense. We
feared for Mrs. Bohanon when *momma mia* found out she had reported her bambino to the police. She claimed our dog was running
wild through the neighborhood, which wasn't true. We did walk
him without leash down the alley, but he pretty much stayed on the
path. The confrontation with Mrs. Bohanon was a stream of invec-
tives that we had never heard before from our mother. After that,

Mrs. Bohanon gave Palmina Modesto a wide berth.

When Schultz went to that Happy Hunting Ground filled with squirrels, my mother grieved; her life was diminished profoundly. She had lost a presence that was both companion and child. She had lost a friend, whose look said, "If I could, I would bite every sorrow until it fled" (Barbara Ras). She could never replace him.

Father, Shiva the Ambivalent

My father was not smitten with Schultz as the rest of us were. That is not to say that he ignored him or was cruel to him. He came from a tradition where dogs had their place and were never allowed on the furniture or fed beneath the table or slept in a human bed. Because from the very beginning we never adhered to any of these restrictions in the least, he did what a wise parent would do and capitulated entirely. In some ways, he just didn't get how a dog could have such free reign within a family.

However, he did his duty like a soldier when it came time to put Schultz down. The rest of us had neither the courage nor the emotional capacity to deal death to our dog. As a veteran of WWII, Dad knew how to kill and move on. We knew it had to be done because Schultz was blind, deaf, and confused, but we could not carry out this most difficult kindness. Dad did. And he surprised himself afterward by crying all the way home.

I don't believe we ever realized how deeply Schultz affected our father until he became really old in his 90s, and it was difficult to get him to wax on any topic. But when we talked about the antics of Schultz, he always became animated and enthusiastic. Obviously, the little guy went deeper into Dad's psyche than we had supposed.

Food Chain of Command

Hunger Strike

Please don't ask me about what you should feed your dog. Whatever science says, I will only contradict with anecdotal information. During Schultz's long and healthy life (we had to put him down at age 19), he ate a wide variety of food, almost everything — except dog food. My mother, on one of the rare occasions that she took our dog to the vet, was told that she shouldn't give Schultz human food; it would shorten his life and lead to all sorts of illnesses. Mom came home resolved to correct this situation, as nothing could arouse her to action as possible harm to her youngest child.

The game was afoot. She purchased a variety of dog foods both dry and wet. The first day of his new diet Schultz gave his bowl a cursory sniff, then drank a little water and moved on. The second day was the same as was the third. Surely, mother thought, she could outlast the will of an animal. But Schultz's fast was as unremitting as an IRA prisoner. Of course, my mother was the first to break with "Well, if he's going to die, he's going to die." That was the last time we tried to force dog food on our brother.

Schultz had the best of human food. Since we ran a restaurant, he had an endless supply of steak and steak bones. As Catholics, eating our fish sticks on Friday (Catholics during this time could not eat meat on Friday), we would look longingly at the dog's bowl filled with fillet mignon. As a German breed, he was true to his heritage by gobbling down sauerkraut. However, he would have nothing to do with the Italian side of our family, refusing to eat spaghetti. Often Mom would give him an egg or two to keep his coat shiny. This in itself would not be interesting, but he would like his eggs scrambled with bacon crumbled in AND with toast and coffee. Yes, he needed his cup of Joe to get his day started. When he had this breakfast, I always thought he would pick up a brief case and go to work.

He worked us at our kitchen table like a sheep dog, pressing on our feet with one paw for a morsel. He knew the feet to press on. Larry and Dad were not susceptible to begging; Mom, Kirby, and I were the real suckers. If he really liked something that we were eating, he would give us the double-paw press, exerting a surprising amount of pressure on our insteps.

Finally, he had the worst of human food — ice cream, chocolate, cookies, and cake. I am at a loss to attest to the toxicity of these foods on Schultz's constitution. He ate them all with gusto and without any signs of sickness, weight gain, or rotten teeth. I have people scream at me when I proffer their dog an edge of a cookie. "Are you crazy! Do you want to kill him? Sugar is poison to dogs!" I immediately apologize and back-off quickly. But I'm not a true believer that any harm will come to their beloved pet. Dogs have been simpatico with humans and human diets for a long time. Even we as humans had to adjust to foods that we were not naturally built to eat — grains, for instance. Dogs weren't built for dog food either.

Conditioned and Unconditioned Behaviors

To Sleep, Perchance to Breathe

If you haven't guessed up to this point that Schultz slept with us, your deductive skills need sharpening. It was his habit to visit multiple beds in the night. He would tire of one person's bed and then make his way to another, bumping against the side of the mattress. Since he was too short to jump into our beds, we'd haul him in. Why we put up with this behavior remains in question. We would not have put up with being awakened constantly in the night by any other family member. But for Schultz, there was unconditional acceptance of this habit. In some ways, I think it prepared me for having a child and never thinking twice about letting her slip into bed with me in the middle of the night.

Once he was pulled into bed, he would burrow into the far regions of the blankets. Often in winter, we worried about him breathing under so many covers, but he was bred for such behavior. *Dachshund* in German means "badger dog," and their short legs and long bodies were designed to go down tight holes to flush badgers, foxes, and rabbits. Schultz liked tight enclosures. Usually in the morning, we'd have to drag him out of a pile of blankets because he did not get up with us. When we unwrapped him like a baked potato, he lay there limp and torpid, radiating heat. We clucked around him until he was able to turn over and face the day. The only Pavlovian trigger that *might* arouse him from his den of warmth was the sound of the toaster.

The Nose Knows

One of the most intriguing things about dogs is the acuity of their senses. Schultz could hear our mother's car returning home a block away. We couldn't hear a thing, but we trusted Mom would soon arrive as he stood by the back door wagging his tail. As far as the nose goes, I always enjoyed watching Schultz on walks pull up suddenly to the invisible and make a dash into the brush. Sure enough, a rabbit would be flushed out on the far side of the brush pile.

Our favorite game to play with Schultz's nose was to take out Mother's fox fur while Schultz was outside. We'd wave its odor all over the living room and then put it away. When Schultz came into the room, he would pause as if he were slapped and then lift up his nose and trace our meanderings with the fur around the room. What must it be like to have 300 million olfactory receptors in your nose compared to the six million receptors we have as humans? We are creatures that are eye-oriented. We *see* mostly to understand. Do you smell what I'm saying?

Dog Delusions

Schultz was a calm dog. He wasn't yappy, which I despise in a dog, and he wasn't prone to being fearful about too many things. Many dogs are inconsolable during thunderstorms, but Schultz liked to perch on his pillow in the window to watch lightning displays and listen to thunder. The mail carriers did not get him into a froth as they do for many dogs, whose barks might be translated into a haiku:

> *The mailman's coming!*
> *The mailman's coming! Coming*
> *to murder us all!*

Strangely, the gas meter was in our basement. When the meter reader came around every few months, he seemed to raise Schultz's ire as he entered the house. I remember an occasion, when upon opening the back door to let the meterman in, Schultz shot out over three backsteps like a torpedo. It was his first attempt to bite anyone. Thankfully he missed to keep his record pure. He never bit a person or another dog his entire life. He did, however, like to chase autumn leaves, hold them down with his front paws, and rip out their stems like spines — such ferocity!

Just because Schultz was calm did not mean that he didn't require attention. When we began looking at TV as a family (we did not watch much TV as a family in the early days), he protested this new kind of focus in the family by sitting up in front of the TV. We broke down like a stack of dominoes. But he soon adjusted to lying on the couch with us, snuggling between a person and the pillows.

The greatest drawback of Schultz's need for family attention was that we could not leave him alone. He would howl until he was hoarse and wouldn't stop until someone from the family returned. He could never be trained to stop this behavior. If we were savvier at the time, we should have medicated him when we went away. My fanciful speculation as to the cause of this behavior was that when we left, he suddenly became conscious that he was an animal. He looked down to see he didn't have hands but claws and paws. He looked at his legs to find them covered in fur. It was like the movie transformations of a human turning into a werewolf. This is why he howled in terror. Only in our presence could he keep the delusion of his humanity.

Backward Forward

Since Schultz, I have had one other dog, Buddy, who was the family dog for me, my wife, and my daughter. As with Schultz, Buddy was a champion, lover-boy of the family. In the debate between dog lovers and cat lovers, I really can find no comparison: dogs will die for you; cats, if they were big enough, would eat you. This does not mean that I hate cats — I do not. I enjoy some of their antics, and I have breathed in their contentment as they purred on my lap. But their intelligence is limited as is their display of emotion.

We have many therapy dogs, but fewer therapy cats. We have dogs entertaining us on stage doing tricks. We have dogs protecting the house and leading the blind, while cats lie on the windowsills, twitching their tails. Some admire cats' independence and find dogs needy for attention. But I respond, "That's what social creatures do. We humans are not solitary creatures, and we are needy in much the same way dogs are for attention." The emotions of a dog are more in tune with human emotions than a cat's, even though I realize cats have their intuitive knowledge of their owners' moods.

Can dogs think? Do dogs understand language? Are their emotions real? I would say "yes" to all these questions, but I wouldn't begin to know the extent of these answers. If I don't know what goes on in a dog's mind, I could say the same for my wife, and even myself at times. Often, I wonder how much humans really think at all and how often we use free will, even though it's available to us. The world we live in certainly does not reflect governance by a thinking species. How we are able to let the planet go to hell as we consume and be merry certainly does not rise that far above a dog's intelligence. As for me, I shall use dogs as an example of purity of motive and transparency. I would be reluctant to claim my superiority to them, and I would be unswerving in saying they have made me a better person.

The Worship of Dog

"Dogs are better than human beings because they know but do not tell."

—Emily Dickinson

who knew
in our evolution
as smooth as we are
how much we would miss fur
its comfort
its gleam in the sun
its sensation on our hands
more stimulating than prayer

who knew
indelicate claws
could open such fine cracks
burrow deep into loneliness
nudge a man to hope
convert a soul from numb to feel

self-consciousness is not grace
it does not wriggle
it does not leap when fetching joy
its ambivalence hesitates before
rolling in the grass
gnawing a bone to marrow
mating naked outdoors
playing the fool

the oneness we seek
in our religious paths
the dog has sniffed out long ago
with a martyr's loyalty
a votary's obedience
a priest's sacrament of flesh and blood

I am sorry, dear God,
your sacred name
is best prayed backwards
and your most effective incarnations
that dwell among us
speak no words

EPILOGUE
LIGHTING OUT FOR THE TERRITORY

"A thing that happens and is not told ceases to exist and perishes." - Olga Tokarczuk

What is this world coming to? I believe I can safely say not home. Not even the planet as home. What will become of us if we do not have homesickness, if we do not have that migratory urge to return to our birthplace and the birthplace of our ancestors? Is there any significance to this lack of bonding to a place that many have today?

In my own geographical region, Mark Twain in *Huckleberry Finn* initiated the theme of not returning home. Literature before this traditionally had heroes return to their roots after their encounter with the outside world. Critics agree that *Huckleberry Finn* is a flawed work, and the flaws are in the last 80 or so pages when Tom Sawyer re-enters the story. Twain loses his voice amidst the buffoonery of freeing Jim when he was already free. But the most disturbing part and the part indicative of a new age coming is that Tom and Huck do not return home as heroes, but "light out for the territory."

By the time we reached my generation in the 50s and 60s, "lighting out for the territory" became the norm. Unlike my father's generation, whose six brothers and sister all stayed in town, married, and had their children, my generation was encouraged by the post war economy and culture to go elsewhere to succeed. Only one of all my first cousins — and he's 91 — remains in Quincy. [He has died since the publication of this book.] Over a hundred and twenty years of Settle history along the banks of Mississippi has been carried downstream. There are no conversations for me of "My father knew your father," "I met my wife at the Settle Inn," "Your uncle sang at our wedding," or "I heard your grandfather was a bodyguard for Leo Monckton." Connectivity is what makes history come alive, and when you leave your home place, you live in an impoverished present.

My brothers and I are spread out from coast to coast — Larry in San Diego, Kirby in San Francisco, and me in Charlotte, NC. When we return to Quincy for reunions or funerals, we find that our elementary and high school friends have mostly moved away. Those who remain Quincyans have children that live elsewhere. The question for me at age 73 is "Would my life have been better if I had returned to live my middle years in Quincy?"

As I'm sure you realize, whatever answer that I give can only be speculative, but that does not preclude that I can reach some definite conclusions. For instance, if I would have returned to Quincy, I would not have taken over The Plaza Restaurant, my father's business. This succession would have put me square into a long tradition of Settle's running bars and restaurants and the even longer tradition of sons going into their fathers' line of work. By the time I had reached college age, I had had enough of service work, night hours, and the twilight interiors of bars. So, if I were to stay in Quincy, I know I would not have been a restauranteur, even though the money was better than I would ever make in my entire life.

Also, I know that, at least for a while, I required adventures outside my childhood locale. I had gone to Catholic grade school, high school, and college in Quincy. Quincy College, my *alma mater*, was just across the street from my grade school. The same path I walked to get to school as a kindergartner was the path I walked as a college student. My life was very narrow in its geographical scope, and when I watched the sun set across the river into the flats of Missouri, my heart ached for the Western dream. The steady chord of a train whistle in the night could take me from my bed into all the world, all the mystery that it held, all the women that it held. This restlessness was further exacerbated by the hippie era, where everyone was hitchhiking and travelling in flowered VW buses. I couldn't have resisted being on the road like one of my literary favorites Jack Kerouac.

But once I had got a taste of the outside world, it is not unimaginable that I could have returned to Q-town and pursued my career as a teacher. I had friends who were very happy that they had done so, and I know that I would have loved to have had them around as lifelong colleagues. Did I find the outside world better, deeper, more sophisticated, more cultured, more filled with stimulation than the "provincial" experiences of my hometown? At first, I thought so, but after many years of chasing these illusions, I can now say "no." To think that one will be enriched by travel beyond those who stay in one place is dubious. To think that one will have some intellectual and cultural superiority because you've traveled the world and live in Sri Lanka is also questionable.

I remember when I was in Paris, standing in line to go up to the parapets of Notre Dame Cathedral, an American walked up to me and said, "Is that Notre Dame Cathedral?" When I said "yes," he made a check in a notebook and walked away. I suppose he could claim to others that he'd been there and done that. When I reflected on my "deeper" experience in Paris, I began to question how deep a tourist's experience can really be? I couldn't speak the language, I knew only a smattering about the building from the guidebook, and the photos that I was taking would probably not be revisited. Further, picture-taking itself often interfered with my engaging fully in what I was seeing. To know Notre Dame in any deep and worthwhile sense would be to visit it every day for a month and meditate in the light of its Rose window. Then maybe the spiritual impulse of those who made such a structure could seep into our consciousness.

This is not to say that people shouldn't travel or that travel cannot be beneficial. I have been awed by some of the sites that I've seen, but these have been few and far between. Yes, I would have traveled no matter where I would have lived. But I am now aware that travel can be overrated and full of romantic notions that don't deliver. The phenomenon called "vacation eyes" comes into play. Somehow a pot of geraniums on the front steps of a house in Tuscany is more beautiful than a pot of geraniums on your neighbor's steps. I expected "the wine dark sea" that is the Mediterranean Sea of Homer to be more inspirational than the Atlantic that is four hours from my house. Yet it did not have the music of beating waves, and its beaches were inhospitable to walking, since they were filled with stones.

The river, the autumns, the arts, and the education available in Quincy could have satisfied my imagination. This is not to preclude forays to Chicago and St. Louis to keep abreast of new movements. As a writer, Quincy would have served as well for me as Louisville, Illinois, did for Edgar Lee Masters in his *Spoon River Anthology*. Or for Emily Dickinson in Amherst, Massachusetts, who proved by becoming the Mother of Modern Poetry, you don't have to go far in order to become a writer that shakes the very foundation of your art form.

In speculating about whether I would have been better off leading a life in Quincy, I cannot put my wife and daughter into the equation. I cannot imagine a life without them, and they were certainly a result of living elsewhere. But that said, I can imagine before Deborah and Hannah marrying locally and having children that attended the same schools I did with some of the children of my friends. It would have been a very rich interweaving of past and present.

Finally, I can say in all this hypothesizing that I have never found anywhere else on this planet that I could label as "home" as Quincy, Illinois. When I visit, I am immersed in a reef of sensations, memories, thoughts, and emotions. Like some birds, I was imprinted by my early, unfiltered experiences. The morning cacophony of birds in all the places I have lived never match the bird sounds of home. I don't know what it is, but the cry of a blue jay seems so primal to me that I truly believe that I heard that sound in my crib. The landscape of Quincy seems to evoke memories in me that are pre-verbal, and as an adult wandering Quincy streets, I am accosted by frissons that I am unable to explain. This is the psychic material of home.

I have regrets not living my life with my childhood friends. One thing I learned in order to be a mobile American is to abandon friendships and relationships with great facility. The cliché, "out of sight, out of mind," characterizes my neglectful approach to living "out there." I was never a good letter writer, phone caller, and visitor. I just moved on in my haphazard quest for some kind of transcendence. The enormity of my selfishness first struck me with the death of my friend, Larry Waterkotte. In my cluttered mind, I always thought there would be time to make amends with Larry for not keeping up with him. Then he suddenly died in 2006, and I thought about all that I had missed with him over the years and could never regain.

The Loss of Larry
(for Larry Waterkotte 1946-2006)

In life you were the larger portion —
full-bodied beer and a steak to cover the platter.
we laughed at your lack of self-knowledge
when you spent six months in a seminary.
you, a Franciscan! maybe Friar Tuck.
but you were destined for fleshier things,
hunting meat and marrying Maid Marian.
being a dad, not a Father.

so many memories crystalline
in my geode skull.
altar boys in red cassocks and white surplices,
close enough to see the martyr's bones.
sanctus, sanctus, sanctus,
we rang the holiness of youth,
poured wine into chalices
of transformation.

in high school, with your big arms,
you could've been a bully.
but you preferred the buddy slap on the back
and football huddle.
you were more prone to break up a fight
than start one.
tough and tender
you walked easily in the worlds
of men and women.

then those morning mists in the blind.
steaming coffee rising like incense
to the goddess of hunt.
the gray river awakening in first light.
you called ducks from the sky.

and college evenings on bluffs
overlooking the Mississippi into Missouri.
we passed the wine bottle and watched sunsets.
talked about the mysteries of women
and meaning of stars.
the western prairie stretched out,
painful with possibilities.
the river kept moving with colors calling.

you cooked catfish
and tapped the keg for my twenty-first birthday.
cup in one hand and spatula in the other
you held court over my passage.

one winter night when you were drunk
I tried to hold up your 220 lbs.
the snow was deceptive with ice beneath,
"Be careful," I said just before your feet went out
and dominoed me on my back.
our splayed laughter inflated the moon.

but now,
dealing with this death of yours.
damn it! You always had a knack
for breaking things.
you've broken my heart.
broken it before I could repent for all the lost years.
I've been prodigal with our friendship.
yet somehow I can still imagine your forgiveness
in my own journey home,
you waiting on a hill in the road,
nearby the fire ready and cups full,
game on the grill.

Larry had left Quincy, too, but not in the way I did. Lighting out for the territory is not just a physical thing; it's psychological. Also, my removal from Quincy wiped clean many of my connections with the past. As I once prayed as an altar boy, *mea culpa, mea culpa, mea maxima culpa* (through my fault, through my fault, through my most grievous fault). Definitely, I had sinned.

Today, I mend fences and have tried to establish closer ties to my friends of the past and to Quincy in general. This is far too little that is far too late, but I have found that my friends have found little to forgive me for and that if there is any forgiveness to be had, it is my forgiving myself. And there are reasons to give myself a break. I have always battled depression, which often got in the way of my returning home. When I suffer, I tend to hole up like a wounded beast, not wanting to be a burden on anyone. Secondly, my wife and daughter could not bear the idea of my moving back to Quincy. All they could see when we visited Q-town was a depressing cityscape filled with equally depressing people. They did not have my mythic glasses that saw a city of enchantment — and who could blame them. Even today (if I want to remain married), I can't think about spending my last days in Quincy. Deborah, my wife, would as soon as be sent to Siberia.

But I have my plans to return to the home soil in the end and, thus, fulfill the full circle of my journey. I will be cremated and buried above my father, Edmond Joseph Settle, at Calvary Cemetery. My brother Kirby will be interred above our mother, and Larry with his wife Frances will be next to us. A family again. We'll be amongst the names of people that we knew, and the air will carry the breath of our ancestors. "Tis a consummation devoutly to be wished. To die, to sleep, perchance to dream." And if I dream, I hope to hear the sound of the jay above me and find in the sunlight unspeakable peace. Those who want to remember us can find us in the mist on the river.

To Love Quincy

"It seems as if the right words can come only out of the perfect space of a place you love."

—Ellen Meloy

to love Quincy is to love decay
to love abandoned houses with old bed springs
wallpaper with peeling roses
to love mildew
the musty, fusty
to love gray porches
pitted with holes

to love alley ways
all gravel and rust –
rusty bolts, rusty hinges
rusty barrels for burning trash
to love wooden shed doors
weathered to their arteries
to love moss growing through cracks
to love backyard fruit trees laden
with forbidden fruit

to love Quincy is to love Soldiers' Home
old soldiers nodding on benches
cannons that cannot fire
tanks that cannot rumble
to love the white-toothed cemetery
where the war dead rank equally
to love the swans that glide
on the Illinois-shaped pond
made for veterans
to ponder peace and war

to love Quincy is to love
buckled brick streets
to hear echoes of past commerce
of horses and wagons
to see metal hitching posts
next to parked cars
their metal rings empty
for over a century
to love buildings of local brick
the shotgun cottages
practical dwellings

for generations of practical people
to love the storied brick walls
of old businesses
faded facades still advertising
Ruffs Brewery, Oshkosh B'gosh, Griesedieck Beer
petroglyphs from the past

to love Quincy is to love
the give and take of the river
the floods that deposit
bottomland silt that grows 20-foot corn
to love the endless flow of the river
the constant cutting and changing course
the levees and dams
made by men that presume to control the Old Man
to love the moans of ice sheets
covering the river
groaning the burdens of millennia
to love the mythology of the river
the riverboats churning in mark twain waters
the dreams of Huck and Jim
rafting beneath the Milky Way

to love Quincy is to love the bluffs
crusty layers of calcium deposits
from an extinct ocean
dug out by glacier water
militant in protecting the city
against flooding and tornados
to love the feeder creeks
their modest falls
their limestone beds full of fossils
crinoids and trilobites
the eroded caves and caverns
stalactites stalagmites
dripping centuries from ceiling to floor
until they become united as pillars

to love Quincy is to love corner taverns
the sacramental beer
twilight juke boxes
societies of euchre and pinochle
wet, pocket change next to coasters
to love the bartender
who lives on the second floor

his shot glass ready as philosophy
to restore faith and hope
to love the churches
their bells that ring out eternity
in the midst of secular seconds
gothic spires pointing the way
Sunday apparel
dark wooden pews creaking tradition
hymns wending out windows into the streets

to love Quincy is to love the meandering parks
the quarried stone that line the roads
fitted by Depression workers
the Riverview wall initialed
with loves turned to epitaphs
to love the pavilions of school picnics
the scarred ball fields
the trails that led to secret kisses
to love Quincy is to love
the glades that once bore American Indians
the burial mounds they left behind
the names they left behind
the Illiniwek and the Sauk,
the arrowheads and spearheads
that surface in plowed fields
the pieces of chert to start fire
the ancient campsites containing
bone fragments from the hunt

to love Quincy is to never be current
to be stuck in amber
to be content to grieve
to commune with ghosts
to love porch rockers and funeral fans
to see faces behind faded curtains
to love wooden screen doors
to know your neighbor
to walk beneath the Big Dipper at night
to love ice cream and Sunday drives
to be familiar with generations
to watch history rise and fall
like sand bars in the river

Martin Settle

ACKNOWLEDGMENTS

I do not believe I could ever have launched this book without the contributions of a few people. I had valuable feedback from Barbara Lau. Tireless feedback, editing, and querying from Elissa Colich. Carolyn Koetters provided research on Quincy as a gambling capital. Finally, to my brothers, who know how to keep a story alive, I give my deepest thanks; we are a triumvirate that makes life worth living and worth recording.

Special thanks to Elissa Colich for editing, suggestions, and all around support; John Amen, John Grooms, Michael Cassidy, and John Adams for reading and reviewing the manuscript. These people are the necessary core to move forward with a book.

Additional thanks to Kate Ontko, Judy Settle, Frances Boltz, Kirby Settle, Larry Settle, Ralph Settle Jr. and Wayne and Rita Settle – all of these people added stories and pictures for this book. Finally, Carolyn Koetters for her research and contact with the Quincy Historical Society.

ABOUT THE AUTHOR

Martin Settle lives in Charlotte, NC, where he taught English at the University of North Carolina at Charlotte. Since his retirement in 2010, he has published eight books. His early years were spent in Quincy, Illinois, which provided critical experiences for his teaching and writing careers. Living on the Mississippi River near the hometown of Mark Twain, Settle was infused with the adventures of Tom Sawyer and Huckleberry Finn and hoped to be a writer like Twain. Besides Twain's tall tales, Settle found material for his writing in his colorful father and relatives, who ran bars, told jokes, recited doggerel, bounced customers, and gambled. Finally, Quincy itself has been a profound source of inspiration and imagination for Martin Settle. While a stranger may see a city in decay in the rust belt, Settle remembers only the enchantment of a city lost in time.

For further information about Martin Settle and his publications:

W: martinsettle.com
F: martinasettle
I: martinanthonysettle

www.ingramcontent.com/pod-product-compliance
Lightning Source LLC
Chambersburg PA
CBHW021705120626
46545CB00004B/1417